The medir

GW00506018

Bengali proverbs
and their echoes in other cultures

4

Mondira Sinha-Ray,
MA (Cal.), Ph.D (London)

30126 01706682 7

Published by Mondira Sinha-Ray
Publishing partner: Paragon Publishing, Rothersthorpe
First published 2009
© Mondira Sinha-Ray 2009

Cover: '**Biral Tapasvi**' (the meditating cat) by Jamini Roy.
Gouache on card, 1940s (private collection, Nirmalya Kumar).

Comments and suggestions about this book will be highly appreciated
and any reports of errors may kindly be sent to:
mondira@hotmail.com

The rights of Mondira Sinha-Ray to be identified as the author of this
work have been asserted by her in accordance with the Copyright,
Designs and Patents Act of 1988.
All rights reserved; no part of this publication may be reproduced,
stored in a retrieval system, or transmitted in any form or by any
means, electronic, mechanical, photocopying, recording or otherwise
without the prior written consent of the publisher or a licence permit-
ting copying in the UK issued by the Copyright Licensing Agency Ltd,
90 Tottenham Court Road, London W1P 9HE.
This book is sold subject to the condition that it shall not, by way of
trade or otherwise, be lent, resold, hired out or otherwise circulated in
any form of binding or cover other than that in which it is published
and without a similar condition including this condition being imposed
on the subsequent purchaser.

ISBN 978-1-899820-78-8

Publishing services by Into Print
www.intoprint.net
Printed and bound in UK and USA by Lightning Source

Contents

		Page
Prologue		5
Acknowledgements		6
Methodology		7
Legend		8
Chapter 1	aw অ	11
Chapter 2	aa আ	25
Chapter 3	e, ee ই, ঈ	40
Chapter 4	u, rh উ, ঋ	43
Chapter 5	ā এ	47
Chapter 6	o ও	58
Chapter 7	k ক	60
Chapter 8	kh খ	82
Chapter 9	g গ	86
Chapter 10	gh ঘ	97
Chapter 11	ch চ	103
Chapter 12	chh ছ	112
Chapter 13	j জ	116
Chapter 14	jh ঝ	123
Chapter 15	t ট	125
Chapter 16	th ঠ	129
Chapter 17	d ড	131
Chapter 18	dh ঢ	133
Chapter 19	ṭ ত	135
Chapter 20	th থ	142
Chapter 21	ḍ দ	143

Chapter 22 dh ধ   152

Chapter 23 n   ন   158

Chapter 24 p   প   169

Chapter 25 ph ফ   185

Chapter 26 b   ব   188

Chapter 27 bh ভ   205

Chapter 28 m   ম   213

Chapter 29 j   য   236

Chapter 30 r   র   253

Chapter 31 l   ল   259

Chapter 32 s   শ   262

Chapter 33 sh ষ   271

Chapter 34 sh স   273

Chapter 35 h   হ   291

Appendix - Context and background   298

Bibliography   314

Subject Index   317

About the Author   331

৷৷৶৶

Prologue

This book happened purely because of a special request from our son Proshun who showed interest every time I quoted a Bengali proverb and wanted it repeated and explained. On his request, I started recording them. In November 2006, I went to Kolkata to visit family and friends. I took my notebook with me in anticipation of adding a few more proverbs during my stay, to the then grand total of 41. Amazingly, the project became a social pastime, and everyone reached into their memories to add to the collection. The whole thing simply snowballed after that, and the collection now stands at over 1400 entries. In 2007, Biman De kindly introduced me to Dr Sujit Ghosh, a retired Reader of Bengali, West Bengal Universities and a literateur. His enthusiasm and encouragement gave me the confidence that the collection could be made into a book. Dr. Ghosh has since remained steadfast in extending tangible help by editing and as well as much needed encouragement.

This book is not meant to complement or supplement the many existing books – most of them scholarly and some even classic - on Bengali proverbs. Rather, here is an attempt to give the reader a broad and light context. Proverbs are things of the social milieu, and the thought here is to present them in a book that brings alive for the reader such a setting.

Proverbs are products of different ages, and as such, it is necessary to set aside any criteria for exclusion based on bigotry, bias and chauvinisms of various kinds. Even so, off-colour proverbs that cannot be said in polite company – and there are some such proverbs in Bengali – have been left out. Thus, this book is suitable for readers of all ages.

The entries in the (E) category have been gathered from a wide variety of sources, representing English-speaking as well as many other cultures. The idea is to create an atmosphere where the Bengali proverbs are being served at one store in an international food court with many stores from many cultures with different languages.

The images in the book, likewise, are meant to help create for the reader a certain mood. Whatever is the reader's national and cultural background, whatever the life experience, he or she may be able to taste here something of the Bengali life while harkening back to the reader's own culture, and hearing wonderful echoes.

It is not essential to know the Bengali language to enjoy this book. Thus, it is suitable for a very general readership. The reader with at least a beginner's knowledge of the Bengali language can enjoy the book even more fully.

Acknowledgements

I am indebted to the brothers De – Biman De and Bijoy De for their continued and invaluable support. Bibhas De worked tirelessly on all aspects of the book. I am further thankful to Sekhar Maitra, Rabeya Aziz and Shyamal Chatterji for their important contributions; to my two sisters Sunanda Nag and Gopa Sarkar De and to my friend Harjinder Kaur who never stopped encouraging me.

I am thankful to Jishnu Burman & Ayesha Khanom for providing the illustrations.

I am also grateful for the photographs provided by Samir Sinha-Ray, Proshun Sinha-Ray and Bibhas De.

ঔকঁ

Methodology

The collection in this book consists of proverbs as well as commonly used idioms, phrases and fragments of poetry and lyrics. Some fragments of poetry and music that are well-known, but do not necessarily constitute colloquialism, are also included to convey the surface richness and the inward beauty of the language.

Each proverb entry (in the Bengali script) is followed by its literal meaning, its interpretive meaning and an equivalent entry in English wherever applicable. Some related entries in other cultures have also been added. The word 'equivalent' here should be understood to include 'similar to', 'opposite of', 'compare with', etc.

While compiling the collection, it was felt that a great deal of the beauty and the significance of proverbs lie in the connection between the literal meaning and the interpretive meaning. This connection is not always obvious, and often stems from the specific Bengali experience. Sometimes this Bengali experience has eminated from social customs and practices from ancient and rural Bengal. For this reason, the literal meaning has been kept as faithful as possible, while liberties have been taken with the interpretive meaning. In other words, the literal meaning is the anchor, like the roots of a tree. The interpretive meaning is the foliage. Depending on the context of a conversation and the people engaged in the conversation, the same proverb can often serve a wide range of intents and purposes. Furthermore, the meaning of proverbs has been illustrated with cartoons and photographs to aid visual imagination.

Also, proverbs often have variation in the exact wording. In such cases, rather than try to be comprehensive, the more common and popular form has been chosen.

In many cases, the proverb requires a 'background story' for the uninitiated. Some such stories have also been provided in the Appendix.

৪৩৫২

Legend

|1-1| Identification of the proverb for cross-referencing.

L: Literal translation of the proverb that preserves the surface meaning.

I: Interpretive meaning(s) of the proverb.

E: Equivalent (similar, opposite, etc.) proverbs, idioms or colloquialisms in English-speaking and other cultures.

*:   An asterisk indicates that there is a background story for this proverb in the Appendix.

"...":   Material in quotes refers to well-known poem or song fragments. These are not further identified as to their sources.

Alt.:   Alternative interpretation.

Cf.:   Compare with...(similar in theme, but not necessarily the same).

Ct. :   Contradictory proverb.

x |1-1| : Cross reference to |1-1| .

Reference codes

The following sources have been used and entries are labelled (choronologically) as appropriate. See Bibliography for further details.

KH   Khanar Bachan, date unknown

RL   Long, Rev. James (1868)

SD   De, Sushil Kumar (1890)

BDG   Das Gupta, Bidhubhushan (1956)

MHP   Pathan, Mohammed Hanif (1985)

SB   Basak, Sudeshna (2007)

MW   Warrington, Matt (2008)

Language origins

For source of different language proverbs, see Bibliography.

[*Sans.*]: Indicates the language of the original proverb when other than Bengali (*Hin.* = Hindi; *Old Beng.* = Old Bengali; *Sans.* = Sanskrit)

[*Chi.*]: Indicates the original language source of the entry under the category E when different from English.

Adyg. = Adyghe	*Mal.* = Malaysian
Afr. = African (Swahili, etc)	*Mao.* = Maori
AfAm. = African American	*Mex.* = Mexican
AmInd. = American Indian	*Mon.* = Mongolian
Ara. = Arabic	*Nep.* = Nepalese
Aze. = Azerbaizani	*Per.* = Persian
Bur. = Burmese (Myanmarese)	*Pol.* = Polish
Chi. = Chinese	*Port.* = Portugese
Dan. = Danish	*Rus.* = Russian
Dut. = Dutch	*Spa.* = Spanish
Fin. = Finnish	*Swe.* = Swedish
Fch. = French	*Syr.* = Syrian
Ger. = German	*Tib.* = Tibetan
Grk. = Greek	*Tur.* = Turkish
Hai. = Haitian	*Uyg.* = Uyghur
Hun. = Hungarian	*Vie.* = Vietnamese
Ind. = Indian	*Yid.* = Yiddish
Indo. = Indonesian	
Inu. = Inuit (Eskimo)	
Jap. = Japanese	
Jew. = Jewish	
Kir. = Kirghiz	
Lat. = Latin	
Lyb. = Lybian	

See bibliography for further details.

৩৩

1-1 অকাল-কু ষ্মাণ্ড   RL,SD,SB

L: An out-of-season pumpkin (tasteless, flavourless!).
I: A good-for-nothing person.
E: Nogoodnik.
A bad egg.
A bad bird.

1-2 অকালের তাল বড় মিষ্টি x 24-26   SD

L: An out-of-season Taal fruit is very sweet to eat.
I: Rarity makes a thing more desirable.
E: Apples taste sweetest when they are going.
    cf. Every vegetable has its own time *[Rus.]*.

1-3 অকূলে কূল পাওয়া   SD

L: To espy the shore in an endless sea.
I: To have in reach or sight the end of a hopeless situation.
E: To see the light at the end of the tunnel.

1-4 অকেজোর তিন কাজ বড়, ভোজন, নিদ্রা, ক্রোধ দড়   SD

L: An idle person has three important preoccupations: eating, sleeping and raging wildly.
I: A useless person never engages in any activity helpful to others.
E: An idle man is the devil's bolster *[Ita.]*.
The one who has nothing to do has no time *[Uyg.]*.
Idlness is the mother of all vices *[Rus.]*.

1-5 অগ্নিতে ঘৃতাহুতি দেওয়া x 28-38

L: To add the oblation of ghee (clarified butter) to a sacrificial fire.
I: To stoke a fire. To inflame a situation.
E: To add fuel to fire.
To fan the flame.

1-6 (সীতার) অগ্নিপরীক্ষা * x 34-53

L: Trial by fire (of Sita).
I: An ordeal of fire.
E: An ordeal of fire.

1-7 অঘটন ঘটায় বিধি x 3-10   SD

L: God makes mishaps happen.
I: Behind even a bad development, there is God's hand.
E: All in God's hand.

1-8 অঘটনঘটনপটিয়সী

L: A female who is adept at doing the undoable.
I: One who can make the difficult or the impossible happen.
E: Making the impossible possible.
cf. Even the most resourceful housewife cannot create miracles from a riceless pantry [Chi.].

1-9 অচিন দেশের নচিন কাঠুরে

L: An unknown firewood gatherer from an unknown land.
I: A completely unknown but mysterious or fascinating person.
E: A rare bird upon the earth and very like a black swan [Lat.]
A stranger is like a white fowl [Afr.].

1-10 অজাত পুত্রের নামকরণ x 35-3   SD

L: Giving a name to a yet-to-be-born son.
I: You are making firm plans around events that are yet to happen.
E: We have no son, and yet are giving him a name [Spa.].
Don't sell the bear's fur before you hunt it [Spa.].

1-11 অর্জুনের বিশ্বরূপ দেখা *

L: Arjun's glimpsing of the many forms of Lord Krishna and through these, the Universe.
I: Glimpsing or grasping something of multi-faceted magnificence, almost miraculously.
E: cf. "Now I have become Death, the destroyer of worlds."
-Bhagabad Gita

1-12 অজ্ঞানে করে পাপ, জ্ঞানে মনস্তাপ ✽   RL,SD

L: One sins unknowingly, and repents when he realizes it.

I: One makes error when he acts without thinking, and regrets later when he realizes it.

E: Act in haste, repent at leisure.

1-13 অতি আশ সর্বনাশ   x 1-22;2-24   SD

L: Too much craving leads to ruination.

I: Wanting too much leads to disappointment.

E: Avarice begets sin.

      One who wants too much holds onto nothing *[Ital.]*

      Shear them but do not skin them *[Dut.]*

1-14 অতি চতুরের ভাত নাই, অতি সুন্দরীর ভাতার নাই   x 1-18

                                             SD

L: Too crafty a person ends up without meals, too beautiful a girl ends up without a husband.

I: Overconfidence or over-qualification may not be a positive.

E: Too beautiful looks snatch the eyes *[Jap.]*

      He who marries a real beauty is seeking trouble *[Afr.]*

      If you want to be happy for he rest of your life,

      Never make a pretty woman your wife *[West Indian Caplyso]*.

1-15 অতি চালাকের গলায় দড়ি   SD,BDG,SB

L: Too crafty a person ends up on the gallows.

I: Too much cunning machination can do you in.

      Alt. Getting caught in a trap one lays for someone else.

E: Too much cunning overreaches itself.

      Smart bird gets trapped in its beak *[Aze.]*.

1-16 অতি দর্পে হতা লঙ্কা ✽   x 1-19   RL,SD, BDG,SB

L: Excessive bravado ruined the great kingdom of Lanka.

I: Excess, even in noble pursuit, can be ruinous. Hubris can be ruinous.

E: Pride goes before fall.

      An arrogant army will lose the battle for sure *[Chi.]*

1-17 অতি পিরিত যেখানে, কীর্তি ঘটে সেখানে   SD

L: Where there is intense doting going on is where there is an affair brewing.

I: If there are the makings of a scandal, then there probably will be a scandal.

E: Where there is smoke there is a fire.
Cf. Wherever there is mischief, there is sure to be a priest and a woman in it [Ger.].

1-18 অতি বড় রাঁধুনী না পায় ঘর, অতি বড় সুন্দরী না পায় বর
x1-14   SD,SB

L: Too fine a cook cannot find a household to cook for, too pretty a woman cannot find a man to marry. ✶

I: An overly qualified person can be 'priced' out of the market

E: cf. Beware of beautiful women as you would of red pepper [Jap.].

1-19 অতি বাড় বেড়ো নাকো ঝড়ে পরে যাবে,
অতি ছোট হয়ো নাকো ছাগলে মোড়াবে। x1-16   RL,SD,SB

L: Don't grow too tall (like a tree) for the storm can fell you, don't remain too short (as a shrub) for the goat can devour you.

I: The middle course is always the safest course. ✗

E: The middle path.
A reed before the wind lives on, while the mighty oaks do fall [Chi.].
Don't be sweet, lest you be eaten up; don't be bitter, lest you be spewed out [Jew.].
Don't lie down in low places, flood will take you; don't lie in high places, the wind will take you [Tur.]. ✶

1-20 অতি ভক্তি চোরের লক্ষণ   RL,SD,BDG,SB

L: Too much religiosity is the indicator of a thief.

I: Pretension of excessive goodness usually hides something bad.

E: Too much courtesy, too much craft.

1-21 অতি মেঘে অনাবৃষ্টি x24-17;26-19 SD

L: Too much cloud followed by no rain.
I: Great portents do not necessarily produce the hoped outcome. Over-expectation is futile.
E: All clouds but no rain.
A promise is a cloud, fulfillment is rain *[Ara.]*.
cf. More smoke than flame *[Hun.]*.
Promises a lot gives a little *[Fin.]*.

1-22 অতি লোভে তাঁতী নষ্ট x1-13,24 RL,SD,BDG,SB

L: Excessive greed ruined the (poor) weaver. *
I: Overly greedy reach can backfire.
E: Grasp all, lose all.
Kill the goose that lays golden eggs.
To fry the whole herring for the sake of the roe *[Dut.]*.

1-23 অতিথিদেবো ভব *[Sans.]*

L: Treat your guest as though he were a god. *
I: Treat your guest as though he were a god.
E: My home is your home *[Spa.]*.
A guest has not to thank the host, but the host the guest *[Rus.]*.
A guest in the house is like God in the house *[Pol.]*.

1-24 অধিক খেতে করে আশা, তার নাম বুদ্ধিনাশা x1-13,22
RL,SD

L: He who greedily wants to eat too much is one who has lost good sense. *
I: Greed leads to downfall. *
E: Grasp all, lose all.

1-25 অধিকন্তু ন দোষায় *[Sans.]* SD,SB

L: No harm in adding a little extra to the requisite amount.
I: For good measure, throw in a little extra. Do a little more.
E: The more, the merrier.

1-26 অনভ্যাসের ফোঁটা কপালে চড়চড় করে   RL,SD,SB

L: The painted dot (symbolizing high status) on your forehead smarts if you are not used to it.

I: It takes time to get used to newfound prosperity: fine things, good life, high status etc.

E: There is no pride like that of a beggar grown rich *[Fch.]*. ✗
When a poor man gets something he boasts of his new wealth *[Afr.]*.

1-27 অনাহ্বানের নিমন্ত্রণ, আঁচালে বিশ্বাস   x16-2   SD

L: An uninvited guest should not believe he is assured a meal until he is actually rinsing out his mouth after the meal.

I: Don't count on a treat that has not been offered to you.

E: There is many a slip between the cup and the lip.

1-28 অনেক সন্ন্যাসীতে গাজন নষ্ট   x5-31   RL,SD,BDG,SB

L: Too many monks presiding can ruin the holy festivity.

I: Too many experts can bungle a project.

E: Too many cooks spoil the broth.
One monk shoulders water by himself, two can still share the labour among them. When it comes to three, they have to go thirsty *[Chi.]*.
Three monks have no water to drink *[Chi.]*.
Where there are six cooks, there is nothing to eat *[Pol.]*.
A baby with seven nursemaids hasn't one eye watching him *[Rus.]*. ✗
The more cooks there are, the more watery the soup will be *[Fin.]*.   The
baby gets lost amongst too many midwives *[Hun.]*.
Too many cooks spoil the meal *[Dan.]*.

1-29 অনেক খাবে তো অল্প খাও, অল্প খাবে তো অনেক খাও   SD

L: If you want to make it (a supply of food) last, eat a little each time; if you want to spend it quickly, eat a lot every time.

I: You can use up a resource quickly or slowly, but the amount available is the same.

E: A little each day is much in a year.

1-30 ইলিশ মাছ   (Hilsa fish)

1-30 অনেক যদি মাছ পায়, বেড়াল কাঁটা বেছে খায়   SD

L: If there is an abundant supply of fish, even the cat discards the bones.

I: When there is abundance, you are apt to pick and choose.

E: If a native of Pemba can get a log he does not relieve himself on the ground *[Afr.]*.
Though you live near a forest, do not waste firewood ⚒
[Chi.].

1-31 অন্তরে বৈরাগীর লাউ বাজে

L: The 'gourd' (a stringed musical instrument made from gourd) of a wandering minstrel hums in his heart.

I: He is a hermit at heart.

E: A saint among us.

1-32 অন্ধকারে ঢিল ছোঁড়া   SD,SB

L: To throw a stone in the dark.

I: To take a chance on something with insufficient information.

E: A stab in the dark.
It takes a heap of licks to strike a nail in the dark *[AfrAm.]*.

1-33 অন্ধের কিবা দিন, কিবা রাত্রি RL,SD,SB

L: What does it matter to a blind man whether it is day or night?

I: Day and night are all the same to a blind person. One way or the other – it makes no difference to me.

E: A nod is as good as a wink to a blind horse.
The blind man's wife needs no makeup. ✶

1-34 অন্ধের নড়ি, কৃপণের কড়ি RL,SD,SB

L: The blind man's cane, the miser's coins. ✶

I: What is important to one. One's total possession.

E: If a blind man does not know his own stick, tell me what else would he know ? ✶

1-35 অন্ধের যষ্টি

L: A blind man's walking stick.

I: The one and the only means of survival one has.

E: A blind person does not forget his walking stick *[Afr.]*.

1-36 অন্ন দেখে দেব ঘি, পাত্র দেখে দেব ঝি SD

L: I will add the ghee after I see what kind of rice it is, I will give my daughter's hand after I see what kind of groom he is. ✶

I: Commit yourself after you have fully assessed the situation.

E: Look before you leap.
Don't sign a paper without reading it, or drink water without seeing it *[Spa.]*.
cf. Look at the mother and marry the daughter *[Hun.]*.

1-37 অন্নচিন্তা চমৎকারা *[Mock Sans.]* RL,SD

L: Thinking about 'rice' (how to earn daily bread) is ornate high thinking yet!

I: A hungry person has no time for high philosophy.

E: *cf.* "The Moon and Sixpence" - *W S Maugham*

18

1-38 অন্নপ্রাশনের ভাত উঠে আসা   SD

L: It makes you throw up the very first rice you ever ate.
I: It is utterly disgusting or revolting!
E: It makes you want to puke!

1-39 অপচয় করো না, অভাবে পড়ো না   x 1-40

L: Don't waste money, don't sink into poverty. ✸
I: Waste not, want not. ✸
E: Waste not, want not.

1-40 অপব্যয়ে লক্ষ্মীছাড়া হয়   x 1-3;29-56

L: Lakshmi (goddess of wealth) abandons the wreckless spender.
I: Profligacy leads to lucklessness.
E: A spendthrift forgets that what is plentiful today may be scarce tomorrow [Afr.].

1-41 অপমান অপেক্ষা মৃত্যু ভাল

L: Death is preferable to dishonour.
I: Death is preferable to dishonour.
E: Death before dishonour.
      Better the trouble that follows death than the trouble that follows shame.

1-42 অপমানের পরাণ সন্মানকে ডরান   SD

L: A person used to insults is apprehensive of praise.
I: A person imured to being neglected is suspicious of sudden attention.

1-43 অপাত্রে দান   x 4-14;26-31

L: To bestow (something) on an unworthy person.
I: Giving to an unworthy person or cause.
E: To cast pearls before the swine.

1-44 অবলা নারী

L: The weak female.
I: The weaker sex.
E: Women have no chief [Afr.]. ·

| 1-45 | অবলার মুখই বল | SD |

L: The only strength a weak woman has is her tongue.
I: The only strength of a defenseless woman is her voice.
E: A woman's weapon is her tongue. ✱

| 1-46 | অবস্থা বুঝে ব্যবস্থা | SD |

L: As is the situation, so should be the remedy.
I: Take the measure that fits the condition/situation.
E: Cut your coat according to your cloth.
Measure for measure.
See the wind, turn the rudder *[Chi.]*.

| 1-47 | অভাগা যেদিকে চায় সাগর শুকায়ে যায় | SD,SB |

L: Whichever direction the unlucky fellow looks in, the ocean dries up on him.
I: Everything seems to go against a luckless fellow.
Alt. A poor man asks in vain for help from a rich man.
E: If your fortune turns against you, even jelly breaks your tooth *[Pers.]*.
A poor man's cow doesn't give birth to twins *[Afr.]*.
Poor Makar, all the pine cones drop on him *[Rus.]*.

| 1-48 | অভাগার সুখ স্বর্গেও নাই | RL |

L: The luckless fellow cannot find happiness even in Heaven.
I: A luckless person is luckless all around and always.
E: Once a loser, always a loser.

| 1-49 | অভাবে স্বভাব নষ্ট | SD |

L: Poverty degrades a person's basic nature.
I: Poverty can change the person that you are.
E: Poverty parts good company.✱
Poverty is a noose that strangles humility and breeds disrespect for God and man *[AmInd.]*.

| 1-50 | অভ্যাসে সয়, অনভ্যাসে নয় x9-25 | SD |

L: It is easier to do something you are habituated to than if you are not.

I: It is easier to do a job if you practice doing it.
E: Practice makes perfect.

1-51 অমাবস্যার চাঁদ SD,SB
L: The moon on a New Moon night.
I: An impossible occurrence, a rarity.
E: Blue moon.

1-52 অমৃতে কার অরুচি? RL,SD
L: Who doesn't have a taste for the nectar of immortality?
I: Exclamation of surprise when someone is not pleased with a most attractive offering.
E: It is astonishing for the neck to refuse to lie down on the bed *[Afr.]*.

1-53 অরণ্যে রোদন RL,SD,BDG,SB
L: Weeping in the wilderness.
I: Raising an alarm where no one can possibly hear you.
E: A cry in the wilderness.

1-54 অরসিকেষু রসস্য নিবেদনম্ *[Sans.]* SD,SB
L: To offer humourous fare to a humourless person.
I: To offer something fine to someone who cannot appreciate the fineness.
E: The worm doesn't see anything pretty in the robin's song *[AfrAm.]*.

1-55 অর্থই অনর্থের মূল RL,SD,BDG
L: Money itself is the root of unhappiness.
I: Money is the root of all evils.
E: Money is the root of all evils.

1-56 অর্থই শক্তি
L: Money is power.
I: Wealth is power
E: Money talks, nobody walks.
With money one may command devils; without it, one cannot even summon a man *[Chi.]*.

With money in your pocket, you are wise and you are handsome and you sing well too *[Yid.]*.

1-57 অর্ধচন্দ্র দেওয়া   RL.,SD

L: To administer the 'half-moon' (to grab someone's neck in a crescent-shaped grip of fingers and push him out).
I: To expel someone. To throw someone out.
E: To show someone the door.

1-58 অর্ধ সত্য মিথ্যা অপেক্ষা ভাল

L: Half-truth is better than lies.
I: A little truth is better than no truth at all.
E: *Ct.* Half the truth is often a whole lie.

1-59 অর্ধেক মানবী তুমি অর্ধেক কল্পনা

L: You are half a mortal woman, and half wishful imagining.
I: A Bengali man romanticising about his love.
E: "How do I love thee..."

1-60 অরাঁধুনীর হাতে পড়ে রুই মাছ কাঁদে,
না জানি রাঁধুনী আমারে কিভাবে রাঁধে ×24-64   RL.SD

L: The Rohu fish about to be cooked is apprehensive of being ruined by a bad cook.
I: Even a victim wants respect.
E: *Cf.* Fish, to taste good, must swim three times: in water, in butter, and in wine *[Pol.]*.
Cf. Even a cat appreciates kind words *[Rus.]*.

1-61 অলক্ষীর নিদ্রা বেশী, কাঙ্গালের ক্ষুধা বেশী   SD

L: A sinister person sleeps a lot, a needy person eats a lot.
I: A person usually does what he is apt to do by his basic nature.
E: A poor man is hungry after eating *[Port.]*.

1-62 অলস মস্তিষ্ক শয়তানের কারখানা

L: An idle brain is a devil's workshop.
I: A person who is not engaged in useful work has the time to think up all kinds of mischief.

E: An idle brain is a devil's workshop.
The devil makes work for idle hands.

1-63 অন্ধ আগুনে তামাক যেমন, ছোটলোককে খোসামোদ তেমন

RL,SD

L: Just as the cinder in the chilam should best burn slowly, so the flattery or praise given to lowly people should best be measured out in small doses.

I: Too much praise given to undeserving people can go to their head.

E: Praise makes good men better and bad men worse.
If you praise the palm wine tapper he will water down the palm wine *[Afr.]*.
A donkey always says thank you with a kick *[Afr.]*.

1-64 অল্পবিদ্যা ভয়ঙ্করী

SD,BDG

L: A little learning is dangerous.

I: Tackling something with insufficient understanding can lead to great disasters.

E: A little learning /knowledge is a dangerous thing.

1-65 অল্প বৃষ্টিতে কাদা হয়, অনেক বৃষ্টিতে সাদা হয়

SD

L: A little rain makes the ground muddy, a lot of rain clears up the sky.

I: What is a bane in a small quantity can be a boon in a large quantity.

E: Small rain lays great dust.
Ct. Little rain calms great winds *[Fch.]*.

1-66 অল্প শোকে কাতর, অধিক শোকে পাথর

SD

L: A small sorrow is depressing, a great sorrow is petrifying.

I: A small sorrow gets you down, but a great sorrow debilitates you completely.

E: Small sorrows speak, great ones are silent *[Lat.]*.

1-67 অশথ কেটে বসত করি, সতীন কেটে আলতা পরি   RL,SD,SB

L: I chop down the great peepul tree to build my home, I slay my co-wife to dye my feet (with her blood).

I: It is dangerous to live under a large tree or with a co-wife
E: It is better to die young than be a co-wife.

1-68   অশ্বথামা হত, ইতি গজ *   RL,SD

L: To shout out loud: "Ashwathama is dead!" Then in an inaudible voice: "Ashwathama the elephant, that is".
I: To utter a lie mumbling. To utter a half fabricated truth.
E: To be economical with the truth.

1-69   অসময়ের বন্ধুই প্রকৃত বন্ধু   x **32-40**

L: A friend in adversity is a true friend.
I: A friend who stands by you in your adversity is a true friend.
E: A friend in need is a friend indeed.
You never really know your friends from your enemies until the ice breaks [Inu.].
You really get to know your friends when trouble comes [Rus.].

1-70   অসারের তর্জন গর্জন সার

L: All a weak person can do (when in a confrontation) is rant and rave.
I: A weak person's only weapon is verbal lashing out.
E: Barking dogs seldom bite.

1-71   অহি–নকুল সম্পর্ক   x **34-40;2-43**
RL,SB

L: The relationship between a snake and a mongoose.
I: A relationship (between two people) as between vicious natural enemies in the wild.
E: At loggerheads.
No love lost between them.

1-72   অহিংসা পরমো ধর্মঃ *[Sans.]*   RL

L: Nonviolence is the supreme religion.
I: Nonviolence is the supreme religion.
E: "Blessed are the peacemakers." *The Bible*

৪০৯

2-1 আইতে শাল যাইতে শাল তার নাম বরিশাল

L: Barishal (a district in Bengal) is where they stick you with a shaal spear (sharpened tree pole) while arriving as well as while departing.

I: It is said of a place where people are habitually cunning rip-off artists.

E: "Ripoff city!"
The scissors hang out there *[Dut.]*.

2-2 আকন্দে যদি মধু পাই, তবে কেন পর্বতে যাই   SD,SB

L: If I can collect honey from the (nearby) Akanda tree, why should I go off to the (far) mountains (to look for honey)?

I: If one can get something easily, why should he work hard for it?

E: *Ct.* The church is near, but the way is icy; the tavern is far, but I will walk carefully *[Rus.]*.

2-2a আকালে কি না খায়   RL,SD

L: What doesn't one eat when the times are tough?

I: Most anything is eaten when there is a famine on.

E: All's good in a famine.
Desperate times call for desperate measures.
In times of famine, sweet potatoes have no skin *[Hai.]*.
No rattans, roots will do *[Indo.]*.

2-3 আকাশকুসুম চিন্তা করা   RL,SD.SB, MW

L: To think on/up/about a flower bud born of the sky.

I: To let one's mind wander off on fanciful thoughts.

E: To build castles in the air.
To daydream.

2-4 আকাশপাতাল তোলপাড় করা   SD,SB,MW

L: To create a stir in heaven and hell.

I: To stir up a great commotion.
E: To raise a hue and cry.

2-5 আকাশ থেকে পড়া   SB
L: To (suddenly) drop from the sky.
I: To be caught unawares. To be surprised.
E: To be caught cold.

2-6   আকাশ ফুটো করে বৃষ্টি   x 28-108
L: Raining (hard) as though the sky has sprung a leak.
I: Raining hard.
E: Raining cats and dogs.
       It is raining ropes *[Fch.]*.
       It's pouring as if out of buckets *[Ger.]*.
       It's raining pipestem *[Dut.]*.

2-7   (মাথায়) আকাশ ভেঙ্গে পড়া   x 26-57
L: As if the sky has collapsed on one's head.
I: Disaster has struck.
E: A bolt from the blue.

2-8   আকাশে তোলা
L: To elevate someone to the sky.
I: To praise someone profusely.
E: To praise someone to high heaven.
       To put someone on a pedestal.

2-9   আকাশে ফাঁদ পেতে চাঁদ ধরা
L: To lay a trap in the sky to catch the moon.
I: To be overly crafty.
E: Even if you are cunning, you will not tie water up in a
       bale of grass *[Afr.]*.

2-10   আকাশে ধুলো ছোঁড়ে, নিজের চোখে এসে পড়ে   x 2-x 12   SD
L: If you throw dust up into the sky, it will only land back in
       your eyes.
I: A foolish act without forethought that backfires.
E: He that blows in the dust fills his eyes with it.
       Stones hurled to the sky. Don't get angry if it hits *[Phi.]*.

2-4   আকাশ থেকে পড়া

2-11   আকাশের চাঁদ হাতে পাওয়া   RL,SD

L: As if the moon has fallen into one's hands.
I: To unexpectedly receive a gift/benefit that one did not
      even dream of being within his reach.
E: To have a windfall.

আকাশের দিকে থুথু ফেললে নিজের গায়েই লাগে ₓ2-10

RL,SD,SB

L: If you spit skyward, it will land right back on you.
I: A foolish act without forethought that backfires.
E: Whoever spits against the wind spits against his own face.
Stones hurled to the sky. Don't get angry if it hits *[Phi.]*.
He who throws a ball, must expect it (back) *[Dut.]*.

2-13 আক্কেল গুড়ুম

L: A sudden overwhelming or suspension of good sense/judgment.
I: Temporary loss of good sense/judgment.
E: At one's wit's end.

2-14 আক্কেল সেলামী

L: Penalty for an action taken from bad judgment or faulty thinking.
I: The price you have to pay for a badly reached decision.
E: *cf.* Pay the piper.

2-15 আগড়ুম বাগড়ুম

L: Aagdoom baagdoom.
I: Meaningless sounds used to describe something. Meaningless or nonsensical or whimsical.
E: Gobbledygook.

2-16 আগুন নিয়ে খেলা   SD

L: To play with fire.
I: To play with fire.
E: To play with fire.

2-17 আগুন পোহাতে গেলে ধোঁয়া সইতে হয়   SD

L: If you want to enjoy the warmth of an open fire, you will have to put up with the smoke.
I: You have to take the bad that comes with the good.
E: Take the bad with the good.
If you can't stand the heat, get out of the kitchen.

He who would gather honey must bear with the sting of bees *[Tur.]*.

cf. He who goes near soot smells of soot *[Fin.]*.

2-18 আগে গরু ওষুধ খায় না, মরণকালে জিহ্বা নাড়ে x34-19 SD

L: The cow doesn't take the medicine when it is offered in a timely manner, but wags its tongue while dying (as if to ask for medicine).

I: A remedy must be applied in a timely manner.

E: A stitch in time saves nine.
If you can do something today don't leave it for tomorrow.

2-19 আগে গেলে বাঘে খায়, পরে গেলে সোনা পায় ✸ SD

L: If you rush ahead of everyone, you will be devoured by the tiger; if you go late, you will find gold.

I: Don't rush into something just to beat the others to it.

E: Slow and steady wins the race.
Cf. Don't go early or late to the well.
Ct. He who gets up early gets the gold *[Fin.]*.

2-20 আগে ত ঘর তবে ত পর x2-40,59,62

L: (Take care of your) home first, the world later.

I: Your first responsibility is to take care of your home/ your own.

E: Home first, the world afterwards.
Self-preservation is the first law of nature.

2-21 আগে তিতা, পিছে মিঠা *ct.* x23-51 RL,SD,SB

L: (At mealtime) first taste the bitter, then the sweet.

I: Save the best for the last.

E: Save the best for the last.

2-22 আগে দর্শনধারী, পরে গুণবিচারী x34-60 RL,SD

L: First people take in your looks, then they judge your qualities.

I: Appearances make the first impression, attributes come next.

E: The coat makes the man.

When you meet a man, you judge him by his clothes;
when you leave, you judge him by his heart *[Rus.]*.

2-23 আগে দাও কড়ি, পিছে দেব বড়ি *x* 2-33   SD
L: You put down the coins, I will give you the pills/medicine.
I: Prove your good faith first.
E: Put cash on the barrelhead.
       Show me the money!

2-24 আগে দাম, পরে কাম *x* 2-23   SD
L: First the bargaining, then the job.
I: Fix the price before starting the job.
E: Let's shake hand on that.

2-25 আগে দুঃখ, পরে সুখ x 11-2   RL,SD
L: Sadness first, happiness later
I: Sadness before happiness.
E: After cloud comes the fair weather.
       Cf. Summer is a lie, winter is a reality *[Tur.]*.

2-26 আগে পাছে লন্ঠন, কাজের বেলায় ঠন্ ঠন্   RL,SD,SB
L: Lanterns are lighted on the back and the front, but hardly
       anything is getting done.
I: Too much showiness, not much substance.
E: All talk and no go.

2-27 আগে ফাঁসি, পরে বিচার   SD
L: First the hanging, then the trial.
I: First the hanging, then the trial.
E: Shoot first, ask questions later.
       "Let's get on with the hanging!"-*Saying in Amrican Wild West*

2-28 আগের হতে পিছে ভাল যদি ডাকে মায়ে   KH,RL
L: Calling from behind is better than calling from the front
       only if it is your mother.
I: Mother's action supercedes everybody else's.
E: *Cf.* If anyone weeps for you, it will be your mother; others
       will only pretend to weep *[Tur.]*.

2-29 আঙুল ফুলে কলা গাছ RL,SD,SB,MW

L: The finger is swollen as thick as the trunk of a banana tree.

I: Said of a greatly self-inflated person. A person given to great puffery.

E: An upstart.
Nouveau riche *[Fch.]*.

2-30 আঙুর ফল টক্

L: Grapes are sour.

I: Grapes are sour.

E: Sour grapes.
'Sour' said the fox about rowanberries *[Swe.]*.
The cat which did not reach the sausage said: 'Anyhow, it is Friday' *[Rus.]*.
"What's all the fuss?" said the crane, after the eel had slipped away. "I never liked fish anyway." *[Afr.]*.
Sour, said the fox about the rowan berries, not being able to reach *[Fin.]*.

2-31 (মায়ের) আঁচল ধরা x 28-73

L: Clinging bashfully to the spare end of mother's sari.

I: To hide behind a safe cover.

E: Hide behind mother's skirt.

2-32 আছে গরু না বয় হাল, তার দুঃখ চিরকাল KH,RL,SB

L: If your cow does not plough, you are doomed forever.

I: Useless assets cannot make you happy.

E: *Cf.* The crops are great in the strength of the ox.

2-33 আজ নগদ কাল ধার * x 2-23 SD

L: Cash today, credit tomorrow.

I: Only cash is accepted.

E: In God we trust, all others pay cash.
If a man speaks of his honour, make him pay cash.
No loans today but tomorrow *[Spa.]*.

জও গেল, কালও গেল x 2-37

...day goes by, tomorrow goes by...
Describes a lazy person.

E: A slow-coach.

আড়ে আছে, বহরে নাই x 5-46

L: A piece of cloth having good length but short in width.
I: Something that is adequate in one way but inadequate in another respect.
E: *Cf.* Long hair, short brain.

আটঘাট বেঁধে অগ্রসর হওয়া

L: To move ahead after tying down everything.
I: To cover all contingencies before starting a project.
E: To cover all angles.
Batten down the hatches.

আঠারো মাসে বছর x 2-34   RL,SD

L: (For him) eighteen months make a year.
I: The way of a procrastinator.
E: To let the grass grow under one's feet.

আঁতুর ঘরে নুন খাইয়ে মারা x 34-21   SD,MHP

L: To kill a baby right at birth by feeding it salt.
I: To nip in the bud.
E: To nip in the bud.

আঁতে ঘা লাগা

L: One's pride being hurt or ego being bruised.
I: He is offended. One's ego is bruised.
E: It got his goat.

আত্মনং সততং রক্ষেৎ [*Sans.*] x 2-20,59,62   RL,SD

L: Always preserve yourself.
I: Always look after yourself first.
E: Self-preservation is the first law of nature.

2-41 আত্মারাম খাঁচা ছাড়া

L: Mister Soul has escaped from its cage.
I: To die (figuratively) from being afraid or startled.
E: One's heart is in one's mouth.

2-42 আদা নুন/ জল খেয়ে লাগা   SD.SB

L: To fortify oneself for a tough task with a snack of gingerroot and saltwater.
I: To vigorously apply oneself to a task.
E: To put one's shoulder to the yoke.
   To roll up one's sleeves.

2-43 আদায় কাঁচকলায় সম্বন্ধ   x1-71;34-40   RL.SD,SB

L: A relationship as between gingerroot and green plantain (considered unmixable).
I: Strongly inimical or quarrelsome relationship between two people.
E: At daggers drawn.
   At loggerheads.

2-44 আদার ব্যাপারীর জাহাজের খবরে কাজ কি?   RL,SD

L: What possible need could a gingerroot vendor have of the shipping news?
I: How does this even remotely concern him?
E: What's that got to do with the price of cheese?
   What business does a dog have in the shop of the blacksmith? *[Tur.]*.
   I have an aunt who plays the guitar *[Spa.]*.

2-45 আদরে বাঁদর হয়   x 2-46   SD

L: Too much indulgence turns a child into a monkey.
I: Overindulgence spoils a child.
E: Spare the rod and spoil the child.
   Who does not beat his own child will later beat his own chest. *[Per.]*.
   Spare the birch, hate the child *[Fin.]*.

2-46 আদর দিয়ে মাথা খাওয়া x 2-45

L: To spoil somebody's head with excessive affection.
I: Overindulgence spoils a child.
E: Overindulgence spoils a child.

2-47 আদ্যিকালের বদ্যিবুড়ো x 27-32   RL,SD

L: A hoary medicine man of yore.
I: A very old man.
E: A man as old as the hills.

2-48 আদুরে গোপাল x 2-7   RL,SD

L: A child that is the object of everyone's affection.
I: Someone (usually a child) that is the object of excessive affection, and behaves accordingly.
E: A spoiled brat.

2-49 আঁধার ঘরের মানিক   RL,SD,SB

L: The luminous gem in a dark room.
I: A bright son in a hapless family. A person who is a bright spot in an otherwise dark situation.
E: The bright spot.

2-50 আনন্দের ফোয়ারা

L: A fountain of joy.
I: An extremely joyous situation.
E: A spring of laughter.
     Let the good times roll *[Fch.]*.

2-51 আপ ভালা তো জগৎ ভালা   RL,SD,BDG,SB

L: If you are good, the whole world is good.
I: To a good person, everything will appear good.
E: To the pure all things are pure.

2-52 আপ-রুচি খানা, পর-রুচি পর্‌না *[Hin.]*   SD,SB

L: Dine to please yourself, dress to please others.
I: Some things you do to please yourself, others you do to please others.

E: Eat to please thyself, but dress to please others.
Eat whatever thou likest, but dress as others do *[Ara.]*.

2-53   আপদ্‌ গেছে

L: Good thing it is behind us! It was a bad deal anyway.
I: Good riddance!
E: Good riddance!

2-54   আপন কোলে ঝোল টানা   RL,SD

L: To draw the gravy boat closer to oneself.
I: To grab everything. To hog.
E: To feather one's nest.
Each draws water to his own mill.
Everyone who stretches a skin on a drum, pulls the skin to his own side *[Afr.]*.

2-55   "পাগল হইয়া বনে বনে ফিরি

আপন গন্ধে মম, কস্তুরীমৃগ সম"

L: Entranced by my own fragrance, like a musk deer I roam the woods.
I: A person too enamored of himself to see beyond.
E: *cf.* Narcissism.

2-56   আপনা মাংসে হরিণা বৈরী *[Old Beng.]*

L: A deer becomes a prey on account of its own flesh.
I: Acquiring enemies because of something or some quality you possess, through no effort of your own.
E: A fox's fur is its own enemy *[Rus.:Uyg.]*.
Elephants are killed for their ivory, birds for their feathers *[Viet.]*.
The eagle was killed by an arrow made from its own feathers *[Arm.]*.

2-57   আপনার মান আপনি রাখি   SD

L: A person is the keeper of his own honour.
I: How you act will decide how people will honour you.
E: Respect yourself that you will be respected by others.

| 2-58 | আপনি আচরি ধর্ম অপরে শিখাও |

L: Practice religion yourself first, then teach others.
I: Practice what you preach.
E: Practice what you preach.
The best mode of instruction is to practice what you preach [Per.].

| 2-59 | আপনি বাঁচলে বাপের নাম | x2-20,62 | SD,BDG,SB |

L: One must survive himself in order for his parental identity to be of any consequence.
I: Self preservation is the foremost task.
E: Self-preservation is the first law of nature.

| 2-60 | আপনি রাঁধি আপনি খাই, আপনি তার বলিহারি যাই | SD |

L: I cook my own food, I eat it, and I admire it.
I: I am quite pleased with my self-sufficiency .
E: "Sometimes I amaze myself!"
Cf. Every cook praises his own broth [Rus.].

| 2-61 | আপনি শুতে ঠাঁই পায় না, শঙ্করারে ডাকে | RL,SD |

L: One who cannot find a bedstead for self, and yet offers Shankara a place to sleep.
I: A person who is himself soliciting something invites others to share it.
E: He who has nothing to spare must not keep a dog.
The mouse, though it could not squeeze into the hole, had a pumpkin tied to its tail [Tur.].

| 2-62 | আপ্ত রেখে ধর্ম, তবে পিতৃকালের কর্ম | x2-20,40,59 |

RL,SD

L: First comes observing one's religion, then comes administering the last rites to one's father.
I: First secure you own future, then perform the rites to secure your father's afterlife.
E: Self-preservation is the first law of nature.
The mouth is nearer than the nose, the stomach is nearer than the brother [Tur.].

2-63 আবোল-তাবোল x35-4

L: Meaningless/nonsensical speech.
I: Playful gibberish.
E: Mumbo jumbo.
Jabberwocky.

2-64 আমড়াকাঠের ঢেঁকি RL,SD,SB, MW

L: A rice-husking pedal made of the Aamra wood (very soft).
I: Something constituted of inappropriate ingredients such that it will not last.
E: Silk purse out of sow's ear.
Cheap meat doesn't make good soup *[Uyg.]*.

2-65 আমাদের তো গঙ্গামুখো পা x35-5

L: We are ready to walk into the Ganges.
I: We are near the end of life.
E: One foot in the grave.

2-66 "আমার কথাটি ফুরোলো, নটে গাছটি মুড়োলো"

L: "My tale is done, the Notay tree is shorn..."
I: So that's the end of the story!
E: "And they lived happily ever after."
The fat lady has sung.
Acta est fabula *[Lat.]*.

2-67 আমার বঁধুয়া আন্‌বাড়ি যায় আমারি আঙ্গিনা দিয়া SD

L: My wife is going to another man's house right through my own courtyard.
I: Someone's cheating me right in front of my eyes!
E: She puts the blue cloak on her husband *[Dut.]*.

2-68 আমার নাম যমুনাদাসী, পরের খেতে ভালবাসি RL,SD,SB

L: Jamunadasi is my name, mooching is my game.
I: Exemplifies selfishness, moochery etc.
E: A freeloader.
To be a skimming ladle *[Dut.]*.

2-69 আমি (মুই) কি হনু, তক্তপোশে শুনু

L: I have truly become somebody, for now I sleep on a wooden platform bed (as promoted from sleeping on the floor).

I: Look how I have come up in the world!

E: "I have arrived!".
Get too big for one's boots.

2-70 আয় বুঝে ব্যয় SD,BDG

L: Spend according to your earning.

I: Match what is going out to what is coming in.

E: Cut your coat according to your cloth.
Stretch your foot only to the length of your blanket *[Afg.]*. Eat according to the limits of your provisions, walk according to the length of your step *[Tib.]*.
When the bait is more than the fish, 'tis time to stop fishing *[AfrAm.]*.

2-71 আলালের ঘরের দুলাল x2-48 RL,SD

L: The much-loved child of rich parents.

I: The spoiled child of rich parents.

E: Spoiled brat.

2-72 আলোর/ প্রদীপের নীচেই আঁধার SD

L: There is darkness just under the lamp.

I: A man who spreads virtue may have trouble in his own home.

E: It is dark under the lamp.

2-73 আষাঢ়ে গল্প RL,SD,SB

L: A story befitting the month of Ashara (a rainy month).

I: A fantastic or fanciful story.
Alt. Traveller's tales.

E: A cock-and-bull story.

2-74 আষাঢ়স্য প্রথমদিবসে * *[Sans.]*

L: On the first day of Ashara (Bengali month).

I: A portentous day (in a positive way).

আসতে যেতে মায়না পাই, কাজ করলে উপরি পাই

L: If I just put in an appearance, I get the full salary; if I actually work, then I get overtime pay.

I: Description of a work-averse person in a lax bureaucracy.

E: Many people quit looking for work when they finally get a job.- *Unknown source.*

2-76 **আসমান জমিন ফারাক** [*Mock Hin.*]

L: Difference as between the earth and the sky.

I: Difference as between the earth and heaven.

E: Heaven and Hell.

2-77 **আহ্লাদে আটখানা হওয়া**   RL,SD,SB

L: To be multiplied eightfold from sudden glee.

I: Show bodily signs of overwhelming glee.

E: To be tickled pink.
    To be on cloud nine.
    Like a dog with two tails.

2-77 আহ্লাদে আটখানা

3.   ই, ঈ

3-1   ইঁচড়ে পাকা/ এঁচড়ে পাকা   x9-38   RL,SD
L: A jackfruit that has ripened before maturing.
I: An unattractively precocious child.
E: *Cf.* A man at five may be a fool at fifteen.

3-2   ইচ্ছা থাকলে উপায় হয়   RL,SD,BDG,SB
L: If there is a will, there is a way.
I: Where there is a will, there is a way.
E: Where there is a will, there is a way.
      cf. If a person has ambition, things will be accomplished *[Chi.]*.

3-3   ইটটি ছুঁড়লে পাটকেলটি খেতে হয়
RL,SD,SB
L: If you pelt a brick, a brickbat will be pelted back at you.
I: If you hurl an insult, it is bound to come back at you.
E: What goes around comes around.
      Tit for tat.
      The forest answers in the same way one shouts in it *[Fin.]*.

3-4   ইঁদুর জানে না বিড়াল কানা   RL,SD
L: The mouse doesn't know the cat is blind.
I: If you don't know your enemy's real strength, you will always be afraid.
E: Know your enemy as you know yourself and you can fight a hundred battles with no danger of defeat *[Chi.]*.

3-5   ইঁদুর মারতে জয়ঢাক   x28-25   SD
L: To kill a mouse to great fanfare.
I: To make much of a small project.
E: Much ado about nothing.
      Cf. Use a sledgehammer to crack a nut.
      Cf. Shooting sparrows with a cannon *[Hun.]*.

3-5   ইঁদুর মারতে জয়ঢাক

3-6   ইল্‌শেগুঁড়ি বৃষ্টি

L: A fine drizzle suitable for catching hilsa fish.

I: A fine, misty drizzle.

E: It's the merry drizzle that makes the grass grow fine
      [Ita.].
      A mackerel sky is never long dry.
      Fish bite best before a rain.

3-7   ইন্দ্রপতন

L: Fall of the great Indra (epic hero and warrior).

I: A momentous setback. Loss of historic proportion.

E: Demise of a great man.
      End of an era.
      When an wise man dies, the heavens lament *[Inu.].*

41

3-8   ইহকাল পরকাল ঝরঝরে করা   SD

L: To ruin one's present life as well as next life.
I: To bring up a child badly.
E: Raise a brat.

3-9   ঈদের চাঁদ   SD,SB

L: The Eid Moon.
I: Something that comes at the end of a long wait.
E: He is like an Eid Moon *[Ind.]*.

3-10   ঈশ্বর যা করেন মঙ্গলের জন্য   x 1-7

L: What God brings about is all to the good.
I: God does not do anything harmful.
E: What God wills is for the good.

Kolkata mid 1940s: Rush hour in Central Business District.

৬৩৫

4. উ, ঋ

4-1 উড়কি ধানের মুরকি আর সরু ধানের চিঁড়ে x[7-4] SD

L: Murki (puffed rice) made from fine rice paddy and chira (flattened rice) made from long grain rice.
I: Simple harvest foods that are the best among their class.
E: *Cf.* A stew of loaches over rice from the first crop *[Jap.]*.

4-2 উড়ে এসে জুড়ে বসা SD,SB

L: To fly in out of nowhere and hold court.
I: A rank outsider claiming a major role in some developing event (without having had any prior involvement in it).
E: "Who made you the leader?"

4-3 উড়ে বলে কি বামুন নই?

L: Just because I am an Oriya (native of Orissa), can I not be a Brahmin as well?
I: There may be high caste in many different races.
E: Because a man is born in a stable that does not make him a horse.

4-4 উড়ো খই গোবিন্দায় নমঃ *[Mock Sans.]* RL,SD,SB

L: The khoi (rice-popcorn) that got blown away by wind might as well be chalked up to votive offering to Lord Govinda.
I: Chalk up to a noble sacrifice something that has been inadvertently lost/wasted.
Alt. To be forced to do a good deed, compelled by circumstances.
E: Let that which is lost be for God *[Spa.]*.

4-5 উটের পিঠে কুঁজ উট জানে না x[11-3] SD,MHP

L: The camel does not know that it has a hump on its back.
I: People are not aware of their own shortcomings.

E: If a baboon could see his behind, he'd also laugh *[Afr.]*.
A camel does not see her own hump *[Grk.]*.

4-6   উঠন্তি মুলো পত্তনেই চেনা যায়   RL,SD,BDG

L: You can recognize the budding radish from its leaf.
I: There are early signs of what a growing thing will turn out to be.
E: Morning shows the day.
Child is the father of the man.

4-7   উত্তম-মধ্যম দেওয়া   RL,SD

L: To administer to someone both the best and the mediocre
I: To give a sound beating.
E: To beat someone black and blue.

4-8   উদোর পিণ্ডি বুধোর ঘাড়ে   x21-1   RL,SD,BDG,SB

L: To perform the funeral ceremony for Budho (by mistake) when Udo is the one who has died.
I: To ascribe something wrongly. To assign credit/blame to the wrong person.
E: Loading Tim's donkey with Jim's luggage.

4-9   উনিশ বিশ   x29-50   SD,SB

L: Nineteen and twenty.
I: A very small insignificant difference.
E: Nine is near ten *[Afr.]*.

4-10   উনো বীজ, দুনো ফসল

L: A small amount of seeds gives twice the crop.
I: A smaller amount may magnify more beneficially.
E: Less seed more harvest.
Small seeds, great harvest.

4-11   উনো ভাতে দুনো বল, অধিক ভাতে রসাতল

L: Eat a little rice and your strength will double, eat a lot of rice and you will be dragged down.

I: Eat in moderation for good health. Eat less and get more strength.
E: Eat few and go to bed early.

4-12 **উপকারীকে বাঘে খায়**
L: The one who comes to rescue (the prey of a tiger) gets devoured by the tiger.
I: The helping hand gets burned.
E: The helping hand gets burned.
No good deed goes unpunished.
Save a thief from hanging, and he'll cut your throat.
Milk is repaid with poison *[Indo.]*.

4-13 **উপরোধে/ অনুরোধে ঢেঁকি গেলা** RL,SD
L: To swallow an entire rice-grinding vessel just because someone requested you to do it.
I: To make extraordinary accommodation just because it has been requested of you.
E: To bend over backward.

4-14 **উলুবনে মুক্তা ছড়ানো** RL,SD,BDG,SB
L: To scatter pearls among the reeds.
I: To mindlessly squander something of great value.
E: To cast pearls before the swine.
Don't cast beads before pigs *[Rus.]*.

4-15 **উলুবনে শিয়াল রাজা** x26-9 SD
L: In the jungle of reed, the fox is the king.
I: Someone who is insignificant in the great scheme of things can be important in his own meager own milieu.
E: In the land of the blind, the one-eyed man is the king.
Any sandpiper is great in his own swamp *[Rus.]*.
If there were no elephants in the jungle, the buffalo would be big *[Afr.]*.

4-16 **উল্টা বুঝলি রাম** SD
L: Rama, you've got it the wrong way round!

I: The listener misunderstands you to the extent of getting the exactly opposite message.

E: You've got me all wrong!

ঋণং কৃত্বা ঘৃতং পীবেৎ   SD

L: Enjoy (eat) ghee (clarified butter) even if you have to borrow money (to buy it).

I: Live in the moment. Live it up.

E: Work like you don't need the money; dance like no one is watching; sing like no one is listening; love like you've never been hurt; and live life every day as if it were your last.

We must eat and drink as though every tree were a gallows [Ger.].

৩০২

5.

5-1 **এ কি স্বপ্ন না মায়া না মতিভ্রম ?**
L: Is this a dream, an illusion or a hallucination?
I: A reaction on seeing something unexpectedly wonderful.
E: To pinch oneself.
I can't believe my eyes!

5-2 **এ পাড়ার মেধো, ও পাড়ার মধুসূদন** x9-44
L: In this neighbourhood he is known as Medho, in the next neighbourhood he is known as Madhushudhan.
I: A person of quality is not recognized in his own milieu.
E: A prophet is never honoured in his own land.
A wiseman to the rest of the world, but a nobody at home. *[Ind.]*.
No man is a prophet in his own country *[Fch.]*.
ct. An ass in Germany is a professor in Rome *[Ger.]*.

5-3 **এ বলে আমায় দেখ, ও বলে আমায় দেখ** x11-10   SB
L: If one says,"Look at me!", the other says, "Look at *me*!"
I: A gathering where every individual person or thing looks exceptionally attractive in their own way.
E: *cf.* Pretty maidens all in a row.

5-4 **এক আঁচড়ে বোঝা যায়/ চেনা যায়**   SD,SB
L: One scratch tells it all.
I: It is so transparently hidden that the simplest of probings reveals all.
E: One scratch tells it all.

5-5 **এক কথার মানুষ** x28-28
L: A man of unambiguous speech.
I: A man who is true to his word.
E: A man of his word.

A man of worth never gets up to unsay what he said yesterday.
An honest man's word is his bond *[Dut.]*.
His words is as good as a tied knot *[Rus.]*.
To a person who has true humility, words are vows *[Chi.]*.

| 5-6 | এক কানে শোনে অন্য কানে বেরোয় | RL.SD,SB |

L: He listens through one ear, and expels through the other.
I: He does not register what he is being told.
E: In one ear and out the other.

| 5-7 | এক ক্ষুরে মাথা মুড়ানো | RL,SD |

L: A single razor used to shave all the heads (in a group).
I: To treat everyone in a group exactly the same way.
E: *cf.* Tarred with the same brush.
    All poor people ain't black, and all black people ain't poor *[AfrAm]*.

| 5-8 | এক গাছের বাকল আরেক গাছে লাগে না | RL,SD |

L: The bark of one tree will not stick to another.
I: You cannot take one person's mantle and put it around another.
E: *ct.* where lion's skin falls short borrow of the fox *[Ger.]*.

| 5-9 | এক গাল মাছি | |

L: A cheek-full of flies.
I: An embarrassing condition.
E: *ct.* A face without freckles is like a sky without stars.

| 5-10 | এক গোয়ালের গরু | SD |

L: Cows from the same corral.
I: Like people.
E: Birds of a feather.

| 5-11 | একচক্ষু হরিণ | SD |

L: One-eyed deer.
I: A person who is vulnerable because he is unable to protect himself fully from all dangers (from all sides).
E: One-eyed doe.

5-12 এক চায় আর পায়   RL,SD

L: One person prays for something, another person receives it. One asks for something and gets something quite different.
I: *Same as above.*
E: *Cf.* One sows another reaps.
Everything goes to him who wants nothing *[Fch.].*

5-13 এক ডাকে চেনা

L: A name so widely known that you have but to say it only once.
I: A famous person.
E: He needs no introduction.

5-14 এক ডালে দুই পাখি, গায়ে গায়ে মাখামাখি   SD

L: Two birds sitting on the same branch, snuggling.
I: Two people being very close to each other.
E: Two peas in a pod.
Like a halved pinang *[Indo.].*
Like two berries *[Fin.].*
Like two drops of water *[Rus.].*

5-15 এক ঢিলে দুই পাখি মারা x 30-3   RL,SD,BDG,SB

L: To kill two birds with one stone.
I: To kill two birds with one stone.
E: To kill two birds with one stone.
Hitting two flies with one swat *[Dut.].*

5-16 এক দেশের বুলি, আরেক দেশের গালি   RL,SD

L: Common verbiage of one country can be abusive language in another country.
I: Common verbiage of one country can be abusive language in another.
E: Pardon my French!

5-17 এক পথের পথিক

L: Travellers of the same road.
I: Fellow traveller. Sharers of the same path/goal/destiny.
E: In the same boat.

5-18 এক পা এগোনো, সাত পা পেছনো x26-30

L: Take one step forward, then slip seven steps back.
I: To lose ground while trying to advance.
E: One step forward, two steps back.

5-19 এক পা জলে এক পা স্থলে   RL,SD

L: One foot on land the other in water.
I: Undecided person.
E: Sitting on the fence.

5-20 এক বাক্যে ধূলিসাৎ

L: To consign something (a plan, a proposal etc) to dust with one fell pronouncement.
I: To summarily dismiss something.
E: To put the kaibosh on.
    Dismiss out of hand.

5-21 এক মাঘে শীত যায় না   RL,SD,BDG,SB,MW

L: One Magh (a Bengali winter month) does not a winter make.
I: Bad time returns.
E: One swallow does not make a summer.
    Cf. One crow does not make winter *[Tur.]*.

5-22 এক মুখে দুই কথা   RL,BDG

L: Two different statements from the same mouth.
I: Saying contradictory things.
E: To blow hot and cold in the same breath.

5-23 এক যাত্রায় পৃথক ফল   RL,SD,SB

L: The same journey (by two people) has led to different outcome.
I: Things did not turn out the same for two people who followed the same plan/strategy.
E: *cf.* Men and women sleep on the same pillow, but they have different dreams *[Mon.]*.

5-24 এক হাটে কিনে আরেক হাটে বেচতে পারে   MHP

L: He can buy something in one marketplace and sell it in another.
I: A very clever or crafty or shrewd person.
E: He can cheat a fish of its skin [Rus.].

5-25 একতাই বল

L: Unity is strength.
I: Unity is strength.
E: Unity is strength.
United we stand, divided we fall.
Cross in a crowd and the crocodile won't eat you [Afr.].
When on a common boat, cross the river peacefully together [Chi.].
Let us keep close together, not far apart [Mao.].

5-26 একবার ঠকলে ঠকের দোষ, দুবার ঠকলে নিজের দোষ

L: If you get cheated once, it is the cheater's fault; if you get cheated twice, it is your fault.
I: One who does not learn from bad experience is a fool.
E: Fool me once, shame on you. Fool me twice, shame on me.

5-27 একবার না পারিলে দেখ শতবার

L: If you don't succeed the first time, try a hundred times.
I: If you don't succeed, try again.
If at first you don't succeed, try, try, try again.
Even a stone gets rounded by constant rubbing [Ind.].

5-28 এক হাত নেওয়া   SD

L: To administer the way of the arm.
I: To give somebody a good talking to.
E: To get one's digs in.
To give somebody a piece of one's mind.

5-29 এক হাতে ছড়াও দুই হাতে কুড়াও

L: Scatter with one hand, gather with two.
I: Give little, take more.
E: Scatter with one hand, gather with two.

5-30 এক হাতে তালি বাজে না x34-69   RL,SD,BDG,SB, MW

L: You cannot clap with one hand.
I: One cannot do what it takes two to do.
E: It takes two to tango.
You cannot clap with one hand.
It takes two to make a quarrel.
It takes both rain and sunshine to make a rainbow.
A bird will not fly with one wing *[Tur.]*.
One hand cannot clap *[Ara.]*.
Do not let your right hand victimize your left *[Ara.]*.

5-31 এক হেঁসেলে তিন রাঁধুনী, পুড়ে ম'ল তার ফেন-গালুনী x1-28
RL,SD

L: With three cooks (bossing) in one kitchen, the rice-strainer ends up dying from scalding.
I: Too many leaders bungle a project.
E: Too many cooks spoil the broth.
There is not enough room for two elephants to sit in the same shade *[Afr.]*.

5-32 একা রামে রক্ষা নেই সুগ্রীব দোসর * x 5-36
RL,SD

L: Rama alone is a fearsome adversary and he has with him his friend Sugrib to boot (lament of Ravana, Rama's enemy in battle).
I: An already fierce enemy has additional help to boot.

5-33 একাদশে বৃহস্পতি   SD

L: Jupiter in the eleventh house (of the Zodiac).
I: A particularly powerful or fortunate person. A time of all-round harmony and prosperity.

5-34 একুশে আইন x 32-23

L: The twenty-first article of law.
I: A fictitious set of quirky and humorous articles of conduct. Arbitrary rules.
E: *cf.* The law west of Pecos.

5-35 একূল-ওকূল দুকূল গেল   SD

L: The safe refuge of both this shore and the other shore is lost (to him).

I: Both of two options for survival are lost.

E: Up a creek without a paddle.

5-36 একে মনসা তায় ধুনোর গন্ধ x5-32   RL, SD, SB

L: Not only is there present the Goddess Manasa (to keep snakes at bay), but there is the scent of frankincense to boot.

I: Not only is there a strong deterrent, but there is a second one to boot.

E: Plan B.
cf. A second line of defense.

5-37 একের বোঝা দশের লাঠি   SD,SB

L: One man's bundle is ten people's sticks.

I: When more people divide a job amongst themselves, each person's burden is lessened.

E: Fifty lemons are a load for one person, but for fifty people they are perfume [Afr.].

5-38 একং সদ্বিপ্রা বহুধা বদন্তি [Sans.]

L: Truth is one, but saints call it by many names.

I: There is only one God, but many religions.

E: cf. The broad-minded see the truth in different religions, the narrow-minded see only the differences [Chi.].

5-39 একমেবাদ্বিতীয়ম [Sans.] x31-8   SD

L: Unique and without a second.

I: Very unique.

E: Without parallel.
The one and the only.

5-40 একলব্যের গুরুদক্ষিণা   *

L: The honorarium Ekalabya gave his teacher.

I: A tragic personal sacrifice out of a sense of honour.

E: The ultimate sacrifice.

5-41   এত টাকা ক্ষয়, তবু বউ সুন্দর নয়

L: After spending so much money to procure a bride, she turns out not to be pretty.

I: Misguided expectation.

E: Money cannot buy everything.

5-42   এত ভঙ্গ বঙ্গদেশ তবু রঙ্গে ভরা

L: Bengal - splintered so badly - is yet full of such lively colours/ enchantment.

I: In praise of Bengal.

E: *cf.* "O to be in England..."

5-43   এত ভাত বাড়ে যে বিড়াল ডিঙাতে পারে না   SD

L: Rice is served in so high a mound that even the cat cannot jump over it.

I: A very generous serving.

E: To pile it on.

5-44   "এতক্ষণে", অরিন্দম কহিলা বিষাদে *

L: At long last, Arindam starts to speak sadly...

I: Someone belatedly realises that there is something wrong.

E: *cf.* Et tu Brute . . ."

এত ভাত বাড়ে যে বিড়াল ডিঙাতে পারে না

৫-৪৫ ধানের ক্ষেত

5-45

"এমন ধানের ওপর ঢেউ খেলে যায় বাতাস কাহার দেশে"

L: Whose land is this where the wind sculpts such waves on the ricefields? (Poem fragment)
I: Poetic extolling of the beauty of Bengal.
E: *Cf.* Amber waves of grain... *US Anthem.*

5-46 এদিক নেই ওদিক আছে x2-35 SD

L: If he is short on this, he is long on that.
I: Deficient in one area, but overcompensated in another (*usually said in an amusing vein*).
Alt. Said of one who has a proclivity to pursue bad ways and avoid good ways.
E: A peacock has too little in its head, too much in its tail *[Swe.].*

5-47 এয়সা দিন নেহি রহেগা *[Hin.]* SD

L: Such (bad) days will not last forever.
I: Good days will come.
E: Weal and woe come by turns.
This too shall pass.

Every flood will have an ebb.
One day is for us, and the other is against us *[Ara.]*.

Kolkata mid 1940s: Writers' Building was still a prominent
landmark in Kolkata as it is now.

৪৩

6.

ও

6-1 **"ওগো বটবৃক্ষ, সাক্ষী থেকো তুমি"**

L: O Banyan Tree, bear witness...
I: Asking something of lasting symbolism to witness your misery, misfortune etc.
E: *cf.* Rock of Ages, cleft for me – *The Bible.*

6-1 বটবৃক্ষ (Banyan tree)

6-2 ওঝা আনলাম মা'কে ভাল করতে, ওঝা চায় মা'কে বিয়ে করতে

SD

L: I summoned the Ojha (an exorcist) to cure Mother, but he wants to marry Mother.
I: Unintended, unexpected and unwanted consequence.

6-3 ওঠ্ ছুঁড়ি তোর বিয়ে   RL,SD

L: Wake up, lass, it's your wedding!
I: A sudden call to feverish action.
E: To catch someone on the hop.
   Cold call.

6-4 ওল বলে মান কচু তুমি নাকি লাগ x12-5   SD

L: Ol (arum, a tuber) says to Maankochu (another such
   tuber), I hear you have a stinging taste.
I: To find in another person a fault which you too have.
E: Pot calling the kettle black.
   People who live in glass-houses should not throw stones.

6-5 ওস্তাদের মার শেষরাতে   SD

L: The star musician plays late at night (near the end of the
   evening's performance).
I: The best part will come at the end.
E: Save the best for the last.
   Cf. The opera isn't over until the fat lady sings.

6-6 ওয়ান পাইস ফাদার মাদার [*Mock Eng.*]

L: One pice (a very small-denomination British India coin) is
   as valuable (to me) as my father and my mother.
I: The motto of a very stingy person.
E: Penny-pincher.

59

7-1 ক–অক্ষর গোমাংস x24-81 RL,SD,SB
L: (To him) the letter Ka is (to be avoided) like beef.
I: (He is) a most illiterate person. Learning is unholy to someone.
E: He doesn't know the three R's.

7-2 কই'র তেলে কই ভাজা x9-1;28-46
L: Frying koee fish in its own oil.
I: Leveraging a situation. Making something enhance itself.
E. A wedge from itself splits the oak tree.

7-3 কই মাছের পরাণ SD
L: The life of a koee fish.
I: Something that cannot be ended easily (koee fish do not die easily in the fisherman's net).
E: The nine lives of a cat.
   Cf. Like a kerakap leaf on a rock, unwilling to live, unwilling to die *[Indo.].*

7-4 কচি পাঁঠা বৃদ্ধ মেষ, দইয়ের অগ্র ঘোলের শেষ x4-1 RL,SD
L: A young goat, an old lamb, the first spoonful of yogurt, the last sip of buttermilk.
I: The finest of treats for the palate. The finest in a class of things.
E: Old wood is best to burn, old horses to ride, and old wine to drink.
   Young girl and a coffee hot *[Fin.].*

7-5 কড়ায় গণ্ডায় মিটিয়ে দেওয়া
L: To repay someone to the last kara and gonda (smallest denomination coins).
I: To pay back in full.

E: Done and dusted.
Paid in full.

7-6 কড়িকাঠ গোনা   SD

L: To count out the rafters.
I: To idle away time. To think stray thoughts.
E: To count sheep.
To carry the day out in baskets *[Dut.]*.
To gaze at the stork *[Dut.]*.

7-7 কড়ি দিয়ে কিনব দই, গয়লানী মোর কিসের সই?   SD

L: If I am paying for her curd, why do I need to befriend the milkmaid?
I: When you are paying for something, you are not receiving any favours. Rightful exchange is the issue.
E: Do not mix business with pleasure.

7-8 কড়ি দিয়ে কিনলাম, দড়ি দিয়ে বাঁধলাম   SD

L: Bought (as a cow) with cowrie shells, tied up with a rope (as to a hitching post).
I: To purchase a bridegroom by cash dowry and to bind him with the power of money. To acquire something and secure it properly.
E: *cf.* Signed, sealed and delivered.

7-9 কড়িতে বাঘের দুধ মিলে

7-9 কড়িতে বাঘের দুধ মিলে   RL,SB

L: If you have the cowries (money), you can even buy tiger's milk.

I: Money can buy anything. Money makes the mare go.

E: Money talks, nobody walks.
     If you have money, you can make the devil push your grindstone *[Chi.]*.
     A rich man has even the devil to lull his children *[Pol.]*.
     He has (even) the bird's milk *[Grk.]*

7-10 কত ধানে কত চাল বুঝবে   RL,SD,SB

L: You will find out how much rice is got from (threshing) an amount of rice paddy.

I: You will finally gain some essential life lesson the hard way.

E: You will learn which side of your bread is buttered.
He knows how many grains to a bushel of wheat.

7-11 কথা কাটাকাটি

L: Fencing with words.

I: Quarrel. Harsh exchange of words.

E: To have words.

7-12 কথা চালাচালি করা

L: To carry words back and forth.

I: To spread rumours.

E: Loose words are picked up like gold coins *[Rus.]*.

7-13 কথা ঘোরানো

L: To make a sentence take a turn.

I: Cleverly change the thrust of what is being said.

E: To back-pedal.

7-14 কথায় কথা বাড়ে, ভোজনে পেট বাড়ে   SD

L: Words lead to more words, eating leads to a bigger belly.

I: Talking begets more talking, acting leads to a tangible result.

E: Actions speak louder than words.

7-15 কথার খেই হারানো

L: To lose the thread of one's speech.

I: To suddenly forget what one was about to say.

E: Losing one's thread.

7-16 কথার ঘা সয় না, হাতের ঘা সয়   RL,SD

L: Blows from the hand are bearable, blows from words are not.

I: Spoken words can cause deep hurt.

E: *ct.* Sticks and stones may break my bones, but words will never hurt me.
ct. Hard words break no bones.

cf. In a good word there are three winters' warmth; in one malicious word there is pain for six frosty months [*Inu.*]
ct. A bark does not wound [*Fin.*].
Soft word don't scratch the tongue [*Fch.*].

7-17 **কথার খেলাপ**

L: A breach of one's word.
I: Not keeping one's word/ promise/ pledge.
E: Going back on one's word.

7-18 **কথার ফুলঝুড়ি** x28-92

L: A sparkle of words.
I: Voluminous, decorative talk.

7-19 **কথার মারপ্যাঁচ** SD

L: Clever twists and turns of words.
I: Verbal jugglery.
E: Jiggery pokery.

7-20 **কথার লাগাম নেই**

L: Speech without reins.
I: Careless/unrestrained speech.
E: Talkng through the back of one's head.

7-21 **কন্টকেনৈব কন্টকম্** [*Sans.*] x7-44 SD, MW

L: To use a thorn to extract a thorn.
I: To remove an impediment with the help of the same impediment.
E: To set a thief to catch a thief.

7-22 **কনে দেখা আলো** SB

L: Bride-viewing light (The light by which a groom first views the bride - near twilight).
I: The twilight hour (poetically).
E: Twilight.

7-23 কপালগুণে গোপাল মেলে RL,SD

L: Luck can attain the favour of Gopal (God).
I: The lucky gets everything he wants.
E: Luck rules everywhere.
If you were born lucky, even your rooster will lay eggs *[Rus.]*.
Throw a lucky man in the sea, and he will come up with a fish in his mouth *[Ara.]*.

7-24 কপাল যদি মন্দ হয়, দূর্বা ক্ষেতে বাঘের ভয় SD

L: An ill-fated person might have to fear the attack of a tiger even in flat grassland.
I: If your luck has given out, you may face danger even in the safest of situations.
E: The day a monkey is destined to die all trees become slippery *[Afr.]*.

7-25 কপালে/ ভাঁড়ে নেইকো ঘি, ঠক ঠকালে হবে কি RL,SD,SB

L: If ghee is not in your lot, no point in rattling the pot (of ghee, to coax out any residual amount).
I: If something is not in your lot, all efforts to get it will be to no avail.

7-26 কপালের লিখন না যায় খণ্ডন x27-3;31-7 SB

L: What is written on the forehead cannot be crossed out.
I: You cannot change your destiny.
E: No flying from fate.
It is written.
He that is born to be hanged shall never be drowned *[Spa.]*.

7-27 কম জলের মাছ বেশী জলে ঠাঁই পায় না SD

L: Shallow-water fish cannot take to deep waters.
I: A person cannot adjust to surroundings better/richer than their own.
E: *cf.* A fish out of water.

7-28 কয়লা শতবার ধুইলেও ময়লা ছাড়ে না   SD

L: Even if you wash coal a hundred times, it remains black.

I: The character of a bad person is as unchangeable as the colour of coal.

E: Dirty water does not wash clean *[Ita.]*.

No matter how much you wash a black person, you are wasting your soap *[Grk.]*.

Rain beats a leopard's skin, but it does not wash out the spots *[Afr.]*.

7-29 কর্তার ইচ্ছায় কর্ম   RL

L: What the headman wills is what will happen.

I: The person in charge decides.

E: The master may do as he pleases.

The master's will is law.

7-30 কর্মে কুঁড়ে ভোজনে দেড়ে

L: Lazy at work, but eats half as much again at mealtimes.

I: Does not earn his keeps.

E: Slow at work, quick to eat.

Laziness spreads a mat for hunger *[Afr.]*.

Eating is sweet, digging is weariness *[Afr.]*.

7-31 কলকাঠি নাড়া

L: To manipulate the control stick (as of a machine).

I: To engage in machinations.

E: To pull strings.

The puppet master.

7-32 কলকে না পাওয়া   SD

L: To not have the hubble-bubble passed to you (in a circle of people smoking in the living-room, e.g).

I: To be counted less than equal in a peerage.

E: He is not a card-carrying member.

7-33 কলসীর জল গড়াতে গড়াতে তলানীতে ঠেকে   SD

L: A pitcher of water is eventually emptied from (people) taking drinks.

I: If you continue to draw from a stock, it is bound to run out.
E: Drop by drop, the lake is drained out.
Always taking out of the meal-tub, and never putting in, soon comes to the bottom *[Spa.]*.
Constant dipping will empty the gourd of honey *[Afr.]*.

7-34 কলুর বলদ x11-18 RL,SD

L: An oil-trader's ox (employed to transport vats of oil).
I: Someone who does mindless and routine drudgery - day in, day out - without any gain for himself.

7-35 কলের পুতুল SD

L: A mechanized/wind-up doll.
I: A puppet.
E: A puppet.
A wind-up doll.

7-36 কষ্ট না করলে কেষ্ট মেলে না SD,BDG,SB

L: You cannot gain the favour of Kesto (Krishna) without working hard for it.
I: You have to work to get what you want.
E: No pains, no gains.
Nothing ventured, nothing gained.
A timid merchant neither loses nor makes profit *[Tur.]*.

7-37 কষ্ট বই ইষ্ট নাই SD

L: No favours of God without hard work.
I: No hard work, no benefit.
E: No cross, no crown.

7-38 কষ্টি পাথরে যাচাই করা

L: To test someone or something on a touchstone.
I: Test of purity. To ascertain the true value of someone or something.
E: Touchstone.
Acid test.

7-39	কাঁকলাসের মতন চেহারা

L: An appearance resembling a chameleon.
I: A very lean person.
E: All skin and bone.
Like death warmed up.

7-40	কাঙ্গালকে শাকের ক্ষেত দেখানো	SD

L: To show the pauper the spinach fields.
I: To show a needy person the place of plenty.
E: Offer to help a pauper, and he will cling to you.

7-41	কাঙ্গালী-বিদায় করা *

L: To say goodbye to (send away) the gathered destitute (with ritual offering of alms).
I: Distribution of alms to the poor.
E: *cf.* Soup kitchen.

7-42	কাঁচকলা দেখানো

L: To hold up a green plantain (as a message) to someone.
I: To deprive. To derisively turn down someone expecting something from you.
E: To thumb one's nose.

7-43	কাঁচা বাঁশে ঘুণ ধরা	SD

L: Termites infesting green bamboo stalks.
I: Unexpected and untimely decay/ disease.
E: To be spoilt in early youth.

7-44	কাঁটা দিয়ে কাঁটা তোলা x7-21	RL,SD,SB

L: Use a thorn to remove another thorn.
I: For a tough problem, use an equally tough measure.
E: One nail drives out another.
To set a thief to catch a thief.
Use a wedge to knock out a wedge *[Rus.]*.
Fight poison with poison *[Chi.]*.

7-45	কা কস্য পরিবেদনা *[Sans.]*	RL,SD,SB

L: Who is going to mourn whom?
I: No one to mourn him.
E: *cf.* A guest mourner does not wail as though his heart is broken *[Afr.]*.

7-46	কাকপক্ষীতে না জানতে পারা

L: To let not even the crow know (a secret).
I: To keep a secret most closely.
E: "Mum's the word!"
cf. My hut is on the outskirt, I don't know a thing *[Rus.]*.

7-47	কাকডাকা ভোর

L: The crow-call morning.
I: Early morning.
E: Crack of dawn.

7-48	কাকতালীয় ব্যাপার *	RL

L: The crow-palm fruit connection.
I: To assign a cause-and-effect relationship to coincidental events.
E: *cf.* If the cock crows on the dung heap, the weather will change or stay the way it is *[Ger.]*.

7-49	কাকের মুখে কৃষ্ণকথা	RL,SD,SB

L: The chanting of the good name of Krishna emanating from the crow's mouth.
I: High words from most unlikely low quarters.
Devil quoting scriptures.
The Bible as read by the devil *[Fch.]*.

7-50	কাগজে কলমে

L: Done with paper and pen.
I: In writing.
E: In black and white.

7-51	কাগটা দেখে মারল তীর বগটা গেল মরে

L: (He) shoots the arrow at the crow, and the crane is felled.
I: To not only miss the mark, but hit the wrong target.

E: Many a shot goes into the heather.
Trap made for some one, but got trapped someone else *[Ind.]*.

7-52 কাগের ঠ্যাং, বগের ঠ্যাং SD

L: Handwriting that resembles the walk of a crow or a crane (with inked feet) walking on a piece of paper.
I: Bad or unintellegible handwriting.
E: Higgledy piggledy writing.

7-53 কাজ আটকালে বুদ্ধি বাড়ে

L: When you are stuck in your project (without a solution), your brain rises to the occasion.
I: Necessity is the mother of invention.
E: Necessity is the mother of invention.

7-54 কাজও নাই, কামাইও নাই SD

L: If there is no job, then there is no absenteeism.
I: If there is no job, absence from job is meaningless.
E: No head, no headache.
He who doesn't plough won't make a crooked furrow *[Rus.]*.

7-55 কাজের মধ্যে দুই, খাই আর শুই RL,SD,SB

L: There are only two things to do, eating and sleeping.
I: For lazy people only two things are important, eating and sleeping.
E: *Cf.* Idle people have the least leisure.

7-56 কাজের সময় কাজী, কাজ ফুরোলে পাজি RL,SD,SB

L: When someone needs you for a task, you are the Esteemed One; as soon as you are finished, you are a scoundrel.
I: To get rid of one after he has served his purpose.
E: Ingratitude is the law of the world.
The father donated the vineyard to the son, the son didn't give bunch of grapes to the father *[Tur.]*.

7-57 কাঞ্চন দিয়ে কাঁচ কেনা   RL

L: To pay for glass with gold.
I: To pay handsomely for something worthless.

7-58 কাটা ঘায়ে নুনের ছিটা (দেওয়া)   RL,SD

L: To sprinkle salt on an open wound.
I: To inflict pain on someone already wounded.
E: To rub salt into the wound.
     Add insult to injury.
     To rub it in.
     Spread salt on the scar *[Uyg.].*

7-59 কাঠখড় পোড়ানো   SB

L: To burn firewood and hay.
I: To spend a great deal of effort and money on something.
E: To burn mid-night oil.
     To spare no effort.

7-60 কাঠবিড়ালীর সাগর বাঁধা *   RL,SD,SB

L: The squirrels building a bridge across the ocean.
I: Sum total of small efforts can be significant.
E: "Little drops of water, little grains of sand
     Make the mighty ocean, and the present land."
     Spits from the public becomes a lake *[Uyg.].*
     The man who removes a mountain begins by carrying
     away small stones *[Chi.].*
     If everyone gives one thread, the poor man will have a
     shirt *[Rus.].*

7-60 Old Howrah Bridge on River Hooghly, Kolkata.

7-61 কাঁঠালের আমসত্ত্ব x34-72   SD,SB

L: Mango jerky made from jackfruit.

I: Something elegant made from a poor substitute ingredient.

E: Silk purse out of sow's ear.
Iron wheel made of wood *[Hun.]*.

7-62 কান ঘুরিয়ে নাক দেখানো x35-18
SD

L: To point to one's nose with one's arm circled back round the ears.

I: An unnecessarily roundabout way of expressing something simple.

E: Shall we kill a snake and carry it in our hand when we have a bag for putting things in?

7-63 কান টানলে মাথা আসে   RL,SD,SB

L: If you pull someone by the ear, the head will follow.

I: Catch the associate to get to the key person .

7-64 কান শুনতে ধান শোনা   SB

L: Someone says "kaan" (ear), and you hear "dhaan" (rice paddy).

I: To mishear something in a way that changes the meaning completely.

7-65 কানা গরু বামুনকে দান   RL,SD,SB

L: To make a gift of a blind cow to the Brahmin (a priest).
I: To get something done by giving somebody a worthless thing in return.
E: To make sacrifice of a diseased sheep.

7-66 কানা ছেলের নাম পদ্মলোচন   RL.,SD

L: A blind boy is named Padmalochan (Lotus Eyes).
I: Name and character are at variance. A humorously inappropriate naming of something or somebody.
E: A porcupine speaking to its baby says, "O my child of velvet." *[Afg.].*
       Every beetle is a gazelle in the eyes of its mother *[Afr.].*
       The crow said, 'Oh! My snow-white child' *[Tur.].*

7-67 কানু ছাড়া গীত নাই   SD,SB

L: All the songs are about Kanu (Krishna).
I: Harping on the same tune. Focused on a single subject.
       Alt. Someone trying to establish his superiority in every area.
E: The bear knows seven songs and they are all about honey *[Tur.].*

7-68 কানে তালা দেওয়া

L: To lock up the ears.
I: Not to care about other's words.
E: To turn a deaf ear to.

7-69 কানে দিয়েছি তুলো, পিঠে বেঁধেছি কুলো   RL.SD,SB

L: I have plugged up my ears with cotton wads and tied a husking tray on my back.
I: To make oneself impervious to other people's words or opinions.

7-70 কায়েন মনসা বাচা [Sans.]

L: With body, mind and voice.
I: (To do/ pursue something) with single-minded devotion.
E: Full speed ahead.

7-71 কার ঘাড়ে কটা মাথা?   SD,SB

L: How many heads do any of you have on your shoulder (to be lopped off)?
I: Who is audacious enough (to have their head lopped off).
E: Who will bell the cat?

7-72 কার শ্রাদ্ধ কেবা করে, খোলা কেটে বামুন মরে   SD

L: Who is performing the last rites when the Brahmin (the priest) is busy cutting the shell of the banana plant?
I: The person whose responsibility it is to do something is not worried, and others are worrying about it.
E: Who's minding the store?

7-73 কারণ বিনা কার্য হয় না   SD

L: There is no effect without cause.
I: There is no effect without cause.
E: No smoke without a fire.

7-74 কারও পৌষ মাস, কারও সর্বনাশ   RL,SD,BDG,SB

L: One's harvest month (Po'ush) is another's complete devastation.
I: The same thing can be a bane to one and a boon to another.
E: One man's loss is another man's gain.

7-75 কালনেমির লঙ্কাভাগ *   RL,SD

L: Kalnemi's share of Lanka.
I: Making elaborate plans about something that is not yet yours.
E: To sell the skin before one has caught the bear.
   To count one's chickens before they are hatched.
   Don't share the skin while it's still on the bear [Pol.].

Don't worry about eggs that haven't been laid *[Ger.].*
Don't undo your bootlaces until you have seen the
river *[Inu.].*

7-76 কালবৈশাখীর ঝড় *

L: The fierce and portentous monsoon rainstorm of (the month of) Boishakh.
I: A dark and portentous phenomenon.
E: An omen.

7-77 কালাপানি পার হওয়া

L: To cross the black waters of the ocean to the Andamans (prison camp).
I: To be banished.
E: To be sent up the river.

7-78 কালার কাছে বলা আর অরণ্যে কাঁদা x 1-53   RL

L: To tell something to the deaf and to weep in a forest.
I: An ineffectual cry for help to someone or somewhere where help cannot materialize.
E: Cry in the wilderness.

7-79 কালি কলম পাত, তবে হয় লেখার জাত   SD

L: To write properly, you need ink, a pen and something to write on.
I: To do something well, you need all the right implements.

7-80 কালে না নোয়াইলে বাঁশ, বাঁশ করে টাস্ টাস্   SD,SB

L: If you do not bend a bamboo stalk in time (before it is mature), it snaps back (and does not yield).
I: If you do not teach (discipline, obedience etc.) at an appropriately young age, it will be too late afterwards.
E: Best to bend while it is a twig.
  If it does not bend as a sapling, will it when it is a tree? *[Ind.].*
  A young branch takes on all the bends one gives it *[Chi.].*
  If you refuse to be made straight when you are green, you will not be made straight when you are dry *[Afr.].*

A colt you may break, but an old horse you never can[*Fch.*]
Whilst childhood the rod has to be bended *[Fin.]*.
ct. You can bend an old tree, if you do it gradually *[Rus.]*.

7-81 কালের মন্দিরা
L: The cymbals of great Time.
I: The march of time.
E: The march of time.

7-82 কালো জগতের আলো
L: A person with a dark complexion (usually not preferred) lights up the world.
I: Someone out of favour may in fact be a beneficial person.
E: The blacker the berry the sweeter the juice *[AfrAm.]*.

7-83 "কি যাতনা বিষে বুঝিবে সে কিসে, কভু আশীবিষে দংশেনি যারে"
L: How would one know the pain from a snake bite if he has never been bitten?
I: You cannot understand hardship until you have faced it yourself.
E: Never criticize someone until you have walked two moons in his moccasins *[AmInd.]*.
The torment of the grave is known only by the corpse *[Afr.]*.

7-84 কিনতে পাগল, বেচতে ছাগল   RL,SD
L: One is in a mad rush to buy something, but is as harried as a goat when he tries to sell it.
I: It is much easier to buy something than to sell it. You pay a steep price when buying something, but do not get anything close to it when selling.
E: The buyer needs a hundred eyes, the seller but one.

7-85 কিম্ভুতকিমাকার   RL.SD
L: Grotesque and ugly.
I: Of strange and ugly form.
E: Ugly as a mine horse *[Hun.]*.

7-86 কিল খেয়ে কিল চুরি করা   RL,SD,BDG,SB

L: To receive blows, and remain quiet about it.
I: To quietly absorb an insult in order to save face.
E: To pocket an insult.

7-87 কিলিয়ে কাঁঠাল পাকানো   SD

L: To make a (green) jackfruit ripen by pounding on it.
I: To try to do the impossible by injudicious means. Trying
     to get result in vain before time.
E: To beat something into shape.
     You cannot rush a mango tree to ripen mangoes *[Ind.].*

7-88 কিস্তি মাত করা   SD

L: To check-mate.
I: To check-mate.
E: To check-mate.

7-89 কিষ্কিন্ধা কাণ্ড *   SD

L: The chapter of the epic Ramayana about the exploits of
     the monkeys in the battlefield.
I: A noisy, runaway melee.

7-90 কীটস্য কীট *[Sans.]*   SB

L: Smallest of insects.
I: An insignificant person.
E: A bit of a nobody.

7-91 "কুকুরের কাজ কুকুরে করেছে, কামড় দিয়েছে পায়;
তা বলে কুকুরে কামড়ানো কি মানুষের শোভা পায়"?

L: The dog has done what dogs do, bitten you in the leg. But
     that does mean that man should bite him back.
I: Don't get down to the level of your enemy.
E: *Ct.* Man bites dog.

7-92 কুকুরকে নাই দিলে কুকুর মাথায় ওঠে/ চড়ে x2-45 SD,SB

L: Indulge the dog and he will be dancing on your head.
I: Don't indulge those who should be kept in their place.

E: Jest with an ass, and he will flap you in the face with his tail.

7-93   কুকুরের পেটে ঘি সয় না   x11-15   RL,SD,SB

L: Ghee doesn't agree with a dog's stomach.

I: Fine things do not become a person who is not habituated to them. It harms to offer valuables to someone who is not accustomed to it.

E: An ass does not appreciate fruit compote *[Tur.]*.

7-94   কুকুরের লেজ ঘি দিয়ে ডল্‌লেও সোজা হয় না   RL,SD,SB

L: A dog's tail would not straighten even if you massage it with ghee.

I: You cannot change a person's basic nature.

E;   Straighten not the dog's tail even in a bamboo hollow.

7-95   কুটোটি নাড়ে না   SD,SB

L: Does not even move a twig.

I: Very lazy.

E: Lazybones.

7-96   কুড়ি পেরোলেই বুড়ি   SD

L: You are an old lady as soon as you have crossed twenty.

I: Youth is short-lived for females.

E: *Cf.* A woman over thirty who will tell her exact age will tell anything.

7-97   কুঁড়ের অন্ন হয় না

L: An idle person gets no rice (meals).

I: One has to earn his food.

E: You won't work, you shan't eat.
No bees, no honey; no work, no money *[Spa.]*.
No mill, no meal *[Spa.]*.
Earn and dine or else fast *[Tur.]*.

7-98   কুপুত্র যদিও হয়, কুমাতা কখনও নয়   SD

L: The son can be bad, but never the mother.

I: The mother is always without blemish.

E: The son may be bad, but the mother never.

7-99 কুমীরের সঙ্গে বাদ ক'রে জলে বাস   SD

L: You pick a quarrel with the crocodile, and then make water your home.

I: One cannot live quarreling with the local power.

E: It is hard to sit in Rome and strive with the Pope.

7-100 কুম্ভকর্ণের নিদ্রাভঙ্গ *   RL,SD,SB

L: The awakening of Kumbhakarna.

I: An event that takes a great deal of effort.

7-100 কুম্ভকর্ণের নিদ্রাভঙ্গ

7-101 কুম্ভীরাশ্রু ফেলা

L: To shed crocodile tears.

I: To show false (hypocritical) sorrow.

E: To shed crocodile tears.
Fox is sad for rabbit's death [Uyg.].

7-102 কুরুক্ষেত্র কাণ্ড *   RL.SD,SB

L: An affair like that of Kurukhestra.
I: To make an unnecessarily big fuss.
E: To make a federal case of something.

7-103 কুসংবাদ বাতাসের আগে/ ঘোড়ার আগে ছোটে

L: Bad news travels faster than the wind / a horse.
I: Bad news spreads fast.
E: Ill news runs apace.

7-104 কূপমণ্ডুক/ কুঁয়ার ব্যাঙ   SD

L: A frog that lives in the confinement of a well.
I: Narrow-minded person. A person who is ignorant
     because he is confined to a small perimeter.
E: A frog in a well-shaft seeing the sky *[Chi.]*
     Like a frog trapped under a coconut shell *[Indo.]*.
     The tortoise in its shell says, 'What a big place I live in'
     [Tur.].

7-105 কৃষ্ণের জীব   SD

L: A creature of Lord Krishna.
I: God's creature, one that should be treated with kindness.
E: God's creature.

7-106 কেঁচে গণ্ডূষ করা   x24-36   SD

L: To start again upon rinsing one's mouth (while dining).
I: To start again from the beginning.
E: To go back to Square One.

7-107 কেঁচো খুঁড়তে সাপ বেরোনো   SD,SB

L: A (deadly) snake pops out from the hole while digging for
     earthworm (fish bait).
I: A perfectly innocuous inquiry accidentally reveals some-
     thing completely unexpected and of a dark nature.
E: The seeking for one thing will find another.

7-108 কোকিল করে বাস, কাক করে বাসা RL,SD

L: The crow weaves a nest, the cuckoo lives in one (which he did not make).

I: The difference between passionate engagement and superficial action. Difference between toilers and parasites.

E: Men make houses, women make homes.

7-109 কোথাকার জল কোথায় গড়ায় RL,SD

L: Water from one place can find its way to other (strange) places.

I: An incident might lead to a surprising end.

E: Queer where a crooked path will sometimes take you [Rus.].

7-110 কোম্পানী কা মাল, দরিয়ামে ডাল [Hin.] x 24-22 RL,SD

L: If it belongs to the company, (you may even) pour it out into the river.

I: You can be extravagant in spending someone else's money/ resources to the point of wasting.

E: A borrowed mule soon gets a bad back [Syr.].

7-111 ক্ষুধার মত খাদ্য নেই, ঘুমের মত বিছানা নেই

L: No food as good as hunger, no bed as good as sleepiness.

I: Whatever satisfies your need best is the most desirable.

E: Hunger is the best sauce.

7-112 ক্ষেপা খুঁজে ফেরে পরশপাথর

L: The mad man roves, looking for the Philosopher's Stone.

I: A foolish person chases unrealistic (dreamy) goals.

E: Chasing the rainbow.

ৡৣঌ

8-1 খর নদীতে চর পড়ে না   SB

L: A fast-flowing river produces no sandbars.
I: A dynamic state avoids problems that result from stagna-
       tion.
E: A rolling stone gathers no moss.

8-2 খড়ম পায়ে দিয়ে গঙ্গা পার   MHP

L: To cross the Ganges wearing wooden sandals.
I;   To do the impossible.
E: There is no flying without wings [Fch.].

8-3 খড়ের গাদায় সুঁচ খোঁজা

L: Search for a needle in a haystack.
I: Wasting time on an insignificant problem that has no real
       solution.
E: Search for a needle in a haystack.
       Looking for fleas in the straw [Grk.].

8-4 খলের ছলের অভাব হয় না

L: There is no end to the trickery of a deceitful person.
I: A deceitful person is resourceful in his art.
E: He that waits to beat a dog will easily find a stick.

8-5 খাওন দেওয়ার মুরোদ নাই, কিল মারার গোঁসাই

L: A great one when it comes to beating up (his family), but
       has no ability to provide (for them).
I: An over aggressive master who has no competence to
       maintain his dependants.
E: Cf. If with the right hand you flog a child, with the left
       draw him to your breast [Yid.].
       Lentils are still in the market and the Brahmin is beating
       the wife (for the failure to cook them properly) [Ind.].

8-6 খাচ্ছিল তাঁতী তাঁত বুনে, কাল হ'ল তার এঁড়ে গরু কিনে

RL,SD

L: The weaver was making a decent living from his loom, but was doomed when he chose to invest in a worthless cow.

I: One should trade in his own profession.

E: Let the cobbler make the shoes.
Schoolmaster, stick to your books; farmer, to your pigs *[Chi.]*.

8-7 খাজনার থেকে বাজনা বেশী

SD,SB

L: The music is louder than the revenue.

I: The extravagance exceeds the meager income.

E: We celebrated at the wax door, and all the time the honeycomb was empty within *[Afr.]*.
The peg is greater than the stake *[Indo.]*.

8-8 খাটে খাটায় দ্বিগুণ পায়, বসে খাটায় অর্ধেক পায়

RL,SD

L: He who works as well as supervises (other workers) makes twice the wages; he who only supervises gets half the wages.

I: The leader should put his shoulder to the yoke also.

E: *Cf.* Lead by example *[Lat.]*.

8-9 খাবার সময় মস্ত হাঁ, উলু দেবার বেলায় মুখে ঘা

RL,SD,SB

L: When it is time to eat (at the festivities), one opens his mouth wide; when it is time to ululate (as a festive ritual), one feigns a soar mouth.

I: Not wanting to pay one's dues, but wanting the reward.

E: Industrious when it comes to food, lazy when it comes to work *[Uyg.]*.
Most people like short prayers and long sausages *[Ger.]*.

8-10 খাল কেটে কুমীর আনা

SD

L: Dig a canal to lead the crocodile in (from the river) to your own backyard (pond).

I: To bring calamity upon oneself by one's own foolish action.

E: To bring on calamity by one's own imprudence.

8-11 খালি কলসীর বাজনা বেশী/ বড়   RL,SD,SB

L: An empty pitcher makes loud noise.
I: Vapid people are more vocal.
E: Empty vessel sounds much.
Where the stream is the shallowest, greatest is the noise.
Empty barrel clacks the most *[Fin.]*.
An empty drum gives loud sound *[Indo.]*.

8-12 খালের জল বিলের জল এক

L: Water from the canal and water from the marsh is same.
I: No difference in water wherever it is found. Flood the great equalizer eliminates the distinction between different bodies of water.
E: Green leaves and brown leaves are from the same tree.

8-13 খিচুড়ি পাকানো   RL,SD,BDG

L: To make a khichuri (kedgeree) of things.
I: To make a jumbled mess of everything.
E: To make a hodgepodge of things.

8-14 খিদে থাকলে নুন দিয়ে খাওয়া যায়   SD

L: If you are hungry, you can eat (rice) with salt alone.
I: When your need is great, you will make do with whatever is on hand.
E: Hunger is the best sauce.
Hunger is the best chef *[Hun.]*.
If the camel is willing to eat, it will stretch its neck to the thorn *[Uyg.]*.

8-15 খেটে খাওয়া যাদের বরাত, কাটবে না তাদের দুখের রাত SB

L: If it is one's destiny to do hard labour for his meals, his night of misery will never end.
I: Once a toiler, always a toiler.
E: Once a toiler, always a toiler.

8-16 খোদায় মালুম

L: Khoda/ God only knows.
I: God only knows.

8-17 খোদার ওপর খোদকারী   SD

L: To out-God God.
I: To be overly smart in trying to alter the course of some
     natural development.
E: You can't outsmart God –*The Bible.*

8-18 খোশ খবরের মিথ্যাও/ ঝুটাও ভাল   SD

L: Entertaining or delightful news is welcome even if it is not
     true.
I: Good news is pleasing, even if it proves to be false.
E: *Cf.* Even if it's not true, it's a good story *[Ita.].*

8-19 খোসামোদে কে না ভোলে

L: Who doesn't fall for flattery?
I: Flattery will get you anywhere.
E: Flattery will get you everywhere.

৳০৫

9-1   গঙ্গাজলে গঙ্গাপূজা   x 7-2   SD,SB

L: Using an oblation of Ganges water to worship the River (goddess) Ganges.

I: To make an offering to please somebody, from out of that person's own resources.

9-2   গজকচ্ছপের যুদ্ধ বা লড়াই   SD,SB

L: The battle between and elephant and a tortoise.

I: A battle between two vastly unequal parties. A relentless encounter between unequals

E: Battle between David and Goliath.

9-3   গড্ ডলিকাপ্রবাহ   x 27-38   SD,SB

L: A herd of sheep following the leading ewe. A continuous flow.

I: Blind obedience to authority or custom and convention. A multitude of blind followers or their act of following en masse.

E: If one sheep leaps over the dyke, all the rest will follow. *Cf.* Unless you're the lead sledge dog, the view is pretty much the same *[Inu.]*.

9-4   গতস্য শোচনা নাস্তি   *[Sans.]*   RL,SD,BDG,SB

L: No use repenting over what has already happened.

I: No sense in regretting what is done.

E: Don't cry over spilt milk.
Let bygones be bygones.
Let the dead past bury its dead.
Do not rip up old sores.
A mill cannot grind with the water that is past.
What has been is gone *[Finn.]*.
What is there of crying when the birds ate the whole farm *[Ind.]*.

| 9-5 | গঙায় এঙা দেওয়া | | SD |

L: To appear to participate in a collective chorus by uttering only the ending sound.

I: To cleverly avoid doing work (in a group work) by presenting an appearance of working.

| 9-6 | গণ্ডারের চামড়া | | SD |

L: The skin of a rhinoceros.

I: Thick skin. Impervious to admonitions, insult etc.

E: Thick skin.

| 9-7 | গণ্ডেপিণ্ডে খাওয়া |

L: To eat full up to one's throat.

I: To overeat.

E: To stuff oneself.

| 9-8 | গদাইলস্করী চাল/ গজেন্দ্রগমন | | SD |

L: Acting like Mr. Godai Lashkar / Pace like the elephant king.

I: A slothful/ extremely sluggish person.

E: Slow coach.

Slower than molasses in January.

| 9-9 | গভীর জলের মাছ | | RL,SD,SB |

L: Deep-water fish.

I: A very shrewd person.

E: A tough customer.

The silent dog is the first to bite.

| 9-10 | গয়ার পাপী মুক্তি পায় না | | RL,SD |

L: A resident of Gaya (where everybody else comes to rceive absolution) who sins does not receive absolution.

I: One who is at the centre of activity does not benefit from it.

E: Closest to the temple, farthest from God.

9-11 গর্জন আছে বর্ষণ নাই   x29-7   SD

L: There is the roar of thunderous cloud, but no rain.
I: Noisy build-up with no actual follow through.
E: Big boast, small roast.

9-12 গরম ভাতে বিড়াল বেজার

L: The cat is unhappy that the rice is hot (too hot to eat).
I: When you are used to getting something the easy way, the slightest impediment makes you unhappy.
E: Sit a beggar at your table and he will soon put his feet on it *[Spa.]*.
     Don't tell a peasant how well cheese goes with pears *[Ita.]*.

9-13 গরীবের কথা বাসি হলে মিষ্টি লাগে   RL,SD

L: A poor man's advice tastes sweet when stale
I: An advice ignored because it was considered to be from an unimportant person may turn out to have been beneficial in retrospect.
E: Little enemies and little words must not be despised.

9-14 গরীবের ঘোড়া রোগ

L: A poor man has "horse disease" (addiction to horse racing).
I: Having a hobby that one can ill afford.

9-15 গরীবের রাংতাই সোনা   SD

L: For a poor man, aluminium foil has to do for gold.
I: You have to make yourself happy with what you have got.
E: A poor man is fain of little.

9-16 গরু খোঁজা করা   SD

L: To look for the lost cow.
I: To do a very extensive and diligent search.
E: To search high and low.

9-17 গরু থাকতে না বয় হাল, তার দুঃখ চিরকাল   RL

L: If he does not till his land while he has a cow, he will

88

always be miserable.

I: A person who cannot make use of available resources in a timely manner is doomed forever.

E: Make hay while the sun shines.

9-18 গলদ্ঘর্ম কলেবর

L: Body all covered in sweat.

I: Sign of having engaged in great effort.

E: Sweating bullets.

9-19 গলাধঃকরণ করা

L: To swallow something reluctantly.

I: To come to terms with something difficult or humiliating to accept.

E: Swallow one's pride.
Eat crow.
Eat humble pie.

9-20 গলায় কাঁটা ফুটলে বেড়ালের পায়ে পড়া   RL,SD,SB

L: When a fishbone is stuck in your throat, you plead with the (lowly) cat (to help take it out).

I: To seek help in a difficulty from one normally despised.

E: A drowning man clutches a straw.
A drowning man grips to his own hair *[Grk.]*.

9-21 গলায় গলায় ভাব

L: So friendly that they always have their arms round each other's neck.

I: Very friendly.

E: Hand in glove.
Bosom friends.

9-22 গল্পের গরু গাছে ওঠে x27-24   RL,SD

L: In a story, a cow is allowed to climb a tree.

I: In a fantasy, anything can happen.

E: "Anything can happen in a story – you can even meet a baboon shopping in town" – *Encouragement to young writers.*

9-23 গড়ার চেয়ে ভাঙ্গা সহজ

L: It is easier to tear down than to erect.

I: It is easier to destroy than to build.

E: It is easier to pull down than to build up [Lat.].

9-24 গাঁয়ে মানে না আপনি মোড়ল   RL,SD,SB

L: He fancies himself the headman even though the village does not acknowledge this.

I: A self-appointed leader whom no one acknowledges.

E: "I am the King of the mountain".

9-25 গাইতে গাইতে গায়েন, বাজাতে বাজাতে বাইন x1-50;30-13
RL,SD,SB

L: A great deal of singing makes a singer, a great deal of playing (an instrument) makes a musician.

I: To learn a skill you must practice a lot.

E: Practice makes perfect.
Practice makes master [Dan.].
Whilst doing one learns [Dut.].

9-26 গাছে কাঁঠাল গোঁফে তেল   RL,SD,BDG,SB

L: To apply oil to one's moustache (so that the sap would not stick to it) while the jackfruit is still up on the tree.

I: To make wishful preparation to enjoy something that is not yet yours to enjoy.

E: To count one's chickens before they are hatched.
Make not your sauce before you have caught the fish.
First catch the hare.
Don't bargain for fish that are still in water.
There is neither cotton nor thread, yet weavers are fighting [Ind.].
You don't have a wife or conception but you have named your son Somalingam [Ind.].
To be a hen feeler [Dut.].
Don't say 'hop' until you jumped over [Rus.].

9-27 "গাছে তুলে দিয়ে বধূ কেড়ে নিল মই" RL,SD,SB

L: The wife helps him up a tree with a ladder, then removes the ladder from under him.

I: To goad someone to do something, and then not stand behind him when he is helpless; to leave one stranded.

E: To leave someone in the lurch.
To send somebody up a creek without a paddle.
To leave someone holding the baby.

9-28 গাছে না উঠতেই এক কাঁদি x28-111 RL,SD

L: To get a bunch (of bananas) even before climbing the tree.

I: An unexpected benefit that falls on your lap even before starting your efforts to secure it.

E: A windfall.

9-29 গাছেরও খায়, তলারও কুড়ায় SD

L: He eats fruit from the tree as well as from (those fallen on) the ground.

I: Enjoys benefit twice over.

E: To have the cake and eat it too.
To have it both ways.
You can't have the bacon and the pig [Fch.].

9-30 গাধা পিটিয়ে ঘোড়া হয় না RL,SD

L: You cannot beat a donkey into (the shape of) a horse.

I: You cannot force an inferior thing to serve a superior purpose.

E: You cannot make a silk purse out of sow's ear.
You cannot turn a buzzard/ a dolt into a sparrowhawk [Fch.].

9-31 গায়ে জ্বর আসা SD

L: To catch fever.

I: To feel apprehensive to the point of physical discomfort at the thought of some impending (unpleasant or dreadful) experience.

E: Cf. To be on tenderhooks

9-32 গায় তো ভাল, কিন্তু থামতে জানে তো?

9-32 গায় তো ভাল, কিন্তু থামতে জানে তো?
L: He sings well, but does he know when to stop?
I: One should know when to stop
E: Too much of a good thing can be bad.

9-33 গায়ে পড়ে ভাব করা   SD
L: To cosy up to someone to make friends.
I: To overzealously seek someone's friendship.
E: To kiss up to someone.

9-34 গায়ে ফুঁ দিয়ে বেড়ানো   SD
L: To move about while blowing air (pleasingly) on oneself.
I: To move about freely and indifferently, avoiding respon-
     sibilities.
E: Footloose and fancy free.

9-35 গায়ের কালি ধুলে যায়, মনের কালি মরলে যায়   MHP
L: Filth from the body goes away with washing, filth in the
     mind only goes away with death.
I: It is not easy to change inherent bad nature.
E: Rain beats a leopard's skin, but it does not wash out the
     spots *[Afr.]*.

9-36 গায়ের গন্ধে ভুত পালায়   RL,SD
L: One's body odour is so foul that even ghosts are repelled.
I: The body odour is unbearable.
E: "Stinketh mightily".

9-37 গায়ের ঝাল মেটানো/ ঝাড়া   RL
L: To assuage the burning sensation in one's body.
I: To satisfy one's grudge by venting, fulminating etc.

9-38 গাল টিপলে দুধ বেরোয় x3-1   RL,SD
L: If you squeeze his cheeks, milk comes out (reference to an
     infant).
I: Said when a young person acts like an adult.

9-39 গালে চুনকালি দেওয়া   SD
L: To smear choon (white lime paste) and ink on one's
     cheeks.
I: To put someone to shame or disgrace.
E: To affix the scarlet letter.

9-40 গুড়ের গন্ধে পিঁপড়ে আসে   SD
L: The smell of jaggery attracts ants.
I: Your wealth attracts unwanted people.
E: Where there is sugar, there are bound to be ants *[Mal.]*.

9-41 গুরুচণ্ডালি দোষ SD

L: The guru (holy man)-chandal (a shabby indigent) incongruity.

I: The practice of mixing up formal or ornate elegant words with colloquial or slang ones in the same text. To mix the sublime and the mundane.

9-42 গুরুমারা বিদ্যা x24-70 RL,SD

L: Dexterity in excelling the master.

I: To surpass one's teacher in knowledge and learning.

E: The scholar may waur (be better than) the master.
Many a pupil has gained more wealth than his master
[Grk.].

9-43 গৃহিণী সচিব সখা প্রিয়শিষ্যা ললিতকলাবিধৌ [Skt.]

L: The wife is the trusted assistant, friend and the favourite disciple in the pursuit of the fine arts.

I: Your wife is your partner in every respect.

E: The Better Half!

9-44 গেঁয়ো যোগী ভিখ পায় না x5-2 RL,SD,BDG,SB

L: Nobody gives alms to the mendicant ascetic in his own village.

I: A wise man to the rest of the world, but not recognized as such in your immediate surroundings.

E: A prophet is never honoured in his own land.
A wiseman to the rest of the world, but a nobody at home
[Ind.].

9-45 গোঁফ দেখলেই শিকারী বিড়াল চেনা যায় SD

L: A hunting cat can be easily recognized by his moustache.

I: A telltale sign that reveals the true (crafty) nature of a person.

E: You can tell a true cowboy by the type of horse that he rides.

9-46 গোঁফে তা দেওয়া SD

L: To twist the ends of a (handlebar) moustache with one's fingers.

I: To display nonchalance, self-contentment or self-confidence.

E: To be sitting at the top of the world.

9-47 গোড়া কেটে আগায় জল RL,SD

L: To water the tip of a plant after severing its roots.

I: To try foolishly to revive something after administering such a foul measure as is sure to destroy it completely.

E: *Cf.* To close the stable door after the horse has bolted.

9-48 গোড়ায় গলদ x26-65 SD

L: The fault is at the very root.

I: The fault is at the very root.

E: Rotten to the core.
To make a mistake right off the bat.

9-49 গোদের ওপর বিষফোঁড়া RL,SD,SB

L: A poisonous boil growing over a gout.

I: Heaping of sorrow upon sorrow. Additional danger and pain.

E: Misfortune never comes alone.
Cf. It never rains but it pours.

9-50 গোবরগণেশ RL,SD

L: A Ganesh made of cow-dung.

I: A dull-headed man. Fat and lazy, mentally retarded man.

E: A schlemiel *[Yid.]*.

9-51 গোবরে পদ্মফুল x21-45 RL,SD,SB

L: Lotus blooming in a bed of cow-dung.

I: A great man, a beautiful girl or a handsome boy born in a low birth.

E: Diamond in the rough.
Primrose in a dunghill.

9-52 গোলাপেও কাঁটা আছে x11-9

SD

L: Even a rose has thorns.

I: Even in great beauty, there is hidden danger.

E: No rose without a thorn.
Every medal has its back *[Fch.]*.
No roses without thorns *[Dan.]*.

9-53 গোলে হরিবোল দেওয়া RL,SD

L: To say (just the refrain word) 'Haribol' in a (huge and noisy) gathering of chanting people.

I: To take advantage of a confusion. To exacerbate a mass confusion.

E: To fish in troubled waters.

9-54 গোল্লায় যাওয়া SD

L: Go to zero.

I: Reduce to nothing,

E: Go to dogs.

৮৩৫৯

10. ঘ

10-1 ঘটকালি করতে গিয়ে বিয়ে করে এল   RL,SD
L: To go to arrange a marriage and end up marrying one.
I: To help oneself to something that one was trusted to
procure for someone else.

10-2 ঘটে বুদ্ধি না থাকা
L: To have no smarts in (one's) water pitcher.
I: Said of not-too-bright a person.
E: Not the sharpest tool in the shed.
A few sandwiches short of a picnic.

10-3 ঘরপোড়া গরু সিঁদুরে মেঘ দেখলে ডরায়   RL,SD,BDG,SB
L: A cow that has been once burned out of his shed fears
even a crimson cloud.
I: After one terrible experience, a person sees fear in any-
thing even remotely reminiscent of it.
E: A burnt child dreads the fire.
Once bitten, twice shy.
Birds once saved fear all bushes.
Once burned by milk, you will blow on cold water *[Rus.]*.
Having been bitten by a snake, he is afraid of a rope *[Afg.]*.
A scalded cat flees from cold water *[Spa.]*.
The one burnt by (hot) milk drinks even cold buttermilk
with precaution *[Ind.]*.
Onece bitten by a snake, forever nervous at the sight of a
coiled cord *[Chi.]*.
Who has burnt is scared of fire *[Hun.]*.
They don't talk about ropes in the house of a man hanged
[Rus.].

10-4	ঘরে আগুন দেওয়া

L: To set fire to someone's house.
I: To ruin one's domestic happiness.
E: To be a home-wrecker.

10-5	ঘরে বসে রাজা উজীর মারা	SD

L: An ordinary person sitting in his ordinary home, talking big - as if he is peer to kings and ministers.
I: A person full of hot air.
E: To solve all the problems of the world.

10-6	ঘরের লক্ষ্মী পায়ে ঠেলা x35-27	SD, SB

L: To (disrespectfully) push away Lakshmi (the household goddess of wealth) with one's feet.
I   To not value the good fortune that one already has achieved. To neglect the existing beneficial situation.

10-7	ঘরের ভাত খেয়ে বনের মোষ তাড়ানো x34-55	RL,SD,SB

L: To eat the daily meal served at home, and then set out to shoo away wild buffaloes.
I: To needlessly venture out of one's secure life and find something spurious to do just to feel useful.
E: He who scrubs the head of an ass wastes his time and effort *[Ital.]*.
     Eats food at home and lays eggs outside *[Uyg.]*.

10-8	ঘরের শত্রু বিভীষণ *	SD,SB

L: Bibhishan, the enemy within your own home.
I: An enemy within a family or group.
E: A thousand enemies outside the house is better than one within.
     Snake in the grass.
     Judas.

10-9	ঘস্‌তে ঘস্‌তে পাথরও ক্ষয় হয়	RL,SD

L: Constant rubbing wears out even a stone.
I: Persistent action, even with small effect, can have great impact over a period of time.

E: Constant dripping wears out the stone.
Little strokes fell great oaks.
The path is made by walking *[Afr.]*.

10-10 পুকুর ঘাট (Bathing place or a landing place)

10-10 ঘাটে এসে নাও ডোবানো   SD
L: To scuttle the boat right near the jetty.
I: To spoil some project just as it was being completed.
E: To upset the apple cart.

10-11 ঘাম দিয়ে জ্বর ছাড়া   RL,SD
L: A profuse sweating at last relieves the fever completely.
I: An emphatic end of a bad streak. To feel relief at last.
E: To have an end of troubles.

10-12 ঘাস কাটা কঠিন কাম, ঠস্‌কি ঠস্‌কি পরে ঘাম

L: Mowing the grass is such hard work that it makes one drip sweat.

I: Even a trifling work makes one all tired (when he is not used to it).

10-13 ঘুঘু দেখেছ ফাঁদ দেখনি   SD,SB

L: You have seen the pigeon (the bait), but not the trap!

I: You are advancing too greedily to see the danger ahead.

E: *cf.* The fish sees the bait not the hook, man sees not the danger – only profit *[Mon.]*.

10-14 ঘুঁটে পোড়ে গোবর হাসে   x 6-4; 12-5   RL,SD

L: As the dried dung-cake (a household cooking fuel) burns, freshly dropped cow-dung smiles in amusement.

I: To relish watching someone's ill fate that is sure to befall you one day.

E: To smile at another's woe.
    Mock not the fallen, for slippery is the road ahead of you *[Rus.]*.

10-15 ঘুঁটের মালা পরানো

L: To put a garland of dried cow-dung cakes around someone's neck.

I: To insult one in public for some misdeed.

E: To tar and feather someone.

10-16 ঘুষ পেলে আমলা তুষ্ট   RL,SD

L: Bureaucrats are gratified by bribes.

I: Every man has his price.

E: Every man has his price.
    Bribery makes a bureaucracy run.

10-17 ঘোড়া চিনে কানে, আর দাতা চিনে দানে   SD

L: A horse is known by his ears, a donor by his giving.

I: A quality should be judged by its proper indicator.

E: A man is judged by his deeds, not by his words *[Rus.]*.
    Judge not the horse by his saddle *[Chi.]*.

A good archer is not known by his arrow, but by his aim
[Tur.].

10-18 ঘোড়া ডিঙ্গিয়ে ঘাস খাওয়া   RL,SD,SB, MW
L: To reach over a horse to eat grass.
I: To defy one's immediate superior.
E: To go over the head of.

10-19 ঘোড়া দেখলে খোঁড়া হয়   RL,SD
L: As soon as one sees a horse, one pretends to be lame.
I: To make excuses not to work when there is somebody to
        do it for you.

10-20 ঘোড়ার ডিম   RL,SD,BDG,SB, MW
L: Horse's egg
I: Absurd thing. Something non-existent. Nil. Nothing.
E: Goose egg.

10-20 ঘোড়ার ডিম?

10-21 ঘোমটার ভিতর খেম্‌টা নাচ   x17-4   RL,SD
L: A sleazy dance behind a veil of modesty.
I: Improper business going on under a noble cover.
E: Coquetry under the disguise of modesty.

10-22 ঘোল খাওয়ানো   SD
L: To make someone drink ghol (buttermilk).

I: To put someone to trouble.

E: To rub someone's nose in 'it.'

10-23 ঘোলা পানিতে মাছ শিকার   x13-9

L: To fish in muddied waters.

I: To exploit a turmoil to extract some gains.

E: To fish in troubled waters.

         Fishing in mucky water *[Indo.]*.

10-24 ঘ্রাণেন অর্ধ ভোজনম্   *[Sans.]*   SD

L: Half the eating is in smelling the food.

I: There are different stages of relishing something.

ৎ৩৫

11-1 চক্‌ চক্‌ করলেই সোনা হয় না SB

L: Just because it glitters, it is not gold.
I: All that glitters is not gold.
E: All that glitters is not gold.
Not all that glitters is gold *[Hun.]*.
Not every glittering thing is gold *[Rus.]*.
Appearance is deceptive *[Fch.]*.

11-2 চক্রবৎ পরিবর্তন্তে সুখানি চ দুঃখানি চ *[Sans.]* x2-25

L: Happy times and sad times change like the turn of a wheel.
I: Weal and woe come by turns.
E: Weal and woe come by turns.

11-3 চক্ষুকর্ণের বিবাদ ভঞ্জন SD

L: Resolving the dispute between the eyes and the ears.
I: Satisfying oneself as to the true nature of something when what is seen and what is heard are at odds.
E: The ears deceive, the eyes not *[Mon.]*.

11-5 চক্ষুদান করা SD

L: Bestowing eye sight. To steal.
I: To cast a glance with a view to stealing.
E: Five-finger discount.

11-6 চরকিপাক ঘোরানো x19-1;26-11 SD

L: To make someone go round like a spinning firework (Catherine-wheel).
I: To extremely harass someone.
E: To run someone rugged.
To make someone jump through the hoops.

| 11-7 | চৈরেবেতি চৈরেবেতি | [Sans.] |

L: Keep walking, always keep walking.

I: Keep moving, do not stagnate.

E: Be not afraid of growing slowly, be afraid only of standing still [Chi.].

The moon moves slowly, but it crosses the town [Afr.].

Allah has said:"Start moving so that I may start blessing." [Afg.].

The air of heaven is that which blows between a horse's ears [Ara.].

The wagon rests in winter, the sleigh in summer, the horse never [Yid.].

| 11-8 | চন্দ্রসূর্যে চাবি দেওয়া |

L: Winding up (as a clock) the sun and the moon.

I: Mocking description of the duties of a person who claims to be very important.

E: The sun sets without thy assistance. — *Talmud*

| 11-9 | চাঁদেও কলঙ্ক আছে | x9-53 | | SD |

L: Even the moon has blemishes.

I: Nobody is faultless.

E: There are lees in every wine.

No rose is without thorns.

There are spots even in the sun.

There is no ivory that is not cracked [Indo.].

| 11-10 | চাঁদের হাট | x5-3 | | RL,SD |

L: A gathering place of moons.

I: Lots of beautiful women gathered in one place.

Pretty maidens all in a row.

| 11-11 | চাচা আপন প্রাণ বাঁচা | | RL,SD,BDG,SB |

L: Uncle save your own life first.

I: Self-preservation comes first.

E: Every man is for himself.

11-12 চালশে ধরা

L: Suffer from the degradation of the eye after the age of forty.
I: To display symptoms of advancing age.
E: "These old bones . . .".

11-13 চালুনী বলে ছুঁচ তোর পেছনে কেন ছেঁদা ×12-5;6-4 RL,SD,SB

L: The sieve asks a needle, 'Why is there a hole at your end'?
I: One who is himself corrupt criticizes a less corrupt person
E: Pot calling the kettle black.
The frying-pan says to the kettle: "Avaunt, black brows!" *[Ara.]*.
One camel does not make fun of another camel's hump *[Afr.]*.
"Your feet are crooked, your hair is good for nothing," said the pig to the horse *[Rus.]*.
'Pot, your bottom is black'. ' Your's is blacker than me' *[Tur.]*.
The donkey called the rooster a bighead *[Grk.]*.

11-14 চালে ভুল করা

L: To make a wrong move
I: To make a wrong move
E: To make a wrong move.

11-15 চাষা কি জানে কর্পূরের গুণ? ×7-93   SD

L: Does the farmer know the fine qualities of camphor?
I: Can an unrefined person understand the value of fine things?
E: what does a monkey know of the taste of ginger *[Ind.]*.
Like cumin in the mouth of an elephant *[Nep.]*.
What farmer doesen't know, he doesn't eat *[Dut.]*.

11-16 চিচিং ফাঁক

L: Open up, Chiching!
I: A secret command that makes a door open.
E: Open Sesame.

11-17 চিত্রগুপ্তের খাতা * SD
L: Chitragupta's Ledger.
I: A legendary chronicle of man's deeds. Everybody's doings are being credited for judgement after death.
E: *cf.* The Pearly Gate.

11-18 চিনির বলদ x7-34 RL,SD,SB
L: A beast of burden (ox) carrying sugar sacks.
I: One who toils to bring amenities to others but cannot enjoy them himself.
E: The ox in the grain heap, Tantalus amidst the waves [*Lat.*].

11-19 চুক আছে বুধ নাই তারে কয় চুকুমবুধাই
I: He who has a foul temper (*chook*) and no good sense (*boodh*) is called a *chookumboodhai*.
I: A quick-tempered person who does not think before lashing out.
E: A headstrong man and a fool may wear the same cap. A fool shows his annoyance at once, but a prudent man overlooks an insult.

11-20 চুরি বিদ্যা বড় বিদ্যা যদি না পড়ে ধরা RL,SD
L: Thieving is a great skill as long as you don't get caught.
I: No art succeeds so well as the art of stealing, only if you escape detection.
E: A thief is a king till he is caught [*Per.*].

11-21 চুল নেই তার টেরি কাটা/ তার খোঁপা বাঁধা RL,SD,SB
L: One who has little hair wants to pompadour it, one who has cropped hair wants to coif it.
I: A person tries to compensate for the lack of something by exaggerating what little he has of it.

11-22 চুলচেরা হিসেব RL
L: Hair-splitting calculation.
I: To be ungenerously mindful of one's own interest down to the smallest detail.
E: Splitting hair.

11-23 চেনা বামুনের পৈতে লাগে না RL,SD,SB

L: The familiar Brahmin doesn't need to show his sacred thread (to prove that he is a Brahmin).
I: If people already know you for who you are, you don't have to prove anything.
E: Good wine / poon needs no bush.
A tiger does not have to proclaim its tigritude [Afr.].

11-24 চেষ্টার অসাধ্য কাজ নেই SD

L: There is nothing undoable if you try hard enough.
I: Try your best, and you will win.
E: If at first you don't succeed, try try try again.

11-25 চোখ চায় সে পায়, চোখ বোজে সে হারায়

L: One who keeps his eyes peeled gets, one who blinks loses.
I: One who is alert can gain opportunity; if not, he loses out on such.
E: He who hesitates is lost.
Opportunity doesn't knock twice.
Opportunity comes but does not linger [Nep.].
He who searches for pearls should not sleep [Lyb.].

11-26 চোখ থাকতে কাণা RL,SD

L: To be blind even as one has his eyes intact.
I: To fail to observe something that is happening right before one's eyes.
E: None so blind as those who won't see.

11-27 চোখ মনের আয়না

L: The eye is the mirror to the mind.
I: The eye reflects what you are thinking.
E: The eye is the witness of the heart [Ger.].

11-28 চোখে ধুলো দেওয়া RL,SD,SB

L: To throw dust into one's eyes.
I: To hoodwink or fool someone.
E: To pull wool over one's eyes.

11-29 চোখে মুখে কথা কওয়া   SD

L: To speak with both eyes and lips.

I: To speak animatedly.

11-30 চোখে সর্ষেফুল দেখা   SD,SB

L: To espy a field of mustard in bloom.

I: To become stunned/ shocked to the point of fainting. To be dazzled on being stricken with fear. To find everything falling to ruin.

E: To have the wind knocked out of you.

11-31 চোখের আড়াল হলেই মনের আড়াল   SD

L: Out of sight is out of mind.

I: Out of sight, out of mind.

E: Out of sight, out of mind.
Present to the eye, present to the mind [Chi.].
Far from the eyes, far from the heart [Ital.].
If the eyes don't see, the heart won't care [Hai.].
Out of eye, out of heart [Dut.].

11-32 চোখের কাজল চুরি করা x28-99

L: To steal the kajal (kohl) from one's eye.

I: To steal something precious right from under one's nose.

E: Take the bread out of somebody's mouth.
He would cheat a heron of her egg, though her two eyes were fixed on him.
He can cheat a fish out of its skin [Rus.].
He steals the mascara from her eyes [Ara.].

11-33 চোখের চামড়া নেই/ চোখের পর্দা নেই   MW

L: There is no skin covering (his/her) eyes.

I: He/she has no sense of shame.

E: Thick skinned.

11-34 চোখের জলে নাকের জলে এক করা   SD

L: Tears and nasal discharge mingling (on one's face).

I: To be visibly and emotionally upset. To be in a distressing quagmire.

E: In a state.

11-35 চোখের মণি

11-35 চোখের মণি x34-13

L: Jewel of one's eyes.
I: A most loved person.
E: Apple of one's eyes.

11-36 চোদ্দ পুরুষ উদ্ধার করা

L: To cause the salvation of someone's fourteen preceding generations.
I: To severely abuse someone verbally.
E: To rip someone apart.

| 11-37 | চোর পালালে বুদ্ধি বাড়ে | SD, SB, MW |

L: One becomes smarter (about securing one's home) after the thief has already fled.
I: Getting wise after the event.
E: To bar the door after the horse has bolted.
To lock the stable after the mare is stolen.
To fill the well after the calf has drowned *[Dut.]*.
Experience is the comb that nature gives us when we are bald *[Bel.]*.
Mustard after meal *[Dut.]*.

| 11-38 | চোরকে বলে চুরি করতে, গৃহস্থকে বলে সজাগ হ'তে | RL, SD |

L: (He) tells the thief to steal, and the home-owner to be on guard.
I: To simultaneously instigate two contending parties against each other.
E: To run with the hare and hunt with the hounds.
To tell the dog to catch, and the rabbit to run *[Aze.]*.
One must spare both the goat and the cabbage *[Fch.]*.

| 11-39 | চোরা না শোনে ধর্মের কাহিণী | RL, SD, SB |

L: A thief does not listen to religious readings.
I: A rogue does not listen to a saint's advice.
E: The devil will not listen to the scripture.

| 11-40 | চোরে চোরে মাসতুতো ভাই | RL, SD, BDG, SB |

L: Thieves are like maternal cousins.
I: There is a kinship among thieves.
E: Birds of a feather flock together.
All thieves are cousins.
A thief knows a thief as a wolf knows a wolf *[Per.]*.
The wolf and the shaman are of one nest *[Inu.]*.
The crow does not take the eye out of another crow *[Grk.]*.
Those who look alike associate together *[Fch.]*.

| 11-41 | চোরের ওপর বাটপারি | RL, SD |

L: Swindling of a thief.
I: One crook deceives another.

E: A swindler robs a thief.
One thief robs another.
cf. It is no crime to steal from a thief *[Spa.]*.

11-42 চোরের ধন বাটপারে খায়   RL,SD
L: The loot of a thief ends up being enjoyed by a swindler.
I: It is not easy to enjoy ill-gotten gains.
E: Ill-got, ill-spent.
Ill gotten goods never thrive.
The receiver is as bad as the thief.

11-43 চোরের মন বোঁচকার দিকে   RL,SD,SB
L: A thief's thoughts are focused on your chest.
I: Selfish people always think only about their own interest.
E: The tongue always returns to the aching tooth.

11-44 চোরের মন পুঁই আদাড়ে   RL,SD
L: The thief's mind is always in the dunghill.
I: The guilty mind is always suspicious.
E: The guilty conscience pricks the mind.

11-45 চোরের মায়ের বড় গলা x24-3   RL,SD
L: The mother of a thief speaks at the top of her voice.
I: Somebody who is guilty speaks with the loud voice of sanctimony.
E: The faulty stands on his guard.
It is the hen which sings which has laid the egg *[Fch.]*.
Goodness speaks in a whisper, evil shouts *[Tib.]*.
He who blabs is the guilty party *[Chi.]*.
The guilty dog barks the loudest *[Ara.]*.

11-46 চোরের লাভ রাত্রিবাস   RL,SD
L: Spending a night in the house is the net gain of the thief (when he could not steal anything).
I: A small gain when the desired big gain did not materialize (he did not steal but had free accommodation for the night).

৩০৯

12. ছ

| 12-1 | **ছলে বলে কৌশলে** | SD |

L: Through trickery, force or tact.
I: By any means.
E: By hook or by crook.

| 12-2 | **ছাই ফেলতে ভাঙ্গা কুলো** | SD,BDG,SB |

L: A broken tray to (scoop up and) discard a pile of ash.
I: To employ an insignificant person to perform something unimportant.
E: Use a gofer.

| 12-3 | **ছাইচাপা আগুন** | SD |

L: Fire hidden under ashes.
I: Some big problem smoldering just under the surface. A latent quality or suppressed feeling.
E: Trouble brewing.

| 12-4 | **ছাত্রানাম্ অধ্যয়নং তপঃ** [Sans.] |

L: Studying is the religion of the students.
I: Studying should be the main preoccupation of students.
E: Those who do not study are only cattle dressed in men's clothes [Chi.].
If you do not study hard when young you'll end up bewailing your failures as you grow up [Chi.].
A jade stone is useless before it is processed, a man is good-for-nothing until he is educated [Chi.].

| 12-5 | **ছুঁচ বলে চালুনী, তোর পেছনে কেন ছেঁদা?** x11-3;6-4 | SD |

L: The needle asks the sieve, Why do you have holes?
I: To be concerned of some shortcoming in others that you too have.
E: Pot calling the kettle black.

One camel does not make fun of another camel's hump [*Afr.*].

'Pot, your bottom is black'. 'Your's is blacker than me' [*Tur.*].

The donkey called the rooster a bighead [*Grk.*].

12-6 ছুঁচ হয়ে ঢোকে, ফাল হয়ে বেড়োয়   RL,SD,SB

L: Goes in (easily) as a (tiny) needle, emerges as a tilling plough.

I: A person who gains your confidence as an innocuous comer to later grow to be a formidable enemy and cause harm.

E: Give him an inch and he will take an ell.

If the camel once gets his nose in the tent, his body will soon follow [*Ara.*].

Evil enters like a needle and spreads like an oak tree [*Afr.*].

Little by little, the camel gets into the couscous [*Afr.*].

12-7 ছুঁচোয় যদি আতর মাখে, তবু কি তার গন্ধ ঢাকে?   MHP

L: If the mole puts perfume on, would it cover his stench?

I: It is difficult to cover up obvious bad behaviour.

12-8 ছুঁচো মেরে হাত গন্ধ করা x28-26   RL,SD

L: To have a foul-smelling hand from quashing a mole to death.

I: To tarnish oneself by undertaking a revengeful task that was not worth the trouble.

E: Sue a beggar and get a louse.

12-9 ছেঁড়া কাঁথায় শুয়ে লাখ টাকার স্বপ্ন দেখা   RL,SD,SB

L: (A poor man) lying on his tattered kantha, dreams of lakhs of rupees.

I: A person of meager means unrealistically dreaming of great riches.

E: He sleeps in the dunghill but dreams of becoming the grand vizier [*Tur.*].

A hungry hen dreams of a barley barn [*Tur.*].

Soak the bread with the soup of a flying duck [*Uyg.*].

Hungry pig dreams of acorns [*Hun.*].

12-10 ছেঁড়া পাতা জোড়া লাগে না x27-15 SD

L: A torn page/ leaf can't be pasted back together.
I: Something that is broken cannot be restored to its original state.
E: You cannot unscramble an egg.

12-11 ছেড়ে দে মা কেঁদে বাঁচি RL,SD

L: Mother, please let me off the hook this time, l will have a good cry (as my punishment).
I: Please let me off the hook.
E: I don't want the cheese, I just want to get out of the trap *[Spa.]*.

12-12 ছেলে শিখবে লেখাপড়া, মেয়ে শিখবে রান্নাবাড়া SB

L: The son should learn to read and write, the daughter should learn to cook.
I: A motto of the male-chauvinistic society of yore.
E: A daughter should be pretty and a son skilled *[Nep.]*.
The son will learn from his father to make a living, the daughter will learn from her mother to cut clothes *[Tur.]*.

12-13 ছেলেরা হীরের আংটি, মেয়েরা মাটির কলসী SB

L: The boys are (valued as) diamond rings; the girls are (treated as) earthen pots.
I: Different value of male and female offspring.
E: *cf.* Your son is your son until he takes a wife, but your daughter is your daughter all your life.

12-14 ছোট মুখে বড় কথা RL,SD,SB

L: Big talk from a small mouth.
I: To greatly exceed one's place.
E: To exceed one's place.

12-15 ছোটলোকের কথা, কচ্ছপের মাথা

L: What the riffraff say is of no more weight than the head of a turtle.
I: This person's words can be dismissed out of hand.

ছ্যাকড়া গাড়ির ঘোড়া

L: The horse that pulls a ramshackle wagon or a jalopy.
I: A person who is not good for much. Slow in work, walk.

Kolkata mid 1940s: Traffic control was an easy matter.

৩৫

13-1 জগদ্দল পাথর SD

L: A very heavy piece of rock (placed on the chest of an offender as punishment).

I: A very heavy and punitive burden that is difficult to get rid of.

E: An albatross around one's neck.

13-2 জগাখিচুড়ি SD

L: A multi-ingredient khichuri (kedgeree).

I: An odd/ incongruous mix of things

E: A hodgepodge.

13-3 জড়ভরত SD

L: Inactive or indolent Bharat (a hero of the Ramayana).

I: An incapacitated person. A person unwilling to take an active role when called for.

13-4 "জননী জন্মভূমিশ্চ স্বর্গাদপি গরীয়সী" [Sans.] RL,SD

L: Mother and motherland are nobler than even heaven.

I: Mother and motherland are nobler than even heaven.

E: " My country 'tis of thee . . . I sing."
Heaven is at the feet of mothers [Ara.].
God could not be everywhere and therefore he made mothers [Jew.].
There is no love like mother's nor place like homeland [Tur.].

13-5 জন্ম মৃত্যু বিয়ে, তিন বিধাতা নিয়ে SD

L: Birth, death and marriage - these three things concern God.

I: The vital events of life are God's domain.

E: Marriage and shroud come from heaven [Spa.].

Born, baptized or in the earth laid – always the priest has to be paid *[Rus.]*.
Only three things in life are certain birth, death and change *[Ara.]*.

"জন্মিলে মরিতে হবে, অমর কে কোথা কবে"

L: If you have been born, you will have to die, who can ever be immortal anywhere?

I: Death is inescapable.

E: "Where-so-ever ye be, death will overtake you, even though ye be in lofty towers" -*The Qoran*.
St. Luke was a saint and a physician and he died.
Death is a black camel that lies down at every door, sooner or later you must ride the camel *[Ara.]*.

13-7 জরু, গরু, ধান, তিন রাখ বিদ্যমান

L: A wise man safeguards three things especially: his wife, his cattle and his rice fields.

I: If you do not keep under control your wife, your cows and your rice fields, they will either create problems for you or be stolen.

E: Having a good wife and rich cabbage soup, seek no other thing *[Rus.]*.
May you have kindness in your heart, a plump woman in your furs, and seal meat in you larder *[Inu.]*.

13-8 জল আর তেল, ঢেলে দিলেই গেল   SD

L: Water and oil - once poured it is gone for ever.

I: Some things, once done, cannot be undone.

E: Think before you act.

13-9 জল ঘোলা করে মাছ শিকার x10-23   SB

L: To fish after muddying the water.

I: To achieve something on the sly.

E: To fish in muddied water.
To fish in troubled waters.
In troubled water there's good fishing *[Rus.]*.

13-10 জলবৎ তরলম্ *[Sans.]*

L: As liquid (clear) as water.
I: Something made abundantly clear. Very easy.
E: Clear as crystal.
It hangs like a privy over a ditch *[Dut.]*.

13-11 জলে কুমীর, ডাঙ্গায় বাঘ   RL,SD,BDG,MW

L: (To be caught between) a crocodile in water and a tiger on
the land.
I: To be caught between two dangerous options.
E: Between the horns of a dilemma.
Between the devil and the deep blue sea.
Between a rock and a hard place.
Between Scylla and Charybdis.
Hobson's choice.
Between the hammer and the anvil *[Pol.]*.
If you spit downward, you hit the beard, if you spit
upwards the moustache *[Tur.]*.

13-12 জলে তেলে মিশ খায় না   RL,SD

L: Water and oil do not mix.
I: Dissimilar things do not mix. Some things do not work
well together. Two people who cannot get along.
E: Oil and water do not mix.
Like water and oil *[Indo.]*.

13-13 জলে বাস করে কুমীরের সাথে বিবাদ   SD,SB

L: Pick a fight with the crocodile while living in water.
I: To act in an unwise way to make your circumstances work
against you.
E: It is ill sitting at Rome and striving with the Pope.

13-14 জলের আরেক নাম জীবন

L: Another name for water is life.
I: Water is life-giving. One cannot live without water.
E: Water of life.

13-15 জহরীই জহর চেনে

L: A jeweller can (best) recognize a jewel.

I: He can judge something best who has some knowledge about it.

E: The donkey recognizes the tracks of a horse *[Mon.]*.

13-16 জানু, ভানু, কৃশানু, শীতের পরিত্রাণ   KH,RL,SD

L: The sun, your knees and open fire – these are your protection against bitter cold.

I: To escape bitter cold, sit in the sun or near a fire with your head tucked between your knees.

E: The head and feet keep warm, the rest will take no harm.

13-17 জাবর কাটা

L: To chew the cud.

I: To talk about things past. To ruminate or reminisce. To be nostalgic.

E: Walk down memory lane.

13-18 জাহান্নামে যাওয়া

L: To end up in hell.

I: To come to a ruinous end.

E: To go to dogs.

13-19 জিগির তোলা

L: To raise a loud clamour/ hue and cry.

I: To spread a viewpoint noisily.

E: Get on a soapbox.

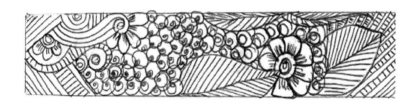

13-20 জিলিপির প্যাঁচ

13-20 জিলিপির প্যাঁচ x24-79   SD
L: The intricate/ tortuous coiling of the sweetmeat jilebi.
I: Crookedness and duplicity.
E: Sly as a fox.

13-21 জীব দিয়েছেন যিনি, আহার দেবেন তিনি   RL,SD
L: He who has created life will also provide food.
I: God will look after our practical needs.
E: God never sends mouth but He sends meat.
God gave teeth, He will give bread.
God gave burdens, also shoulder *[Yid.]*.

13-22 জীবনমরণ সমস্যা
L: Life-and-death situation or problem.
I: A very precarious problem.
E: Life-and-death situation.

13-23 "জীবনের ধন কিছুই যাবে না ফেলা"
L: Nothing of the wealth (knowledge, lesson etc) one gathers in life will go to waste.
I: Every life experience counts for something.
E: Everyday of your life is a page of your history *[Ara.]*.

13-24 জীবিকা নির্বাহ করা

L: To carry on with one's livelihood.
I: To manage to earn a living.
E: To earn a living.

13-25 "জীবে প্রেম করে যেই জন, সেই জন সেবিছে ঈশ্বর"

L: One who cares for the living is serving the God.
I: If you want to be virtuous, care for your fellow men.
E: Serve your fellow men.

13-26 জুতো মেরে গরু দান   RL,SD, SB

L: Strike someone with a shoe (symbolic of utter disrespect), then offer a cow as a solace.
I: Try to compensate someone after insulting him.
E: Steal a goose and give the giblets in alms.
    He gives him roast meat and beats him with the spit *[Per.]*.

13-27 জুতো সেলাই থেকে চণ্ডী পাঠ

L: From mending shoes to reading from the Chandi (the scripture).
I: (Being able to do everything) from the most mundane to the most sublime. Efficient in all kind of jobs.
E: Jack of all trades.

13-28 জুতোর আবার পাখনা   SB

L: Shoes having wings.
I: Audacity of the lower class people.

13-29 জুতোর সুকতলা খুইয়ে দেওয়া

L: To wear out the soles of one's shoes.
I: To have to do a great deal of legwork because of the callousness of the bureaucracy.
E: To get the runaround.

13-30 জোঁকের মুখে নুন পড়া   SD

L: To apply salt to the mouth of a leech.
I: To apply a fatal countermeasure to a threat.
E: To make someone curl away and die.

13-31 জোয়ারের জল, নারীর যৌবন

L: The youth of a woman is as effusive as a rising tide.
I: The surging and ephemeral nature of youth.
E: *cf.* Time and tide for no man bide.

13-32 জোর যার মুল্লুক তার x26-78; 29-45

RL,SD,BDG,SB,MW

L: The one with the muscle bosses over the territory.
I: The powerful prevails.
E: Might is right.

Kolkata mid 1940s: Individual's picture being taken was not such a common occurance.

14-1 ঝড়ে কাক মরে, ফকিরের কেরামতি বাড়ে *   SD,SB
L: The stork is felled by the storm, but the Fakir gets the credit.
I: Misplaced or mis-claimed credit for an action.
E: The pot cooks, the plate gets the name.

14-2 ঝাঁকের কই ঝাঁকে যায়   RL,SD
L: A stray koee fish always returns to its shoal.
I: A stray member of a collective has an affinity for that collective.
E: The sheep returning to the flock.
     Birds of a feather flock together.
     The same kind of bird will fly together *[Fin.]*.

14-3 ঝাড়া হাত পা   SD
L: Hands and legs shaken clean.
I: One with no encumbrances.
E: Free as a bird.

14-4 ঝি জব্দ শিলে, বৌ জব্দ কিলে
L: To subdue the maid, make her grind (spices) on a stone slab; to subdue the wife/ daughter-in-law, beat her up.
I: Use appropriate technique to bring people under control.
E: A woman, a dog, and a walnut tree, the more you beat them, the better they be.

14-5 ঝুনো নারকেল
L: A fully mature coconut.
I: A tough, shrewd, cunning person.
E: A tough nut to crack.

14-6 ঝোপ বুঝে কোপ মারা RL,SD, BDG

L: (In hunting) smite with your axe the right clump of shrubs (where the prey is hiding).

I: To sense where the opportunity is, and zero in.

E: To make a beeline for.

14-7 ঝোলে অম্বলে এক করা SD

L: To mix up (on your dinner plate) the gravy and the sour soup.

I: To mix up unrelated or dissimilar issues.

E: Apples and oranges.

14-8 ঝুড়িঝুড়ি মিথ্যা কথা বলা

L: To tell basketfuls of lies.

I To tell basketfuls of lies.

E: Lying through one's teeth.
The tongue indeed has no bone *[Indo.]*.

৬৩৩

124

15.

15-1 টাকা উড়ে যায়, থাকে না

L: Money flies away, doesn't accumulate.
I: Money is difficult to accumulate.
E: Riches have wings.

15-2 টাকা গাছে ফলে না

L: Money doesn't grow on trees.
I: One has to work hard to earn money.
E: Money doesn't grow on trees.
 Money is not found under a horse's hoof/ feet *[Fch.]*.

15-3 টাকা থাকলে বাঘের দুধ পাওয়া যায় x 7- 9;15-7

L: Money can buy even tiger's milk.
I: Money makes the unattainable attainable.
E: Money talks, nobody walks.
 If you have money, you can make the devil push your grindstone *[Chi.]*.
 A rich man has even the devil to lull his children *[Pol.]*.

15-4 টাকা থাকলেই মানুষ হয় না

L: Having money doesn't make one a decent human being.
I: Being wealthy is not synonymous with being a good person.
E: Money doesn't make the man.

15-5 টাকা সঙ্গে নিয়ে যাওয়া যায় না

L: You cannot take the money with you.
I: All your wealth will matter not when you are dead.
E: You can't take it with you when you die.
 A shroud has no pockets *[Ger.]*.
 Death don't see no difference 'tween the big house and the cabin *[AfrAm.]*.

The greatest Tsar must be put to bed with a shovel at last *[Rus.]*.

15-6 টাকা নেবে গুনে, পথ চলবে জেনে SB
L: When you receive money, count it well; when you travel, know your road well.
I: In any situation, be aware of the right things to watch out for.
E: To know the road ahead, ask someone coming back.

15-7 টাকায় কি না হয় x15-3
L: What is it that money can't do?
I: Money makes everything possible.
E: 'Tis the money that sets the world going round.
If you have money you can make the devil push your grind stone. *[Chi.]*

15-8 টাকায় টাকা হয় / টাকায় টাকা আনে SD,BDG
L: Money begets money.
I: If you have money, you can make more money.
E: Money begets money.
Money comes to money *[Fin.]*.
Money goes where money is *[Spa.]*.

15-9 টাকার বলে দুনিয়া চলে/ টাকায় পৃথিবী চলে SD
L: Money makes the world go round.
I: Money decides everything.
E: Money makes the world go round.

15-10 টিপ্পনী কাটা
L: To make a concise comment.
I: To make a sarcastic remark.
E: To get one's digs in.

15-11 টেক্কা দেওয়া / টেক্কা মারা SD,SB
L: Play the ace / to plonk down an ace.
I: To top everybody/ everything else.
E: To play the ace.

15-12 টোটো কোম্পানীর ম্যানেজার

L: Manager of Toto Company.
I: The leader of a group of tramps, looking busy.
E: In charge of the river without water *[Uyg.]*.
   cf. An idle wanderer consumes his legs *[Afr.]*.

Specially hand painted wooden seat, one each, for the bride and the groom to sit on during the Bengali Hindu marriage ceremony.

Some ritual items required for performing a Hindu marriage ceremony.

Special gifts from the bride and the groom's family for the in-law's family.

৪০৫৪

16-1 ঠক বাছতে গাঁ উজাড় x31-16   RL,SD,SB

L: If you are culling out the swindlers, you will end up emptying the village.

I: If you are too particular about selecting only the most honest people, you may end up with none.

E: Sift him grain by grain, and you will find him all chaff.
Who sieves too much keeps the rubbish *[Bel.]*.

16-2 ঠকের বাড়ির নেমন্তন্ন, না আঁচালে বিশ্বাস নেই x1-27

L: If you are invited to a swindler's house, you should not believe you are assured a meal until you are actually rinsing out your mouth after dinner.

I: Don't trust untrustworthy people until the job is done.

E: There is many a slip between the cup and the lip.
Cf. He that will cheat at play will cheat you any way.
When a thief kisses you, count your teeth *[Yid.]*.

16-3 ঠাকুর ঘরে কে? না, আমি তো কলা খাইনি   RL,SD

L: Q: Who do I hear (stealthily moving) in the worship room?   A: I have not eaten the banana.

I: A guilty conscience makes an innocent question seem to cast suspicion.

E: A guilty conscience pricks the mind.
A guilty conscience needs no accuser.
He who excuses himself accuses himself.
A mind conscious of guilt is its own accuser *[Lat.]*.

16-4 ঠিক দুপুরবেলায় ভূতে মারে ঢেলা   RL,SD

L: Just when it is precisely noon, the ghost pelts a stone.

I: Something strange happens with uncanny punctuality.

E: "Never fails"!

16-5 ঠুঁটো জগন্নাথ *   SD,SB

L: The armless deity Jagannath of Puri.

I: An ineffectual idol. A useless person.

16-6 ঠেকলে বাঘে খায় ঘাস   SD

L: When desperately hungry, a tiger will eat even grass.

I: Desperate situations make you accept what is normally beneath your standards.

E: Desperate situations call for desperate measures.

16-7 ঠেকে শেখা আর দেখে শেখা   RL,SD

L: To learn out of dire necessity or to learn by observing.

I: There are two ways of learning – the easy way and the hard way.

E: You can learn something the easy way or the hard way.
Tell me, I will forget. Show me, I may remember. Involve me, and I will understand [Chi.].
He who is not taught by his mother will be taught by the world [Afr.].
It is when there is a stampede, that a person with big buttocks knows that he carries a load [Afr.].
If skills would be gathered by watching, every dog would become a butcher [Tur.].
Necessity is the greatest teacher [Hun.].

16-8 ঠেলাঠেলির ঘর, গোঁসাই রক্ষা কর   x27-10   SD,SB

L: Gonsai (the Vaishnava priest) please preserve this house where everyone passes responsibility to the other.

I: If people involved will not do their part, outside intervention is needed.

E: Everybody's business is nobody's business.

16-9 ঠেলার নাম বাবাজী   SD

L: Pressure is a hard taskmaster.

I: Pressure compels you to do things like nothing else does.

E: Necessity is the law of life.
The cat in a mesh calls mouse its brother.
Who suffers from diarrhoea, is not afraid of the dark [Afr.]

17-1 ডাইনে আনতে বাঁয়ে ফুরায় x21-17
RL,SD
L: No sooner you gather something on your right, it is used up from your left.
I: To barely make both ends meet.
E: To live from hand to mouth.

17-2 ডানপিটের মরণ গাছের ডগায় RL,SD
L: The rambunctious boy will die upon a tree branch.
I: A reckless person comes by a violent death.
E: He who lives too fast, goes to his grave too soon.

17-3 ডিমে তা দেওয়া
L: To sit on an egg (to hatch it).
I: To nurture something like a mother hen so it will bear fruit.
E: The meat on the spit must be basted *[Dut.]*.

17-4 ডুবে ডুবে জল খাওয়া x10-21 SD
L: Taking dips to drink water while submerged.
I: To do something on the sly. To do something secretly.
E: A sly rogue is often in good dress.

17-5 ডুমুরের ফুল RL,SD,SB
L: Flower of the fig tree.
I: A rare or unseen object.

18-2 ঢাকী (Indian ceremonial drummers)

18-1 | **ঢাক্‌ ঢাক্‌ গুড় গুড়** | SD,SB
L: Cover-up cover-up, hide hide.
I: Hushing up is going on.
E: To sweep something under the carpet/ rug.

18-2 | **ঢাকী সুদ্ধ বিসর্জন দেওয়া** | RL,SD
L: During the immersion ceremony (after the festivity is over), to consign to the river even the drummer along with the image of the god/ goddess.
I: To make an indiscriminate or wholesale sacrifice. To part with everything.
E: *cf.* To throw out the baby with the bath water.

18-3 | **ঢাকের দায়ে মনসা বিকানো** | RL,SD
L: To sell the idol of the goddess Manasa in order to pay the drummers.
I: Misplaced sense of value. The cost of external glamour is much more than the real event.
E: Buy donkey for three bucks, saddle costs five bucks *[Uyg.]*.

18-4 | **ঢাল নেই, তরোয়াল নেই, নিধিরাম সর্দার** ⨯19-7 | RL, SD
L: He has no sword and no shield - such is the guardsman Nidhiram.
I: A worker without his tools of the trade is useless.
E: A carpet knight.

18-5 | **ঢিলটি মারলে পাটকেলটি খেতে হয়** | RL,BDG
L: Pelt a stone, and you will be pelted back with a brickbat.
I: Tit for tat
E: Tit for tat.
To give a Roland for an Oliver.
If you throw a ball, must expect it (back) *[Dut.]*.

টেঁকি স্বর্গে গেলেও ধান ভানে

L: A husker of rice paddy will continue to husk paddy even after going to heaven.

I: Old habits die hard.

E: Destiny follows one everywhere.

The trumpet player dies, and his finger is still playing *[Egy.]*.

The cock is dead, but its eyes remain gazing in the dung heap *[Tur.]*.

Kolkata mid 1940s: Unlike now, tram cars in Kolkata were a real novelty.

৩৩৩

19-1 তন্বী শ্যামা শিখরীদশনা পক্কবিম্বাধরোষ্ঠী
মধ্যে ক্ষামা চকিতহরিণীপ্রেক্ষণা নিম্ননাভিঃ। *[Sans.]*

L: Young and slender, complexion like burning gold, sharp-edged teeth, full lips like a bimba fruit, slim of waist, eyes like a startled doe, deep navel...

I: Specification for a classically beautiful woman.

E: Three traits of a woman: a broad bosom, a slender waist and a short back.
The neck of a swan, the trot of a peacock, the eyes of a falcon and brows like sabres *[Rus.]*.

19-2 তাণ্ডবনৃত্য

L: A frantic or frenzied ritual dance.

I: An out-of-control frenzy.

E: Devil dance.

19-3 তানা-নানা করা

L: To go 'tana-nana' (linger in the prologue of a tune).

I: To stall. Waste time on preliminaries.

E: To hem and haw.
To pussyfoot around.

19-4 তাবড় তাবড় লোক

L: People this big and people that big.

I: Important people.

E: Big cheese.
Muckety-muck.
Bigwigs.

19-5 তার হাতে জল গলে না

L: Water doesn't pass through his fingers.

I: Said of a miserly person.

E: He is tight-fisted.

19-6 তালগোল পাকানো

L: To wrap everything up in round balls.
I: To make a mess of things.
E: To make a hodgepodge of things.

19-7 তালপাতার সেপাই x 18-4   RL,SD,SB

L: A soldier made of palm fronds.
I: An ineffectual warrior. A powerless authority figure.
E: Tin soldier.
Carpet knight.

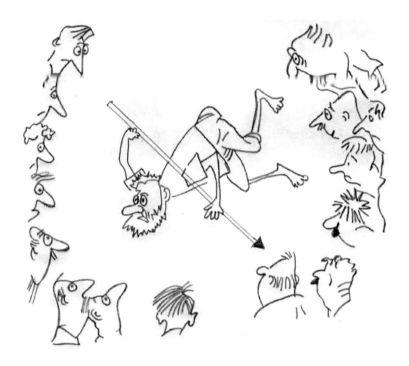

19-7 তালপাতার সেপাই

19-8 তাস, গল্প, পাশা, এ তিন সর্বনাশা   RL

L: Playing cards, gossiping and playing dice - these three things ruin a person.
I: Your idle addictions can ruin you.
E: The best way to throw the dice is to throw them away.

Gaming, women and wine, while they laugh they make men pine.
Wine, women, and tobacco reduce one to ashes *[Ita.]*.
A pack of cards is the devil's prayer-book *[Ger.]*.

19-9 তাসের ঘর
L: A house of cards.
I: An unreal or non-viable construct.
E: A house of cards.

19-10 তিতোর ফল মিষ্টি
L: The leaves are bitter but the fruit is sweet.
I: The source of birth does not determine the result.
E: "Honour and shame from no condition rise".

19-11 তিন মরণের চিন
L: The number three is the mark of death.
I: The number three is a bad omen.
E: *Cf.* Unlucky thirteen.
    Cf. Misfortunes always come in threes.

19-12 তিন কামের ভেটু
L: A utensil having three different uses.
I: An implement which has multiple uses.
E: *Cf.* Three-in-one.
    Cf. All-in-one.

19-13 তিনকূলে কেউ না থাকা   RL,SD
L: Not having any relatives within one's three generations.
I: Someone who has no close relatives.

19-14 তিন খোঁটায় বেগুন পাড়া
L: To pluck an aubergine by joining three sticks.
I: To do something simple in a very roundabout way. A very short person.

19-15 তিল ধারণের জায়গা নেই

L: There is not enough space left even for a sesame seed.
I: Really full.
E: Full to the gills.
     "Standing Room Only."
     House full.

19-16 তিলক কাটিলেই বৈষ্ণব হয় না   x24-83   SD,SB

L: You don't become a Vaishnava just by painting a sandal -
     wood mark on your forehead.
I: You do not become a member of a group just by wearing
     their symbol.
E: It is not the hood that makes the monk.
     There is more to being a Knight than a horse, sword and
     lance.
     An ape's an ape, a varlet's a varlet,
     Though they be clad in silk or scarlet.
     If the beard were all, goats could preach *[Dan.]*.
     All are not cooks who carry long knives *[Ger.]*.

19-17 তিলকে তাল করা   RL,SD,BDG

L: To blow up a (tiny) sesame seed into a (large) palm fruit.
I: To blow out of proportion. To grossly exaggerate.
E: To make a mountain out of a molehill.
     Do not make an elephant out of a fly *[Rus.]*.
     To make an elephant out of a mosquito *[Dut.]*.

19-18 তিলে তিলে মরা

L: To die a little every moment.
I: To die a slow death.
E: Die a slow death.

19-19 তীর্থের কাক   RL,SD

L: A crow in a place of pilgrimage (waiting for food scraps).
I: Someone who wishfully waits to pick up a bit of some-
     thing that he has not been offered. One who waits
     expectantly for others' favours.

E: *Cf.* Never such a small feast, that it won't have spongers on [*Fin.*].

19-20 তুমি অধম তাই বলিয়া আমি উত্তম না হইব কেন?

L: Even though you are mean, why can't I be noble?

I: I don't have to come down to your level.

E: Let others take the low road, I will take the high road.

19-21 তুমি ফের ডালে-ডালে, আমি ফিরি পাতায়-পাতায়   RL,SD,SB

L: You are lurking on the branches, but I am on the leaves.

I: I have a great deal more experience than you.

E: To be one step ahead.
     If you are a wind then I am a hurricane [*Ara.*].

19-22 তুমি যাও বঙ্গে, কপাল যায় সঙ্গে   RL,SD

L: You go to Bengal, your fate follows you.

I: Wherever you go, your fate goes with you.

E: Destiny follows you everywhere.

19-23 তুলো ধুনো করা   SD

L: To fluff up the cotton (by beating on it).

I: Give somebody a good hiding.

E: To dress down somebody.

19-24 তুর্কি নাচ নাচানো   **26-21**   SD,SB

L: To make someone dance the Turkish Dance (like a Whirling Dervish).

I: To make someone jump through the hoops.

E: To make someone jump through the hoops.

19-25 তৃণ হতে হয় কার্য রাখিলে যতনে

L: (Even) grass can be of use if nurtured with care.

I: Even insignificant people have their usefulness if properly cultivated.

E: Keep straw, its time will come [*Tur.*].
     Sometimes you need a pinch of salt too [*Ind.*].

19-26	তেপান্তরের মাঠ

L: A faraway mysterious field from the fairytales.

I: A remote expanse of great emptiness.

E: The back of beyond.

The fields of dream.

9-27	তেল দেওয়া

L: To oil somebody.

I: To obsequiously try to please someone to extract some advantage.

E: To butter someone up.

19-28	তেলা মাথায় তেল দেওয়া	RL,SD,BDG,SB

L: To rub oil on someone's already oily scalp.

I: Giving more to one who has enough already.

Alt. To flatter the rich and denegrate the poor.

E: To carry coals to Newcastle.

Sell ice to the Eskimos.

The devil always evacuate bowel on the biggest pile *[Ger.]*.

Money goes where money is *[Spa.]*.

Take coconuts to sell in the orchard *[Thai]*.

He is taking water to the Danube *[Hun.]*.

One should not go farther than the sea to fish *[Fin.]*.

Don't cross the stream to get water *[Dan.]*.

Carry water to the sea *[Dan.]*.

19-29	তেলে বেগুনে জ্বলে ওঠা	RL,SD,SB

L: To flare up like pieces of aubergine dropped in boiling oil.

I: To flare up in anger.

E: To fly off the handle.

19-30	তোমার ইহকালও নেই, পরকালও নেই

L: You are doomed in this life as well as the next.

I: You are doomed both here and in the hereafter.

E: You are done for.

19-31 "তোমার পতাকা যারে দাও তারে বহিবারে দাও শকতি"

L: He to whom you have entrusted your flag - give him the strength to carry it.

I: (God) give him the resources to carry out his noble task.

19-32 তোমার বয়সের গাছ-পাথর নাই

L: There are no rocks or trees of your age.

I: You are very old.

E: You are an antiquity.
You are over the hill.

19-33 "তোমারে বধিবে যে গোকুলে বাড়িছে সে"   SD,SB

L: 'He who will slay you is now growing in Gokul'.

I: Your downfall is in the making. Events are developing that will bring your downfall.

19-34 ত্রাহি ত্রাহি ডাক ছাড়া   SD

L: To call out "Save me, save me!"

I: To cry for help in desperation.

E: To say Uncle.

19-35 ত্রিভঙ্গ মুরারি   SD

L: (The posture of standing of Lord Krishna with) three bends in his body. (An appellation of Krishna when he piped his flute).

I: Something that is badly or humorously askew. A grotesquely ugly person who cannot keep his body straight.

19-36 ত্রিশঙ্কুর স্বর্গ   SD

L: Trishanku's 'heaven' (a place suspended between heaven and earth).

I: In limbo. In purgatory.

E: Between two fires.
To be suspended between heaven and earth *[Dut.].*

৩৩২

20-1 **থ' হয়ে যাওয়া**

L: To be stunned.
I: To be bewildered. To become peechless from surprise.
E: To be speechless.
     Cat got your tongue?
     Did the flour get to your mouth? *[Fin.]*.

20-2 **থরহরি কম্পন**

L: Shivering like a shaking Hari.
I: To be chaking all over from fear or shock.
E: Shaking in one's boots.
     Shaking like jelly.

20-3 **থাকতে দেয় না ভাত কাপড়, মরলে পরে দান সাগর**   MHP

L: In his lifetime, he does not even get food and clothing;
     when he dies, money is lavished on him.
I: A mistreated person gets a lavish funeral after he dies.
E: When a blind man dies, they say he had almond eyes;
     when a bald man dies, they say he had golden hair *[Tur.]*.
     The living are denied a table, the dead get a whole coffin
     [Mon.].

20-4 **থোঁতা মুখ ভোতা**   RL,SD,SB

L: To flatten an already flat face.
I: To punish someone excessively.
E: Add insult to injury.

20-5 **থোড় বড়ি খাড়া, খাড়া বড়ি থোড়** *   SD,SB

L: (To eat) thor, bori, khara one day; khara, bori, thor the
     next day. (The same three bland ingredients in varied
     sequences).
I: Monotonous routine day in and day out.
E: Same old same old!

21-1 **দই খেলেন রমাকান্ত, বিচারের বেলায় গোবর্ধন** x 4-8   SB

L: It was Ramakanta who stole the curd, but you are trying Gobardhan for the crime.

I: To ascribe someone's fault to someone else.
The blacksmith was guilty, but they hanged the Gypsy *[Pol.].*

21-2 **দণ্ডমুণ্ডের কর্তা**   SD

L: The lord who has the power to impose on you any punish -ment, from beating with a stick to beheading.

I: The absolute ordainer.

E: "Lord High Executioner."

21-3 **দন্তস্ফূট হয় না**   RL,SD

L: Can't sink one's teeth into.

I: Cannot understand or grasp.

E: Can't sink one's teeth into.

21-4 **দরজিপাড়ার নতুন-দা**

L: Natun-da ('the new elder brother') of Darjipara.

I: The neighbourhood braggart (seen as a comic character).

E: *Cf.* Big Man on Campus.

21-5 **দরিদ্র নারায়ণ** *

L: The destitute Narayan.

I: The poor and the destitute given the status of (to be treated as) a deity.

E: "He who is kind to the poor lends to the Lord, and He will reward him for what he has done" — *The Bible*

21-6 **দশচক্রে ভগবান ভূত** x 21-8   RL,SD,SB

L: God becomes a ghost because ten people assert so.

I: Collective opinion can turn a falsehood into a truth.

E: If three people say you are an ass, put on a bridle.
Three people can make up a tiger *[Chi.]*.

`21-7` দশে মিলি করি কাজ, হারি জিতি নাহি লাজ   RL,SD

L: When ten (many) of us work as a team, there is no individual shame if we lose.

I: If many work together in a cooperative way, an individual does not have to shoulder the accountibility.

E: United we stand, divided we fall.
Heavy, we carry together, light, we carry together *[Indo.]*.

`21-8` দেশের বাণী বেদের বাণী x`21-6`

L: The voice of ten people has the power of the voice of the Vedas.

I: The opinion of the crowd rules.

E: What the people believe is true *[AmInd.]*.
Vox populi, vox dei *[Lat.]*.

`21-9` দেশের লাঠি একের বোঝা   RL,SD,BDG

L: Ten walking sticks can be quite a burden for a single person (to carry).

I: An useful implement, when carried in large qantity, can become a burden. A job which is heavy for one person is easy for ten united.

E: Many a little makes a mickle.

`21-10` দহরম মহরম

L: Friendly as during Muharram.

I: Very friendly. Intimate.

E: Bosom friends.

`21-11` দাঁও মারা   SD

L: To strike an unexpected bargain.

I: To secure an unexpected advantage.

E: To make a killing.

21-7 দশে মিলি করি কাজ, হারি জিতি নাহি লাজ

21-12 দাঁত থাকতে দাঁতের মর্যাদা বোঝে না   RL,SD,SB

L: To not appreciate the value of one's teeth while one has still got them.

I: Blessings are not valued till they are gone.

E: The worth of a thing is best known by the want of it.
      You never miss the water till the well has run dry.
      We know the worth of a thing when we have lost it *[Fch.]*

21-13 দাঁতাল ও মাতালকে বিশ্বাস নেই   SD

L: Neither the tusker (elephant) nor the drunkard is to be trusted.

I: Do not trust someone who has the ability to harm you or someone who is not thinking straight.

E: Trust not a horses's heel, nor a dog's tooth.

21-14 (তার) দাপটে বাঘে গরুতে এক ঘাটে জল খায়   RL,SD,SB

L: (He is so fearsome a taskmaster that under him) the tiger and the cow drink at the same waterhole.

I: Said of a very powerful person.

E: A hard taskmaster.

21-15 দায়িত্ব যার চিন্তা তার

L: The person who has the responsibility does the worrying.

I: One with the responsibility has the worries.

E: With great power comes great responsibility.

21-16 দিও কিঞ্চিৎ না করো বঞ্চিত   SD

L: Don't turn away someone empty-handed, give him a little something.

I: When someone requests something, try at least to satisfy him a little.

E: Give a token (gift), never mind if it's a rotten nut [Aze.].

21-17 দিন আনি দিন খাই   x17-1
SD

L: What I earn each day I consume each day.

I: To barely make both ends meet.

E: To live from hand to mouth.
Make ends meet.
To be barely able to reach from one loaf to another [Dut.].

21-18 দিনগত পাপক্ষয়   SD

L: The absolution of each day's sin each day.

I: The daily grind.
Alt. Absolution for some past transgression.

E: The daily grind.

21-19 দিনকে রাত করা   SD

L: To turn day into night.
I: To grossly misrepresent.
E: The liar's mother is a virgin.
       Point at a deer and call it a horse *[Chi.]*.

21-20 দিন নেই, রাত নেই

L: Whether it is day, whether it is night...
I: Something that is going on all the time.
E: Round the clock.

21-21 দিনে দুপুরে ডাকাতি   x[24-64]

L: A robbery right in the middle of the day.
I: A very bold and brash crime or wrongdoing.
E: Daylight robbery.

21-22 দিল্লী দূর অস্ত

L: Dilli (Delhi) is very far.
I: Something is quite out of reach.

21-23 দিল্লীকা লাড্ডু, যে খায় সে পস্তায়, যে না খায় সেও পস্তায়
                                 RL,SD,SB

L: The Dilli (Delhi) Laddoo - he who has tasted it regrets, he
       who hasn't tasted it regrets as well.
I: Something of dubious value.
E: Can't live with them, can't live without them.
       Some wish they had a beard and the ones that do, are
       spitting on it *[Grk.]*.

21-24 দুই দিনকার বৈরাগী, ভাতেরে কয় অন্ন   RL,SD

L: A monk for only days, he starts to call daily rice by its
       Sanskrit name (anna).
I: Newly indoctrinated person is more dogmatic.
E: Convert's zeal.
       Cf. It is not by saying halva, halva, that sweetness will
       come to your mouth *[Per.]*.

21-25 দুই নৌকোয় পা দেওয়া   RL,MW

L: To stand on two boats with one leg in each.
I: To not be able to decide between two options.
E: To sit on the fence.
     Those who have one foot in the canoe, and one foot in the
     boat, are going to fall into the river [AmInd.].
     If you chase two rabbits, you will not catch either one
     [Rus.].

21-26 দুই সতীনের ঘর, খোদায় রক্ষা কর   SD

L: Khoda, please preserve this house with two co-wives.
I: Power-sharing does not work. Only God can help a person
     who has two wives.
E: Two cats and a mouse, two wives in a house, two dogs
     and a bone, never agree in one.
     One woman, what a glory; two women, what a worry!
     [Tur.].
     A day's disease: take brandy. A life's disease: take two
     wives [Rus.].
     Watch out that a black dog does not come in between
     [Dut.].

21-27 দুঃখ বিনা সুখ লাভ হয় কি মহীতে

L: Can one atttain happiness on this Earth without first
     suffering?
I: There is no unmixed happiness.
E: Weal and woe come by turns.
     Get your reward in Heaven.

21-28 দুঃখের পরে সুখ   SB,MW

L: Happiness comes after misery.
I: Good times come after bad times.
E: After cloud comes fair weather.

21-29 দু'চক্ষের বিষ   SD

L: A person who is seen as venom through both eyes.
I: Someone you cannot stand.
E: *Ct.* A sight for sore eye.

21-30 দুগ্ধপোষ্য শিশু

L: A baby still on a diet of milk only.
I: Said in sarcasm of an adult who acts like a child.
E: An overgrown baby.

21-31 দুধ কলা দিয়ে কালসাপ পোষা   RL,SD,BDG,SB

L: To lovingly rear a deadly snake on a rich diet of milk and bananas.
I: To lovingly nurture a potential deadly enemy.
E: To nourish a viper in one's bosom.
  Raise crows and they will peck your eyes out *[Spa.]*.

21-32 দুধালো গাইয়ের লাথিও ভাল   x 29-53   MHP

L: Even the kick of a milch cow is sweet!
I: One can put up with a lot from one's benefactor.
E: Give me the roast meat and beat me with the spit.

21-33 দুধের স্বাদ ঘোলে মেটে না   RL,SD,SB

L: You cannot satisfy the craving for milk with a yogurt drink.
I: You really cannot substitute a derivative for something genuine.
E: A good breakfast is no substitute for a large dinner *[Chi.]*.

21-34 দুমুখো সাপ   SD,SB

L: A two-headed snake.
I: A treacherous and duplicitous person.
E: A double-dealer.
  "White man – he speaks with a forked tongue".

21-35 দুয়ারে হাতি বাঁধা   SD

L: To keep a pet elephant tied in the yard.
I: To be able to afford expensive hobbies.

21-36 দুষ্ট গরুর চেয়ে শূন্য গোয়াল ভাল   RL,SD,BDG,SB

L: Better an empty shed than a wicked cow.

I: Having no asset or help is preferable to having a
     problematic one.
E: Better an empty house than a bad tenant.
     Better a good neighbour than a distant friend *[Dut.]*.

21-37 দুষ্টের দমন, শিষ্টের পালন   SD
L: To subdue the evil, to preserve the good.
I: What a good leader does.

21-38 দেওয়ালেরও কান আছে   SD,SB
L: Even walls have ears.
I: You can never be sure who is eavesdropping.
E: Even walls have ears.
     Fences (ditches) have ears.
     Walls have mice and mice have ears *[Pers.]*.
     There are always ears on the other side of the wall *[Chi.]*

21-39 দেবতার গ্রাস
L: What angry gods want to gobble up.
I: Usually said of a great loss in a natural disaster.
E: An apocalyptic disaster.

21-40 দেবা ন জানন্তি কুতো মনুষ্যাঃ *[Sans.]*   SD
L: Even God doesn't know, how could man?
I: It passes all understanding, human or divine.

21-41 দেমাকে মাটিতে পা পরে না   RL,SD
L: He is so vain that his feet do not touch the lowly ground.
I: A pompous person.
E: A stuck-up person.

21-42 দেশভেদে প্রথাভেদ
L: Customs vary from land to land.
I: Customs vary from land to land.
E: When in Rome, do as Romans do.
     Each country's customs are different, just as each
     meadow's grass is different *[Mon.]*.

21-43 দেহাতিপনা

L: Act like a villager/ country folk.
I: To act provincial.
E: To act like a village bumpkin.

21-44 দেহি পদপল্লবমুদারম্ [Sans.]

L: Place your noble feet (on my head) and bestow glory upon me thus.
I: Please bestow your favours on (lowly) me.

21-45 দৈত্যকূলে প্রহ্লাদ * ₓ9-51   RL,SD,SB

L: Prahlad (a good character) born to the race of demons.
I: A good character born amongst the bad sort.

21-46 দোটানায় পড়া

L: To be pulled between two option.
I: To be torn between two options.

21-47 দোষে গুণে মানুষ   ₓ21-48

L: A man is made of virtues and vices.
I: Both good and bad qualities are to be found in a normal human being.
E: No man is without fault [Tur.].

21-48 দোষে গুণে সৃষ্টি, ঝড়ে জলে বৃষ্টি   ₓ21-47   SD

L: The world is made of vices and virtues, rain is made of storm and water.
I: Every human being is made of good and bad qualities (to one extent or another).
E: It takes both rain and sunshine to make a rainbow.
   No man is without fault [Tur.].

21-49 দ্রৌপদীর বস্ত্রহরণ *

L: Droupodi being disrobed in public.
I: Gross public humiliation of a good person by bad people.

৬৩৫

22-1 ধনে প্রাণে মারা   RL

L: To destroy someone both in wealth and life.
I: To totally ruin somebody.
E: To crush someone within an inch of life.

22-2 ধনে সুখ না মনে সুখ

L: Is happiness of matter of wealth or of the mind?
I: Is happiness of matter of wealth or of the mind?
E: *cf.* Health is better than wealth.

22-3 ধনুকভাঙা পণ   SD,SB

L: The resolve to string a very hard-to-string bow.
I: To make a firm resolution to do something difficult.
E: Bite the bullet.

22-4 ধর লক্ষ্মণ *

L: Laksman, hold this (meaning, eat this food).
I: Offering meals without an explicit request to eat.

22-5 ধরণী দ্বিধা হও * x28-19   SD

L: Mother Earth, please part (and swallow me!).
I: Someone in a state of great public shame or humiliation praying to disappear.
E: I wish I could vanish.
     "Rock of Ages, cleft for me, let me hide myself in thee"
     - The Bible

22-6 ধরাকে সরা জ্ঞান করা   SD

L: To regard the Earth as an earthen pitcher.
I: To be so vain as to belittle everything under the sun.
E: In your pride, you spurn at the world.

22-7 ধরি মাছ না ছুঁই পানি   SD,SB

L: To fish without ever touching the water.
I: Gaining something without risking anything.
E: All cats love fish but hate to get their paws wet.
The cat would eat fish but would not wet her feet.
The cat would eat the fish, but not be ready to wet its paw
[Fin.].

22-7 ধরি মাছ না ছুঁই পানি

22-8 ধর্মপুত্র যুধিষ্ঠির * x22-25   RL,SD

L: Judhisthir (an epic hero), the Son of Dharma.
I: Said in sarcasm of a bad person who pretends to be chaste
or noble or virtuous.
E: Pure as driven snow.

22-9 ধর্মের কল বাতাসে নড়ে   x22-10   RL.SD,SB

L: The wind makes the machinery of Dharma work.
I: Truth cannot be kept concealed.
E: Virtue proclaims itself.

22-10 ধর্মের ঢাক আপনি বাজে   x22-9   RL,SD.SB

L: The drum of Dharma plays itself.
I: Truth will come out.
E: Virtue is its own advertisement.
Truth will out.

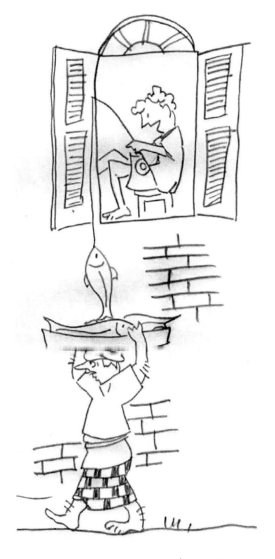

22-7 ধরি মাছ না ছুঁই পানি

22-11 ধর্মের ষাঁড়   SD

L: The Dharma Bull.
I: A person who is as wayward as an ox dedicated to the
       Gods (an ox that roams freely without any restraints and
       is of no use). A do-nothing fellow.
E: A fop.
       A dandy.
       Footloose and fancy free.
       Dharma bum.

22-12 ধান দিয়ে লেখা পড়া করা   RL,SD

L: To pay for one's education with rice paddy.
I: To not pay the proper fees for your education.
E: If you pay peanuts, you get monkeys.

22-13 ধান ভানিতে শিবের গীত   RL,SD,SB

L: Singing praise of Shiva while husking rice.
I: To bring up something completely unrelated to the activity at hand.
E: "What has that to do with Bacchus?"
     When you are discussing about elephants don't talk about yam matters *[Ind.]*.

22-14 ধাপধাড়া গোবিন্দপুর   SD

L: Gobindapur, in the middle of nowhere.
I: A little known ignoble place.
E: Podunk.

22-15 ধামাচাপা দেওয়া   SD

L: To cover something up with an inverted basket.
I: To hush up. Cover up.
E: To deep-six.

22-16 ধামাধরা মানুষ   SD

L: One who carries someone's Dhama (basket).
I: A flatterer or sycophant or yesman.
E: Bagman.
     Yesman.

22-17 ধারেও কাটে ভারেও কাটে   RL,SD

L: (A knife that) cuts both by its sharpness and by its weight.
I: Accomplishing something with a dual advantage.

22-18 ধুতুরা ফুল দেখা   SD

L: To espy Datura flowers.
I: To suddenly become dazed or shocked.
E: Seeing stars.

22-19 ধুলিমুষ্টি ধরিলে স্বর্ণমুষ্টি হয়

L: (When he) picks up a fistful of sand, it turns into a fistful of gold dust.

I: Whatever he sets his hand to turns into gold.

E: Midas touch.

22-20 ধুস্তুরি মায়া

L: A supposedly psychadelic reverie one has upon eating or smoking the fruit of Datura tree.

I: A fanciful reverie. Dazzled delusion.

E: A Walter Mitty-like experience.

22-21 ধরে প্রাণ আসা

L: Life returning to the body again.

I: To recover from some great ordeal, trauma or shock.

E: "I am back in business".

22-22 ধোপা–নাপিত বন্ধ করা

L: To deprive a person of the services of the washerman and the barber.

I: To make an outcast of somebody. To socially boycott by depriving the services of washerman and the barber.

E: To chase someone out of Dodge City.

22-23 ধোপে টেঁকে না

L: Does not survive in the wash.

I: An argument that does not stand on examination.

E: Does not hold in the wash.
Does not stand wear and tear.
Everything, however finely spun, finally comes to the sun [*Dut.*].

22-24 ধোবি কা গাধা/কুত্তা, না ঘরকা না ঘাটকা [*Hin.*] x23-2 SD

L: The washerman's donkey/dog - it belongs neither in the house nor in the landing of the pond.

I: A person who does not solidly belong to a particular place, profession etc.

E: Neither here nor there.

ধোয়া তুলসী পাতা

L: A tulsi leaf (a symbol of purity) that has been washed clean (to boot).

I: Purest of pure (said in sarcasm). Someone who is not honest.

E: Not exactly lily white.

Kolkata mid 1940s: Streets were not so busy.

৳০৵

23-1   ন' মন তেলও পুড়বে না, রাধাও নাচবে না   x34-35,68   BDG

L: Neither will nine maunds of oil be sacrificed burned (for festivities) nor will Radha dance.

I: Said of an once-opulent aristocray now decaying.

E: Gone are those glory days!

23-2   ন যযৌ ন তস্থৌ   [*Sans.*]   x22-24   SD

L: Neither here nor there.

I: Neither here nor there. In a dilemma.

E: Neither here nor there.

23-3   নখদর্পণে রাখা/ থাকা   RL,SD

L: To have knowledge instantly mirrored in one's finger-nail.

I: To hold a great deal of knowledge readily available.

E: To have something at one's fingertips.

23-4   নদী শুকালেও রেখা যায় না   x28-68   MHP

L: Even when a river has dried up, its trace remains.

I: Great men have impact even if they have fallen on hard times.

E: Time passes away but sayings remain.

23-5   নদী এক কূল ভাঙ্গে, আরেক কূল গড়ে   SD

L: As the river erodes one bank, it builds the other.

I: As something is lost, something else is created.

E: If God closes a door, he opens a window.

23-6 "নদীর এপার কহে ছাড়িয়া নিঃশ্বাস
ওপারেতে যত সুখ, আমার বিশ্বাস।"

L: The river bank says sighing, "I think, all the happiness is on the other bank."
I: Everything good is on the other side.
E: The grass is always greener on the other side of the fence.
The neighbour's lawn is greener *[Jap.]*.
Your neighbour's grass is always greener *[Dan.]*.

23-7 নদীর কূলে বাস, দুঃখ বারমাস   RL,SD

L: If you live off and by the river, you suffer throughout the year.
I: You have to live with the inconveniences of the life you have chosen.
E: If you don't want to get flooded, don't build a house next to the sea *[Indo.]*.
ct. A man who lives on the banks of the Niger should no twash his hands in spittle *[Afr.]*.

23-8 ননদিনী রায়বাঘিনী, দাঁড়িয়ে আছে কালসাপিনী   SD,SB

L: (My) husband's sister, a real tigress, is standing there like a deadly snake.
I: Refers to family rivalry between a man's wife and his sister.
E: The co-wife is poisonous and the sister-in-law is a bitter almond *[Ara.]*.

23-9 নন্দন-কানন

L: The Garden of Heaven.
I: An idyllic place.
E: Garden of Eden.

23-10 ন'মাসে ছ'মাসে

L: In nine months or six months.
I: Things happening rarely.
E: Once in a blue moon.

23-7 নদীর কূলে বাস, দুঃখ বারমাস

23-11 নয়ছয় করা   SD

L: To make nines and sixes (of something).
I: To squander away.
E: To make a mess of things.

23-12 নরক গুলজার   SD

L: Big partying in Hell.
I: A loud or raucous party or gathering.
E: Whooping it up.
       Party hearty.

23-13 নরাণাং মাতুলক্রমঃ   [Sans.]   SD

L: It is the nature of man to take after the maternal uncle.
I: Said of a man's inherited traits.

23-14 নষ্টের গোড়া　　　　　　　SD

L:　The root (cause) of what is wrong.

I:　Someone who is responsible at the core for what has gone wrong.

E:　The root of all evil.

23-15 না খায় ভাত, না পিয়ে পানি, যমে মানুষে টানাটানি ×29-21

　　　　　　　　　　　　　　　　RL,SD

L:　He neither eats nor drinks, it is a tug-of-war between Yama and men.

I:　Someone is at death's door.

E:　At death's door.

23-16 না থাকবে বাঁশ, না বাজবে বাঁশী

L:　If there are no bamboos (to make flutes from), then there will be no playing of flutes.

I:　When the raw materials for an implement is not available, you will have to do without that implement.

E:　*cf.* Where the lion's skin falls short, borrow of the fox *[Ger.].*

23-17 না ভাঙে, না মচ্‌কায়　　　　　RL,SD

L:　Neither breaks nor yields.

I:　Unyielding.

23-18 না রাম না গঙ্গা　　　　　　SD

L:　Neither (the deity) Rama nor the (sacred river) Ganga.

I:　To not know anything. To keep mum.

E:　Mum's the word.

23-19 নাক উঁচু করা/ নাক সিটকানো

L:　To turn one's nose up

I:　To sneer at. To act uppity.

23-20 নাকানিচোবানি খাওয়া

L:　To (ineffectually) thrash around in water, with water getting into your nose and mouth.

I: To be roiled by a problem, and to suffer without any effective way out.

23-21 নাকে খত দেওয়া   SD
L: To make a scar mark on the nose (by rubbing it on the ground.)
I: To inflict a symbolic punishment on oneself for doing something, and swear not to do it again.
E: To fall on one's sword.

23-22 নাকে দড়ি দিয়ে ঘোরানো   SD
L: To steer someone by a rope strung through his nose.
I: To harass someone like a domesticated animal.
E: To run someone rugged.

23-23 নাকে মুখে গোঁজা   SD
L: To stuff (food) into one's nose and mouth.
I: To eat hastily. To gorge.
E: To wolf down.

23-24 নাকে সর্ষের তেল দিয়ে ঘুমানো   RL,SD
L: To put mustard oil in one's nose to induce deep sleep.
I: To be unaware / oblivious of one's surroundings.
E: He is logged off.

23-25 নাকের চেয়ে নাকের ডাক বেশী   SB
L: A snoring that is disproportionately loud compared to the size of the nose.
I: A report or hype that is disproportionately big compared to the underlying event or source.

23-26 নাকের জলে চোখের জলে   SD
L: Water (discharge) from both nose and eyes (trickling down one's face and mingling).
I: To be in a distressing quagmire.
E: In a state.

23-27 নাকের বদলে নরুণ পাওয়া SD

L: (To receive) a nail-clipper (in compensation) for one's nose (sliced by the barber).

I: A ridiculously inadequate compensation.

E: Chalk for cheese.
(Give) cat for rabbit/hare *[Spa.]*.

23-28 নাচতে না জানলে উঠান বাঁকা RL, SD, BDG, SB

L: If you don't know how to dance, you blame the floor for being not level.

I: Blaming someone or something else for your own inability or inadequacy.

E: A bad workman quarrels with his tools.
A person who cannot dance blames the stage to be tilted *[Ind.]*.
A bad dancer blames the hem of her skirt *[Pol.]*.
Cannot dance but blames the floor is uneven *[Indo.]*.
Ugly face, the mirror is split *[Indo.]*.
The crippled blames the cobblestones *[Spa.]*.
The bad shooter blames the bullet *[Uyg.]*.
The camel limped from its split lip *[Ara.]*.
He who cannot dance will say, ' The drum is bad' *[Afr.]*.

23-29 নাজেহাল হওয়া/ নাস্তানাবুদ হওয়া

L: To be left in a harried and ineffectual state.

I: To be harassed.

23-30 নাড়ী– নক্ষত্র জানা SD,BDG

L: To know everything about someone, from his pulse-beats to his stars.

I: To know everything about one since one's birth.

E: To know the ins and outs.

23-31 নাটের গুরু

L: The guru of the theatrical production.

I: One who pulls the strings.

E: The mastermind.
The puppet master.

23-32 নাটোরের বনলতা সেন *

L: Miss Banalata Sen from Natore.
I: A mysterious heroine.
E: *Cf.* **"To Helen"** - *Edgar Allan Poe.*

23-33 নানা মুনির নানা মত   SD,BDG

L: Different sages have different opinions.
I: Many men, many opinions.
E: Many men, many minds.

23-34 নান্যঃ পন্থা   [*Sans.*]

L: No other way (except through God).
I: No other way.

23-35 নামে তালপুকুর ঘটি ডোবে না x|২৩-১| RL,SD

L: It is called Taalpukur (a big pond), but you cannot even immerse your tumbler in it.
I: A label that greatly exaggerates the reality.
   Alt. Famous family, now poor.

23-36 নামতা পড়া

L: To rattle off mechanically as if reciting the multiplication table.
I: To narrate something in effortless monotone.
E: To rattle off.

23-37 নাভিশ্বাস ওঠা   SD

L: Breath starting to come from as deep as one's navel.
I: Near death. The last gasp before death.
E: Breathe one's last.

23-38 নারদ নারদ x|1-5|

L: Saying "Narad, Narad".
I: To goad two contending parties on.

23-39 নারীর বল চোখের জল   MHP

L: A woman's strength is her tears.

I: A woman cries easily (and gets her way).

23-40 নারীর শিক্ষা না হলে, সমাজ পিছোয় পলে পলে   SB
L: A society that does not value education of women falls behind apace.
I: A society that does not impart education to women is doomed.

23-41 নিঃশ্বাস ফেলার অবসর নেই
L: To not even get a break for breathing.
I: To be extremely busy.

23-42 নিজের চরকায় তেল দেওয়া   RL,SD
L: To oil one's own loom.
I: Mind one's own business.
E: To oil one's own machine.
If I am not meant to be their keeper, I will let geese be geese *[Dut.]*.
I have neither a male nor a female camel in it *[Ara.]*.

23-43 নিজের ঢাক নিজে পেটানো
L: To beat one's own drum.
I: To brag about oneself. Self-aggrandizement.
E: To blow one's own trumpet.
The sheikh's miracles are related by himself *[Tur.]*.

23-44 নিজের নাক কেটে পরের যাত্রাভঙ্গ করা   RL.SD,SB
L: To slice one's nose to create an ill omen to prevent some-one else from setting out on a journey.
I: To do a greater harm to oneself in an attempt to put another to trouble.
E: Don't cut off your nose to spite your face.
Burn not your house to frighten the mouse.
Dying to spite the graveyard *[Thai]*.
Cf. For some reason Qaseer amputated his nose *[Ara.]*.

23-45 নিজের পায়ে নিজে কুড়ুল মারা   RL,SD,SB,MW
L: To aim the axe at your own feet.

I: To foolishly do harm to oneself.

E: Don't dig your own grave with your own knife and fork.
    To shoot oneself in the foot.
    Never squat with your spurs on.
    Piercing one's shield with one's own spear *[Chi.]*.

23-46 নিজের বেলায় আঁটিসাঁটি, পরের বেলায় চিম্‌টি কাটি   SD,SB

L: You play it safe when the stake is yours, you try various stratagems when the stake is someone else's.

I: When it comes to your own interest, you play it safe;when it comes to others, you take risks or play tricks.

E: Play fast and loose with someone else's money.

23-47 নিতে জানে, দিতে জানে না   SD

L: Knows how to accept (a gift) but not how to give.

I: Said of a tight-fisted person.

E: Sweet's the wine, but sour's the payment.

23-48 নির্ধনের ধন আর কুৎসিতের/ অথর্বের যৌবন

L: Wealth for the poor and youth for the ugly/disabled (neither lasts).

I: Qualities/ attributes that are not natural to a person don't last.

23-49 নিপাতনে সিদ্ধ

L: Irregularly formed (in grammar). Something that is legitimised by the dictate of Grammar.

I: Accepted because of popularity but is otherwise irregular.

23-50 নির্বোধের নাই প্রমাদের ভয়

L: A fool has no fear of making a mistake.

I: A fool is not concerned about mistakes.

E: Who knows nothing, fears nothing.

23-51 নিম হাকিম, খতরা জান *[Hin.]*

L: Bad doctor, imperiled life.

I: A bad doctor is a danger to your life.

E: The ignorant doctor is no better than a murderer *[Chi.]*.

A young doctor means a new graveyard *[Ger.]*.

A half doctor takes your life away; a half Hakim, your faith *[Tur.]*.

23-52 নিমিত্তের ভাগী

L: A part of the cause (of some bad happening).

I: A person who fortuitously shares responsibility for some wrong-doing of another.

E: Bad rap.

23-53 নীচ যদি উচ্চ ভাষে সুবুদ্ধি উড়ায় হেসে   RL,SD

L: When a small man talks big, the wise dismisses him with a smile.

I: A wise man is not bothered by a fool's talk. Silence is the best reply to the fool.

E: Let the dog bark.

Dogs bark, but the caravan goes on.

23-54 নুন আনতে পান্তা ফুরোয় x21-17   RL,SD

L: No sooner you fetch the salt (to make stale rice edible) than you are out of rice.

I: Have trouble making both ends meet.

E: Live from hand to mouth.

23-55 নুন খাই যার গুণ গাই তার x29-39   SD

L: One praises him whose salt one eats.

I: Be grateful or loyal to your provider.

E: One speaks well about the bridge which carries him over.

Be true to your salt .

Whose bread I eat, his song I sing *[Ger.]*.

23-56 নেই কাজ তো খই ভাজ   RL,SD,SB

L: If you have nothing to do, pop some khoi (popcorn).

I: Someone is doing something unnecessary and spurious because he does not have any useful work to do.

E: Busy as a bee.

23-57 নেই মামার চেয়ে কানা মামা ভাল RL,SD,BDG,SB,MW

L: A blind uncle is better than no uncle.
I: Something that is less than whole is better than nothing at all.
E: A squint eye is better than no eye.
Half a loaf is better than none.
A little is better than none.
On a fishing lull, even a crayfish is a fish *[Rus.]*.

23-58 নেবু কচলাবে যত তেতো হবে তত SD,SB

L: The more you squeeze a lemon, the more bitter it gets.
I: Over-discussing an interesting subject may turn it into a dull subject.
E: The orange that is too hard squeezed yields a bitter juice.
Long churning makes a bad butter.

23-59 নেংটার নাই বাটপারের ভয় RL,SD

L: A naked person need not fear a thief.
I: Somebody who has nothing does not fear big losses.
E: A pauper has nothing to lose.

23-60 নেড়া বেলতলায় যায় ক'বার SB

L: How many times does the bald man go under the bel tree?
I: Repetition of anything becomes bitter/uninteresting.

23-61 ন্যাকা সাজা/ ন্যাকামি করা

L: To (conveniently) pretend to be a simple person (who is not understanding something).
I: To feign inability to comprehend something one does not want to confront/discuss.

23-62 ন্যায়-অন্যায় যেভাবেই হউক

L: Do something ethically or unethically, legally or illegally.
I: To do something by hook or by crook.
E: By hook or by crook.
By fair means or foul.

৳৩৫২

24-1 পগার পার হওয়া

L: To cross over the rampart.
I: To flee. Abscond.
E: To hightail it.

24-2 পঙ্গুর গিরিলঙ্ঘন   RL,SD

L: The lame crossing the mountain.
I: A miracle.

24-3 পচা আদার ঝাল বেশী   x7-45   RL,SD

L: Rotten gingerroot has greater pungence.
I: A bad person who is no longer able to do any harm still
    has his evil thoughts.

24-4 পথঃভূতে মিলিয়ে যাও

L: To mingle into the five elements.
I: To die.
E: "Earth to earth, ashes to ashes, dust to dust."

24-5 পথঃাশোর্ধ্বে বনং ব্রজেৎ [*Sans.*]

L: When you have crossed the age of fifty, you should retire
    to the forest.
I: As you grow old, start to withdraw from family life and
    seek a spiritual life. Act your age.
E: Act your age.

24-6 পটল তোলা   SD

L: To harvest potol (a vegetable).
I: To die.
E: To give up the ghost.
    Pushing up daisies.

24-7 পটের বিবি   SD

L: The framed picture of a queen.

I: A picturesque beauty.

E: Fit to be framed.

24-8 পদ্মা নদীর মাঝি

L: A boatman of the river Padma.

I: A romantic icon of the river-faring life.

24-9 পতিহীন যৌবন, সাজগোজ অকারণ   SB

L: If a young woman has no husband, her dressing up is pointless.

I: Why dress up when there is no one to see it?

E: All dressed up and no place to go.

24-10 পথিক পরাণ

L: A wanderer at heart.

I: A traveller at heart. One with wanderlust.

E: Wanderlust.

24-11 পথে কাঁটা দেওয়া   SD

L: To place thorns in one's way.

I: To impede or hinder someone.

24-12 পথে বসানো

L: To make someone squat on the street.

I: To ruin someone.

24-13 পরনিন্দা পরচর্চা

L: Defaming others and gossiping about others.

I: Gossiping.

E: Gossip needs no carriage *[Rus.]*.

      If you want world peace then hold your tongue *[Afr.]*.

24-14 পরনিন্দা অধোগতি   RL,SD

L: Defamation of others is a declivitous act.

I: By defaming others, one degrades oneself.

E: Whoever gossips to you will gossip about you *[Spa.]*.

24-15 পরস্পরের পিঠ চুলকানো

L: To scratch each other's back.
I: To exchange favours, flattery etc.
E: "You scratch my back, I will scratch yours."

24-16 পর্বতের আড়ালে থাকা   x26-8   RL,SD

L: To live in the shadow of a mountain.
I: To lead a sheltered life.
E: Whoever leans close to a good tree is blanketed by good shade *[Spa.]*.

24-17 পর্বতের মূষিক প্রসব   x26-19

L: A mountain giving birth to a mouse.
I: After building up great expectations, something most insignificant is produced.
E: Great boast, small roast *[Chi.]*.

24-18 পর্বতো বহিন্মান্ ধুমাৎ *[Sans.]*

L: If there is smoke over the (distant) hill, it must be on fire.
I: If there is a hint that something is wrong, take note.
E: Where there is smoke, there is fire.
If the wind comes from an empty cave, it is not without reason *[Chi.]*.
No smoke will come out where there is no fire *[Tur.]*.
Bushes don't rattle if there is no fire *[Hun.]*.

24-19 পড়িমরি করে করা

L: To do something so hurriedly that one appears to be falling or dying.
I: To do something in a great rush.
E: A rush job.

24-20 পরে কখনও পরের মর্ম বুঝে না

L: One cannot really feel for another.
I: One cannot really feel for another.
E: Don't judge a man until you have walked two moons in his moccasins *[AmInd.]*.

24-21 পরেছি যবনের হাতে, খানা খেতে হবে সাথে   SD,SB

L: (A Hindu says:) Now that I am in company of Moslems, (I am afraid) I will have to dine with them.

I: Social circumstances may force you to do something you would not do otherwise.

E: Dine with a stranger but save your love for your family [Afr.].

24-22 পরের ঘি পেলে, প্রদীপে দেয় ঢেলে   x7-110   RL,SD

L: When it is someone else's ghee, use it to fuel the lamp (in place of the cheaper alternative, oil).

I: One doesn't value something when it is easily acquired.

E: A borrowed mule soon gets a bad back [Syr.].

24-23 পরের ছেলে পরমানন্দ, যত উচ্ছন্নে যায় তত আনন্দ

L.   The more Paramananda   someone else's son – goes to the dogs, the more it pleases me.

I: To find pleasure in other people's misery.

E: A man can sleep on every hurt but his own.
     If somebody's mother goes mad, it is a good scene to watch [Ind.].
     The best joy is someone else's misfortune [Hun.].

24-24 পরের দোষ আকাশজোড়া, নিজের দোষ ছোট   SD

L: Someone else's fault is as big as the sky, your own fault is but small.

I: You tend to minimize your own fault and maximize other people's fault.

E: He can't see the beam in his own eye, but he's looking for an eyelash in someone else's [Aze.].
     A man who has one finger pointing at another has three pointing towards himself [Afr.].

24-25 পরের ধনে পোদ্দারি   RL,SD

L: To spend someone else's money like a generous banker.

I: To make free with other people's money.

E: Out of another's purse it is easy to be generous.

24-26 পরের পিঠে, বড় মিঠে SD.SB

L: Other people's pancakes are very sweet.
I: When you do not have something someone else has, it becomes more desirable to you.
E: The grass is greener on the other side of the fence.
A neighbour's hen looks as big as a goose, and his wife as young as a girl *[Tur.]*.
cf. Forbidden fruit is the sweetest *[Hun.]*.

24-27 পরের মন্দ করতে গেলে আপনার মন্দ আগে হয়

L: If you try to harm others, harm will come to you first.
I: If you try to harm others, harm will come to you first.
E: Curses, like chickens, come home to roost.
He who does evil to another, has done it to himself *[Tur.]*.
Don't dig a pit for somebody (to fall into), you will end up in it yourself *[Rus.]*.
He who digs a hole for another, falls in it himself *[Fin.]*.

24-28 পরের মাথায় কাঁঠাল ভাঙ্গা RL,SD,SB

L: To crack open a jackfruit on someone else's head.
I: To enjoy at other people's cost.
E: To make a cat's paw of a person.
Use your enemy's hand to catch a snake *[Pers.]*.
Use other's banquet to host own guests *[Uyg.]*.
Don't eat your bread on someone else's table *[Ara.]*.

24-29 পরের মাথায় হাত বুলানো SD

L: To run your hand over someone else's head.
I: To swindle someone.
E: Do not put your spoon into the pot which does not boil for you *[Rom.]*.

24-30 পরের মুখে ঝাল খাওয়া RL,SD,SB

L: To sample hot spices with someone else's palate.
I: To be guided by hearsay.

24-31 পক্ষির আহার

L: The meal of a bird.

I: A very small meal.
E: Bird feed.

24-32 পাঁচ আঙুল সমান হয় না   RL,SD,MW

L: Not all five fingers are of equal length.
I: Things of a kind may be individually different.
E: Your fingers can't be of the same length *[Chi.]*.

24-33 পাঁচমিশালী

L: A medley of five ingredients (as a curry).
I: A mix of diverse things.
E: Hodgepodge.
      Medley.

24-34 পাঁয়তারা কষা

L: To do some warm-up moves before actually engaging in something (wrestling e.g).
I: To continue the preliminary moves in an effort to forestall the actual event. Parading one's power or tactics.
E: Pussyfooting around.

24-35 পাকা ঘুঁটি কেঁচে যাওয়া   x7-106   SD

L: A game piece going from near the finish box back to the start box.
I: Undoing of an almost complete work.
E: To upset the applecart.

24-36 পাকা ধানে মই দেওয়া   RL,SD

L: To run a ladder over a ripe field of rice paddy.
I: To ruin something that has just come to fruition.
E: To upset the applecart.

24-37 পাগলে কি না বলে, ছাগলে কি না খায়   RL,SD,SB, MW

L: What doesn't a mad man say, what doesn't a goat eat?
I: An indiscriminate person can say or do anything.
E: Tell a fool to close the shutters, and he will close them all over the town *[Yid.]*.

24-38 পাছে লোকে কিছু বলে

L: Lest people should talk....

I: A debilitating fear to try anything.

24-39 পাটোয়ারী বুদ্ধি

L: The shrewdness of a wheeling-dealing businessman.

I: A shrewd head for business. Worldly wisdom.

24-40 পাড়া মাথায় করা   SD

L: To lift the whole neighbourhood up on one's head.

I: To disturb the peace of the neighbourhood by crying out.

E: To raise a hue and cry.

24-41 পাততারি গুটানো

L: To roll up one's scrolls.

I: Wind up a household or a business.

E: To leave with bag and baggage.
       To pack it in.

24-42 পাত্রাধার কি তৈল কিংবা তৈলাধার কি পাত্র

L: Is the bottle the container of the oil, or the oil the containner of the bottle?

I: Meaningless, esoteric debate.

E: Ask which was born first, the hen or the egg *[Ita.]*.

24-43 পান থেকে চুন খসা   RL,SD

L: The lime-paste slipping off a betel-leaf.

I: To commit a very negligible offence.

E: Storm in a tea cup.
       Storm in a glass of water *[Dut.]*.

24-44 পান না তাই খান না   SB

L: (He doesn't) eat it simply because (he) doesn't have anything to eat.

I: If one is depriving himself of something, it may be simply because he cannot afford it.

E: Sour grapes.

24-45 পাণ্ডব বর্জিত দেশ

L: A place forsaken by the Pandavas.
I: A desolate, uninteresting place.
E: Po-dunk.

24-45a পান্তাভাতে ঘি নষ্ট   SD

L: Wasting ghee on stale rice.
I: Adding something fine to something commonplace.
    Ludicrous spending of a costly thing.
E: Don't put gold buttons on a torn coat *[Alb.]*.

24-46 পান্তাভাতে নুন জোটে না, বেগুন পোড়ায় ঘি x25-8;32-30 SD

L: He has no salt to add to his stale rice, and dreams of
    adding ghee to roasted aubergines.
I: Unrealistic aspiration of person with limited means.

24-47 পাপের ধন প্রায়শ্চিত্তে যায়   RL,SD,BDG

L: Ill-gotten wealth will be used up in atonement.
I: Ill goten gains do not last.
E: Ill got, ill spent.
    What is got over the Devil's back will be spent under his
    belly.

24-48 পায়ে তেল দেওয়া

L: Oil somebody's feet/ leg.
I: To flatter servilely.
E: Licking somebody's boots.

24-49 পায়ে পড়ে থাকা

L: To lie at someone's feet.
I: To act servile and subservient to someone.
E: *Cf.* People who bite the hand that feeds them usually lick
    the boot that kicks them.

24-50 পায়ের ওপর পা দিয়ে বসে থাকা

24-50 পায়ের ওপর পা দিয়ে বসে থাকা

L: To sit around with legs crossed.
I: To lead a free life of comfort and indolence. To be idle.
E: Tweedling one's thumb.

24-51 পায়েসান্নের পর শুক্তো *ct* x 2-21

L: After the rice pudding comes the watery, bitter vegetable mash.
I: Serving bitter after sweets. One should eat in the correct order.
E: After sweetmeat/ rice pudding comes the sour sauce.

24-52 পালে বাঘ পড়া

L: A tiger pouncing onto a herd (of cows etc).
I: Someone or something spooking or terrorizing a group.

24-53 পালের গোদা   RL,SD

L: The leader of the pack or gang.
I: The ringleader.
E: The ringleader.

24-54 পি. পু. ফি. শো. (পিঠ পুরে, ফিরে শোও)

L: My back is on fire! Just turn over and go back to sleep. (Two lazy people talking in bed using only the initials of the words, while the house is no fire).

I: A humorous example of extreme laziness.

E: *Cf.* A lazy sheep thinks its wool heavy.
Cf. Ain't no use askin' the cow to pour you a glass of milk *[AfrAm.]*.
Ct. The elephant never gets tired of carrying its tusks *[Afr.]*.

24-55 পিতা স্বর্গ, পিতা ধর্ম

L: One's father is his true heaven, his true religion.

I: One's father is the highest person/ idol/ deity to him in every respect.

E: "Honour thy father."

24-56 পিতৃমুখী কন্যা সুখী, মাতৃমুখী পুত্র সুখী   SD

L: A daughter who takes after the father and a son who takes after the mother are the happy offspring.

I: A daughter who takes after the father and a son who takes after the mother are the happy offspring.

E: *ct.* Like father, like son, like mother, like daughter.
Clever father, clever daughter; clever mother, clever son *[Rus.]*.
ct. A daughter does not take advice except for her mother's example, a son does not take advice except for his father's example *[Tur.]*.
Mothers raise their daughters and let their sons grow up *[AfrAm.]*.

24-57 পিত্ত রক্ষা করা

L: To take care of one's liver (prevent bile juices that flow in an empty stomach).

I: To eat.

E: Nosh.

24-58 পিত্ত জ্বলে যাওয়া   SB

L: To feel as if the liver is on fire.

I: To be extremely angry or irritated.

24-59 পিণ্ড চটকানো SD

L: To knead someone's pinda (a round lump made of edibles that is used to perform the Hindu last rites).

I: To dress someone down (usually behind his back). To abuse or slander.

E: Tearing someone apart.
To lay into someone.

24-60 পিণ্ড দান করা x24-59 SD

L: To make a funerary offering of pinda.

I: To perform the last rites.

E: *Cf.* To throw a handful of dust.

24-61 পিপীলিকার পাখা ওঠে মরিবার তরে RL,SD,SB

L: The ant sprouts wings that will lead to their death.

I: A person who does a bad thing to an excess comes to a tragic end.

E: The ant had wings to hurt herself.
When the ant grows wings it is about to die *[Ara.]*.

24-62 পিলে চম্‌কে যাওয়া

L: To be startled down to one's spleen.

I: To be greatly startled.

E: To jump out of one's skin.

24-63 পিরিতে পেত্নীও ভাল x 27-24;29-47 MHP

L: When you are in love, even a petni (a ungainly female ghost) seems desirable.

I: Love is blind.

E: Love teaches even asses to dance *[Fch.]*.

24-64 পুকুর চুরি * x21-21 SD,MW

L: Theft of a pond or lake.

I: A very clever act of thievery. Robbery that is nearly impossible.

E: Daylight robbery.

24-64 পুকুর (a pond)

24-65 পুকুরের রুই মাছ জালে পড়ে কাঁদে,
না জানে গেরস্থের বউ কেমন করে রাঁধে x1-60   SD

L: The Rohu fish of the pond caught in the net weeps,
      anxious about how the housewife might cook it.
I: One who is about to lose everything still wants respect.
E: *cf:* Even the dog knows when he is stumbled on and when
      he is kicked.

24-66 পুঁটি মাছের পরাণ   SD,SB
L: The heartbeat of a Puti fish (a tiny edible fish).
I: A very fragile life.
E: Hanging by a thread.

24-67 পুঁটি মাছের ফরফরানি
L: The thrashing around of a Puti fish (in shallow water).
I: Bragging of a man of little importance.
E: A mule can swim seven deft strokes but the moment he
      sees water, he forgets them all *[Arm.]*.

24-68 পুত্র সম্পদ, মেয়ে আপদ   SB

L: A son is wealth, a daughter is trouble.
I: A son is an asset while a daughter is a liability.
E: "Have you come with a boy or a girl?" *[Aze.].*
    Cf. Marry your son when you will, and your daughter
    when you can *[Dan., Spa.].*

24-69 পুত্রার্থে ক্রিয়তে ভার্যা   *[Sans.]*   SD

L: One marries in order to have a son.
I: One marries for procreation of a male child.
E: It is the woman who bears the man *[Afr.].*

24-70 পুত্রাৎ শিষ্যাৎ ইচ্ছেৎ পরাজয়ম্ *[Sans.]*   x-9-41

L: Deafeat from the son or the disciple is a desirable thing.

I: A good mentor wishes his protégé to surpass him.

24-71 পূনর্মূ ষিকো ভব * *[Sans.]*   SD,SB

L: "Turn into a mouse again!"
I: Revert to the old, ignoble state (from an upgraded state).
E: Back to the pavilion.

24-72 পুরানো কাসুন্দি ঘাঁটা   SD

L: To stir up old Kasundi (an aged mustard sauce).
I: To stir up old, unpleasant matters.
E: If you will stir up the mire, you must bear the smell *[Dan.].*

24-73 পুরান চাউল ভাতে বাড়ে   RL,SD,SB

L: The older the rice, the larger the amount of cooked rice it
    makes.
I: Passage of time has a beneficial effect on certain things.
E: *Cf.* Old wine and friends improve with age *[Ita.].*

24-74 "পূর্ণিমার চাঁদ যেন ঝলসানো রুটি"   x-37

L: The full moon looks like a freshly fired roti (flat bread).
I: Existentialist statement about sublime beauty and stark
    hunger.

E: The rainbow might be better lookin' if 't wasn't such a cheap show *[AfrAm.]*.
       Even honour is not an honour if there is nothing to eat *[Rus.]*.

24-75 পৃষ্ঠ প্রদর্শন করা
L: To show one's back.
I: To flee.
E: To hightail it.

24-76 পেছনে চাকু মারা
L: To stab someone in the back.
I: To betray someone behind his back.
E: Back-stabbing.

24-77 পেছনে লাগা
L: A jackal stalking (a tiger).
I: Shadowy stalkers latching on persistently to someone prominent.
E: To pick up a tail.

24-78 পেটে খেলে পিঠে সয়   RL,SD, SB
L: If someone gives you food, you can stand some beating (from him).
I: You can stand some abuse from the hand that feeds you.
E: Pain is forgotten where gain follows.
       'Give me bread and call me stupid' *[Spa.]*.
       A dog is never offended at being pelted with bones *[Ita.]*.

24-79 পেটে খিদে মুখে লাজ   RL,SD,SB
L: Hungry, but too shy to ask for food.
I: To badly want something, but not wanting to let it show.
E: Refusing and wanting at the same time *[Afr.]*.

24-80 পেটে জিলিপির প্যাঁচ   x **13-20**
L: (His) entrails are coiled up like a jilebi (a pretzel-like sweetmeat with many twists).
I: A person who is very crafty and scheming by nature.

E: The crafty rabbit has three different entrances to its lair *[Chi.]*.

24-81 পেটে বোমা মারলেও ক'অক্ষর বেরোয় না ₓ7-1

L: Not even the first letter of the alphabet, 'Ka', will come out if a bomb explodes in his stomach.

I: Totally illiterate.

24-82 পেত্‌নীতে পেয়েছে

L: The Petni (a female ghost) has got hold (of her).

I: To act in an abnormal way not consistent with one's general nature.

E: To act like a woman possessed.

24-83 পৈতে থাকলেই বামুন হয় না ₓ19-16   SD

L: One is not a Brahmin just because he wears the sacred thread.

I: An outward symbol of virtue does not necessarily make one virtuous.

E: The cowl does not make the saint.
            If you put a silk dress on a goat he is still a goat.

24-84 প্রথম রাত্রে মারিবে বিড়াল *   SD

L: Slay the cat on the first night.

I: To perform a strong symbolic act early on to establish your position of authority so that no one will dare question it again.

E: Beat your wife on wedding day and your life will be happy *[Jap.]*.
            Whip the saddle and give the mule something to think *[Bul.]*.
            Kill the chicken to scare the monkey *[Chi.]*.
            'Daughter, I'm telling you; daughter-in-law, listen' *[Aze.]*.

24-85 প্রদীপের নীচেই অন্ধকার   RL,SD,SB

L: It is dark right underneath the earthen oil-wick lamp.

I: Someone that spreads virtue or good may himself lack these qualities.

E: The cobbler's children have no shoes.

Under the lamp it is dark *[Ara.].*
A diviner cannot accurately divine his own fortune *[Afr.]*

24-86 প্রবাসে নিয়মো নাস্তি   SD

L: When you are abroad, you don't have to observe all the
      (religious) rituals.
I: You don't have to observe the rituals if you are, for some
      reason, unable to.
E: When in Rome, do as the Romans do.

24-87 প্রহারেণ ধনঞ্জয় *   SD

L: To beat someone like Dhananjaya.
I: To give someone a good beating.
E: To beat someone black and blue.

৪৩৫

25-1 ফলেন পরিচীয়তে *[Sans.]*   RL,SD,BDG

L: (A tree is) known by its fruit.
     (An action) is judged by the result.
I: The goodness of an action will be clear from the result it produces.
E: A tree is known by its fruits.
     The rainmaker who doesn't know what he's doing will be found out by the lack of clouds *[Afr.]*.
     Looking at a tree see its fruits, looking at a man see his deeds *[Rus.]*.

25-2 ফাঁক পেলে সবাই চোর   x 34-62   SD

L: Given an opportunity to steal, anyone is apt to steal.
I: Opportunity to be corrupt can corrupt anyone.
E: Opportunity makes the thief.
     Where a chest lieth open, a righteous man may sin *[Chi.]*.

25-3 ফুটো পাত্রে জল ঢালা

L: Pour water into a leaky pot.
I: If you need to explain to a person it should be done at their level of understanding. Pouring money to a destitute family in vain.
E: Tailor your speech to your audience.
     Reading Bhagbat Geeta to a buffalo (is a waste) *[Ind.]*.

25-4 ফুলদল দিয়া কাটিলা কি বিধাতা শাম্মলী তরুবরে?

L: Has God felled the great Shalmoli tree by striking it with a boquet of flowers?
I: Surprise about an impossibility.

25-5 ফুলের ঘায়ে মূর্ছা যায়

25-5 ফুলের ঘায়ে মূর্ছা যায়   RL,SD,SB

L: To faint upon being struck by a flower.
I: To be easily hurt or bruised.
E: Hit me with a feather and knock me over.

25-6 ফুল্লরার বারমাস্যা *

L: The dull annual routine of Phullora.
I: A boring narrative that goes on and on.
E: Litany.

25-7 ফুৎকারে উড়িয়ে দেওয়া
L: To scatter something by blowing on it.
I: To dismiss something out of hand.
E: To pooh-pooh.

25-8 ফেন দিয়ে ভাত খায়, গল্পে মারে দই x 32-30   SD
L: Eating only watery rice (at home), and telling (the world)
    tall tales about eating rice with yogurt.
I: A poor man putting on airs of a rich man.
E: *Cf.* Even let God think that you eat pilaf *[Aze.]*.

25-9 ফেল কড়ি মাখ তেল x 2-23,33   SD,SB
L: Put down the cowrie shells (money), and by all means rub
    oil (all over you, before entering the bathhouse).
I: Pay the price, and the merchandise is yours!
    Alt. Outwardly friendly, but very business-like when the
    chips are down.
E: Show me the money.

25-10 ফোঁপরদালালি করা
L: To act as an uninvited, meddlesome agent.
I: To meddle overbearingly.
E: A buttinsky.

25-11 ফোড়ন দেওয়া/কাটা   SD,SB
L: To add heated oil and spices to a pot of stew, making a
    crackling noise.
I: To throw in a terse remark.
E: Throw little digs.

26-1 বকধার্মিক x26-45 RL,SD

L: The religious heron (pretending to be in deep meditation, to lull fish into coming near him).

I: A deceptive person. A hypocrite.

E: Wolf in sheep's clothing.

26-2 বজ্র আঁটুনি, ফস্‌কা গেরো RL,SD,BDG

L: To wrap something up in thunderously strong turns of rope, then finish with a loose, easily undone knot.

I: To do something with great care, then be careless finishing up, where utmost care is needed.

E: The stitch is lost unless the thread is knotted *[Ita.]*.

26-3 বড় গাছে আগে ঝড় লাগে RL,SD,SB

L: A tall tree is the first to catch the storm.

I: People who have the most visibility will catch the brunt.

E: Oaks may fall when reeds stand the storm.

A big tree attracts a woodman's axe.
The nail that sticks out gets pounded down.

26-4 বলা সহজ করা কঠিন MHP

L: Easy to say, hard to do.

I: Easy to tell others to do something, hard when it comes to doing it yourself.

E: Easier said than done.
It is one thing to cackle and another to lay an egg *[Ecu.]*.

26-5 বড় তো বে (বিয়ে), তা দু পায়ে আলতা SB

L: An insignificant wedding, and yet the bride has painted both her feet with alta (a red dye used for feet on festive occasions).

I: An insignificant occasion requires no fanfare.
E: A petty wedding requires no dressing.

26-6 বড়'র পিরিতি বালির বাঁধ

L: The love (for a lowly person) of the high and mighty is like a dam of sand.

I: If you hobnob with the high and mighty, prepare to be both accepted and slighted.

E: Poor man and the rich man do not play together *[Afr.]*.

26-7 বড় হবি তো ছোট হ' RL,SD

L: If you would be big, first be small.
I: Try being humble before trying to become someone big.
E: He that humbleth himself, shall be exalted.
If you want to build high, you must dig deep *[Mon.]*.
If a man is as wise as a serpent, he can afford to be as harmless as a dove *[AmInd.]*.

26-8 বটবৃক্ষের ছায়া x24-16

L: The shade of the Banyan tree.
I: The nurturing and sheltering cover of the family patriarch.
E: Whoever leans close to a good tree is blanketed by good shade *[Spa.]*.

26-9 বন গাঁয়ে শিয়াল রাজা x4-14 RL,SD,SB

L: In his little domain in the jungle, the fox is the king.
I: Everyone is important in his own little domain.
E: In the land of the blind, the one-eyed man is the king.
The Englishman is king in his own castle.
Where there are no eagles, I am the one, said the grasshopper *[Indo.]*.
(Being) big fish in a small pond *[Dut.]*.

26-8 বটবৃক্ষের ছায়া (Banyan tree: Waikiki, Oahu, Hawaii)

26-10 **বন্যরা বনে সুন্দর, শিশুরা মাতৃক্রোড়ে**
L: Wild things look natural in the jungle, children look natural in their mothers' lap.
I: Each thing looks natural in its own habitat.
E: *cf.* To everything there is a season.

26-11 **বয়সের গাছ পাথর নেই** RL,SD
L: (He is) so old that there are no trees or stones of the same age as him.
I: Hoary with age.
E: As old as the hills.

26-12 **ব্যাক্তি ডুবে যায় দলে, মালিকা পরিলে গলে প্রতি ফুলে কেবা মনে রাখে**

L: The individual gets lost in the crowd, when one wears a garland, is he mindful of each individual flower?

I: We lose sight of the goodness of the individual person when he is a part of many such persons.

26-13 বরের ঘরে মাসি, কনের ঘরের পিসি   RL,SD

L: The groom's maternal aunt, the bride's paternal aunt.

I: Selfish relatives who try to extract the most advantage from the other party (at a wedding, for example).

26-14 বলির পাঁঠা

L: A sacrificial goat.

I: One who is earmarked to be made a scapegoat or to be sacrificed in some way. A victim.

E: Sacrificial goat.

26-15 বসতে পেলে শুতে চায়   RL,SD

L: If you let him sit, he will want to lie down.

I: If you give him a little, he wants a lot.

E: Give him an inch and he will take a mile.
Want two instead of one (slice of bread) and that smeared in butter *[Ind.]*.
You give them a hand and they take your elbow *[Spa.]*.
Give a man some cloth and he'll ask for some lining *[Ara.]*.
Hold food in your hand and the dog will bite it *[Fch.]*.

26-16 বসন্তের কোকিল

L: A spring cuckoo.

I: A pleasure-loving, superficial person.

E: Summer soldier and sunshine patriot.

26-17 বসুধৈব কুটুম্বকম্ *[Sans.]*

L: The whole world is your relative.

I: Said of a person who befriends everyone.

E: *Cf.* All people are your relatives, therefore expect only trouble from them *[Chi.]*.

26-18 বসে খেলে রাজার গোলাও ফুরায়   SD

L: Even the royal treasury is emptied when an idle (jobless) person consumes it.

I: If you spend from a fund and do not work to replenish it, it is bound to run out.

E: Idle consumption empties even a king's treasure.
Drop by drop, the lake is drained out.
Always taking out of the meal-tub, and never putting in, soon comes to the bottom *[Spa.]*.
Constant dipping will empty the gourd of honey *[Afr.]*.

26-19 বহ্বারম্ভে লঘু ক্রিয়া   x1-21;24-17   SD,BDG,SB

L: A tremendously elaborate beginning leads to very little (in the end).

I: After a great build-up, disappointingly little is delivered.

E: Much ado about nothing.
Great boast and small roast *[Chi.]*.

26-20 বংশের শেষ সলতে

L: The last wick (as in an oil-wick lamp) of the family line.

I: The last surviving member of the family line.

E: Sole heir.

26-21 বাঁদর নাচ নাচানো   x11-6;19-24   SD

L: To make someone do the monkey dance.

I: To run someone rugged. To extremely harass someone.

E: To make someone jump through the hoops.

26-22 বাঁদরকে আদর করলে মাথায় ওঠে   x26-22

L: If you indulge a monkey, he will climb over your head.

I: If you indulge an undeserving person, he will take over your life.

E: When apes climb high, they show their naked rumps *[Dut.]*.
Seat a swine at the table, and he will put his feet on it *[Rus.]*.

26-23 বাঁশের চেয়ে কঞ্চিঃ দড়   SD,SB

L: A young bamboo stalk is stronger than the full-grown bamboo.

I: Suppleness or adaptability of the young can be an advantage over the strength of the adult.

E: The chip is tougher than the old block.
The greenhorn is tougher than a veteran.

26-24 বাক্যবাণে জর্জরিত

L: To pierce (someone) with volley a of word arrows.

I: To overwhelm somebody with words. To verbally abuse.

E: Cursing up a blue streak.

26-25 বাঙ্গালকে হাইকোর্ট দেখানো SD

L: To point out as the High Court any imposing city building, to a provincial person.

I: To deceive a simple person.

E: To shave a fool without lather *[Dut.]*.

26-26 বাঘে ছুঁলে আঠারো ঘা RL,SD

L: Once the tiger attacks, you will get at least eighteen wounds.

I: Once an ill fotune befalls you, it will take its full toll. To fall in a trouble which creates many problems.

E: Misfortunes come on horseback and depart on foot *[Fch.]*.

26-27 বাঘের ঘরে ঘোগের বাসা RL,SD,SB

L: The Ghogh (a small animal that eats tiger cubs) has settled down in the tiger's den.

I: Your mortal enemy has found a niche in your own home.

E: A wolf in a lion's den.
It is a bold mouse that makes her nest in a cat's ear *[Dan.]*.

26-28 বাণিজ্যে বসতে লক্ষ্মীঃ *[San.]* SD,SB

L: Lakshmi (the Goddess of Wealth) sits in the place of commerce.

I: The industrious person attains wealth and prosperity.

E: Trade is the mother of money.

26-29 বাতাসের গলায় দড়ি দিয়ে ঝগড়া করা SD

L: To put a noose round the neck of wind and pick a quarrel.

I: To pick a quarrel for quarrel's sake.
E: To shadow box.
To bark against the moon.

26-30 বানর ও তৈলাক্ত বাঁশের অংক * ₓ5-18

L: The maths problem about the monkey climbing an oiled (slippery) bamboo pole.
I: A hard-to-make-progress situation. You advance two steps and fall back one.
E: Slippery slope.

26-31 বানরের গলায় মুক্তার মালা ₓ1-43   RL,SD,SB
L: A pearl necklace round a monkey's neck.
I: Incongruous finery or decoration.
E: A ring of gold in a sow's nostril *[Lat.]*.
To play violin for the water buffalo to listen to *[Thai]*.
Even if a monkey wears a gold ring, it is and remains an ugly creature *[Dut.]*.
Pearls for the pigs *[Dut.]*.

26-32 বানের জলে ভেসে আসা   SD
L: Something that floated in with the flood water.
I: Something that has come to you fortuitously. A person who feels rootless.

26-33 বাপ্‌কা বেটা সিপাইকা ঘোড়া *[Hin.]* ₓ29-76   SD,BDG
L: A son gets his qualities from his father, a horse from the soldier (the rider).
I: Like father, like son.
E: A chip of the old block.
Like father, like son.
The apple doesn't fall far from the tree.
The apple will fall under the apple tree *[Grk.]*.
Dogs don't make cats *[Fch.]*.
Ct. A miser's son is generally a spendthrift.

26-34 বাপের জন্মেও না

L: Not even in the entire time going back to my father's birth!

I: Never in a million years!

E: When pigs fly!

If the sky falls, we shall catch larks.

When the camel's tail touches the ground *[Uyg.]*.

26-35 বাবারও বাবা আছে   MHP

L: Even father has a father.

I: However fierce is the torturer, there is somebody to punish him/ put him in line.

E: To every high mountain, there is a higher one *[Rus.]*.

A master has their master too *[Fin.]*.

26-36 বাবু মরেন শীতে আর ভাতে   SD

L: The Babu (gentleman) has a hard time keeping up appearances in harsh winter and when he has no rice.

I: Keeping up appearances in adverse times is difficult.

E: Honour buys no meat in the market *[Spa.]*.

26-37 বামন হয়ে চাঁদে হাত দেওয়া   SD,SB

L: A dwarf wanting to touch the Moon.

I: Audaciously aspiring far beyond one's means, abilities, station in life etc.

E: Fools rush where angels fear to tread.

Who reaches for the spruce, falls down onto the juniper *[Fin.]*.

An owl craving for the moon *[Indo.]*.

26-38 বামুন গেল ঘর তো লাঙল তুলে ধর   RL.SD,SB

L: Put away the plough as soon as the Brahmin (the boss) goes home.

I: To stop working when no one is supervising.

E: When the cat is away, the mice begin to play.

When the cat is absent, the mice dance *[Grk.]*.

If the cat is not at home, the mice will sing *[Hun.]*.

Without a cat mice feel free *[Rus.]*.

When cat is away from house, the mice dance (on the table) *[Dut.]*.

26-39 বার ভুতে খায়

L: Twelve ghosts consume (someone's wealth or inheritance).

I: Rank outsiders squandering away someone's unguarded wealth, inheritance etc.

26-40 বার মাসে তের পার্বণ   RL,SD,SB

L: Thirteen festivals packed into twelve months.

I: A very full calendar of festivities. A very festive people.

E: *cf.* Party hearty.

26-41 বারে বারে ঘুঘু তুমি ধান খেয়ে যাও   SD

L: You (confounded) dove, time and again you are getting away with eating our rice paddy!

I: You have got away with it once too often!

E: *Cf.* When you go up to the mountain too often, you will eventually encounter the tiger *[Chi.]*.

26-42 বারো হাত কাঁকুড়ের তের হাত বীচি   SD

L: A twelve cubit long squash has a thirteen cubit long seed.

I: Something that exceeds its own container. A son who exceeds the father in some aspect (usually bad).

E: *Cf.* Too big for one's breeches.
   The peg is greater than the stake *[Indo.]*.

26-43 বাসর সাজিয়ে বসে থাকা

L: To sit alone in the middle of a decorated wedding hall.

I: To prepare a stage, only to have no one turn up.

E: "Suppose they gave a war and no one came..."

26-44 বিড়াল নরম মাটি দেখলেই আঁচরায়   MHP

L: A cat always scratches the soft ground.

I: Everybody attacks a person who is soft/ gentle.

E: Beat up on the little guy.

26-45 বিড়াল তপস্বী x26-1

RL,SD,SB

L: The meditating cat (pretending to be harmless, waiting for his prey to approach him).

I: A pretender.

E: Wolf in sheep's clothing.
Like cat drinking milk with eyes closed *[Ind.]*.

26-46 বিড়ালের গলায় ঘন্টা বাঁধবে কে? x28-110

L: Who's to bell the cat?

I: Who is to spearhead a collective assault?

E: Who's to bell the cat?

26-47 বিড়ালের ভাগ্যে শিকে ছেঁড়া SD,SB

L: By a stroke of the cat's luck, the hanging (out-of-reach) food basket falls to the floor.

I: A unexpected stroke of good luck.

E: Like obtaining a fallen durian fruit *[Indo.]*.

26-48 বিদুরের ক্ষুদ * SD

L: Bidur's offering of chipped rice grains.

I: A meager gift made by a poor man with sincere heart.

E: *Cf.* The Little Drummer Boy: "I am a poor boy too,... I have no gift to bring... That's fit to give the King... Shall I play for you... On my drum?"

26-49 বিদ্যা যত দিবে দান ততই বাড়িবে

L: The more you give of your knowledge, the more it will grow.

I: By teaching others, you enrich yourself.

E: As you teach, you learn *[Jew.]*.
If you always give, you will always have *[Chi.]*.
By learning you will teach, by teaching you will learn *[Lat.]*.

26-50 বিদ্যা দদাতি বিনয়ম্ *[Sans.]*

L: Learning makes you humble.

I: Learning makes you humble.

26-51 বিধবার একাদশী,করলে আর ভাল কি, না করলেই পাপ   RL,SB

L: The monthly fasting of the widow: If you observe it there is no benefit, but if you don't it is a sin.
I: A custom, the observing of which has no benefits, but not observing is detrimental.

26-52 বিধি যদি করে মন, তুষ্ট হতে কতক্ষণ   SD

L: If God wills, how long can it take for you to be satisfied?
I: If God is with you, you can succeed. If destiny desires, one can be satisfied any moment.
E: If God wills all winds bring rain.

26-53 বিধির লিখন, না যায় খণ্ডন   x7-26;29-40; 31-7   SD

L: One cannot undo what God has written (as your fate).
I: One cannot ignore fate.
E: Inevitable are the decrees of God.
      "It is written."

26-54 বিবেকের দংশন

L: The bite of conscience.
I: One's conscience troubling him.
E: The prick of conscience.

26-55 বিনা পয়সায় পেলে বিষও খায়   SD

L: He will eat even poison if it is free.
I: Someone who loves free things.
E: When the wine is free even the judge drinks it.
      Even vinegar is sweet when for a freebie *[Rus.]*.

26-56 বিনা সুতার সেলাই

L: Stitches without thread.
I: The relations of love.
E: Bonds of love.

26-57 বিনামেঘে বজ্রপাত x2-7   RL,SD,BDG,SB

L: Lightning and thunderclap without any (foretelling) clouds.

I: A sudden calamity without any prelude or forewarning.

E: A bolt from the blue.

26-58 বিনাশকালে বিপরীতবুদ্ধিঃ *[Sans.]*   SD

L: When one is facing doom, his mind works against him.

I: When one is going under, he makes wrong decisions.

26-59 বিপদ কখনও একা আসে না   SD

L: Misfortune never comes alone.

I: Misfortune never comes alone.

E: Trouble always comes in pairs.
If you have escaped the jaws of the crocodile while bathing in the river, you will surely meet a leopard on the way home.
Trouble never comes alone *[Rus.]*.
A person slips and the ladder falls on him *[Indo.]*.

26-60 বিশ্বাসে মিলায়ে কৃষ্ণ, তর্কে বহুদূর   SD

L: You can find Lord Krishna through blind faith, you cannot find Him through debate/ questioning.

I: God is accessible only through faith.

E: Faith moves mountains.

26-61 বিষ নেই তার কুলোপানা চক্কর

L: A snake who has no venom, but is coiled and has a hood.

I: A futile rage of an impotent person.

26-62 বিষয় থাকলেই ব্যবস্থা হয়

L: If you have the money, you can take care of things.

I: If you have the money, you can take care of things.

26-63 বিষদাঁত ভাঙা   SD

L: To pull out one's poisonous fang.

I: To disarm or neutralise someone. To render someone harmless.

26-64 বিষে বিষক্ষয়/ বিষস্য বিষমৌষধি [Sans.] RL,SD

L: Poison counteracts poison.
I: Something harmful used as its own antidote.
E: One poison drives out another.
Fight poison with poison.

26-65 বিসমিল্লায় গলদ x9-48 SD

L: To make an error right at the Bismillah (the first word of a
Moslem prayer).
I: To make an error right at the beginning.
E: (To make a mistake) right off the bat.

26-66 বীজের মাঝে বনস্পতি

L: The giant tree of the forest is right within the seed.
I: All the makings of a great thing are contained in the seed.
E: Great oaks grow from little acorns.
Child is the father of man.
All the flowers of tomorrow are in the seeds of yesterday.
You already possess everything necessary to become great
[AmInd.]
From the seed grows the tree [Ara.].

26-67 বীরভোগ্যা বসুন্ধরা SD

L: Heroes enjoy the Earth.
I: Heroes enjoy the Earth.
E: Cf. Luck is infatuated with the efficient [Per.]

26-68 বৃহস্পতিবারের বারবেলা x32-11

L: The noon hour of Thursday.
I: An inauspicious time.
E: Neither marry nor travel on Tuesday or Friday! [Ita.].

26-69 বুক ফাটে তো মুখ ফোটে না SD,SB

L: Even though her chest is about to explode (from holding
in something she wants to say), she does not utter a word.

I: Said of someone who endures a lot without complaining. When one is extremely eager to speak out one's mind, one's tongue obstinately keeps mum.

26-70 বুকে বসে দাড়ি উপড়ানো

26-70 বুকে বসে দাড়ি উপড়ানো   SD
L: Sit on someone's chest and rip out his beard.
I: To subjugate and torture someone.

26-71 বুড়ী ছোঁয়া   SD
L: To touch the 'buri' or the marker post (as a sign that you passed through here).
I: To make a quick or symbolic visit.
E: A whistle stop.
       A flying visit.

26-72 বুড়ো পাখি পোষ মানে না   SD
L: An old bird is not tamable.
I: A person who is set in his ways/ habits is hard to retrain.

E: You cannot teach a old dog new tricks.
       An old Moor will never make a good Christian *[Spa.]*.

26-73 বুড়ো শালিকের ঘাড়ে রোঁ   SD

L: Fine soft feather on the shoulder of an old black bird.
I: Youthful fancy or aspiration of an old man.
E: There is no fool like the old fool.

26-74 বুড়োয় বুড়োয় কথা কয়, প্রতি কথায় কাসি,

যুবায় যুবায় কথা কয়, প্রতি কথায় হাসি।   RL

L: When old men chat, you hear lots of coughing; when young people chat, you hear lots of laughing.
I: Every age has its characteristics.
E: Youth looks ahead and old age looks back and middle age looks tired *[Afr.]*.
       Youth (love) and cough can't be hidden *[Grk.]*.

26-75 বুদ্ধি থাকলে শ্বশুরবাড়িতে খেটে খেতে হয় না   RL

L: If you are clever, you won't have to work for your meals at your in-laws.
I: If you are clever, you can get by with minimal work almost anywhere.
E: A fool does a lot of work, a wise man gets off easier *[Fin.]*.

26-76 বুদ্ধিতে বৃহস্পতি   RL,SD,SB

L: A Vrihaspati (Jupiter) in wisdom.
I: A very wise man.
E: A Solomon.

26-77 বুদ্ধির ঢেঁকি   SD

L: (He has) the intelligence of a rice husking pedal.
I: A blockhead. A great fool.
E: A dunderhead.

26-78 বুদ্ধি যার, বল তার x13-32;29-45   SD

L: Whoever is clever is mighty.
I: Whoever is clever is mighty.
E: Knowledge is power.

26-79 বৃদ্ধাংগুষ্ঠ/ বুড়ো আঙুল দেখানো

L: To show one the thumb.
I: A sign of taunt or defiance.
E: To thumb one's nose at.

26-80 বৃদ্ধস্য তরুণী ভার্য্যা [Sans.]   SD

L: An old man's young wife.
I: A May-December marriage.
E: Young maid married to an old man is like a house
thatched with old straw.
The old cat looks for a young mouse [Tur.].

26-81 বেকারের চেয়ে বেগার ভাল   MHP

L: It is better to work without pay than be unemployed.
I: It is better to keep busy than to do nothing or being lazy.

26-82 বেঙের ছাতা   SD

L: The umbrella of a frog (toadstool).
I: An ephemeral appearance.

26-83 বেঙের সর্দি   SD

L: A frog catching a cold.
I: A most unlikely or bizarre malady.

26-84 বেল পাকলে কাকের কি   RL,SD,BDG,SB

L: What does it matter to the crow if the Bel fruit ripens?
(He cannot break into it because of the hard exterior!).
I: Said of someone who becomes jubilant over a situation
that has no benefits for him.
E: It makes no difference to the blind when a circus party
comes to city.
There is nothing to do with a duck if the water is flooding
from the river [Uyg.].

26-85 বৈতরণী পার হওয়া *   SD

L: Crossing the river Vaitarani.
I: Passing away. Going to the Hereafter.
E: To cross the Stygian river.

26-86 বৈষ্ণব বিনয়

L: Politeness befitting a Vaishnava.

I: Greatly humble. Exemplary politeness.

26-87 বোঝার ওপর শাকের আঁটি   RL,SD,SB

L: A bunch of spinach on top of the heavy bundle (load).

I: A small but significant addition to an already ponderous
    burden.

E: The straw that breaks the camel's back.
    The last straw.
    It's the drop of water that makes the jug overflow *[Ara.]*.
    The drop that floods the bucket *[Dut.]*.

26-88 বোবার শত্রু নাই   RL,SD

L: A dumb person has no enemies.

I: He who speaks not, creates no enemies.

E: Silence is golden .
    Into a closed mouth no fly will enter *[Afr.]*.

26-89 ব্রহ্মকর্ম সমাধিনা *[Sans.]*

L: To fulfill the service to Brahma.

I: To eat.

E: There is no god like one's stomach, we must sacrifice to it
    every day *[Afr.]*.

৯০২

27-1 ভগবান যাকে দেন তাকে দু'হাত ভরে দেন
L: Whomsoever God chooses to give, He gives him lavishly.
I: God's favour is unlimited to some.

27-2 ভদ্রলোকের পাতে দেওয়া যায় না
L: Not fit to be served on the dinner plate of a gentleman.
I: Something that is not up to standard. Not presentable.
E: Not servable in polite company.

27-3 ভবিতব্য খণ্ডাবে কে? x7-25;27-11   SD
L: Who will change destiny?
I: Who will change destiny?
E: Fate rules everywhere.

27-4 ভবের হাট
L: The marketplace of the world.
I: The world stage.
E: The vanity fair

27-5 ভয়ে পেটের ভেতরে হাত পা সেঁদিয়ে যাওয়া
L: One's arms and legs retracting into one's belly out of fear.
I: To be greatly afraid.
E: To have one's heart in one's mouth.

27-6 ভস্মে ঘি ঢালা   RL,SD
L: To pour ghee over ashes.
I: To waste valuable resources on something to no avail.
E: Pouring down the drain.

27-7 ভরা কলসীর শব্দ কম
L: A full pitcher makes less noise.
I: A wise person talks less.
E: A loaded wagon makes no noise.

27-8 ভাই ভাই ঠাঁই ঠাঁই   RL,SD,BDG

L: Brothers should best set up separate households.
I: If brothers live together, relations become strained. A prescription for harmonious living.
E: Brothers will part.
    A landmark is very well placed between the fields of two brothers [Fch.].
    Two bears in one cave will not end up well [Mon.].
    Visit each other but don't be neighbours [Ara.].
    From far away and beloved rather than close by and argueing [Grk.]

27-9 ভাগাড়ে গরু পড়ে, শকুনির টনক নড়ে   RL,SD

L: When a cow dies in the corral, the vulture becomes alert.
I: When a selfish person senses opportunity, he zeroes in.
E: Hungry kite sees a dead horse afar.
    Where the carcass is, there shall the eagles be gathered together.
    Where the carcass is, there fly the crows [Dut.]

27-10 ভাগের মা গঙ্গা পায় না   x16-8   RL,SD,BDG

L: A mother of many does not receive the last rites in the Ganges (because no individual child takes responsibility).
I: What belongs to all belongs to none.
E: Everybody's business is nobody's business.

27-11 ভাগ্যং ফলতি সর্ব্বত্র   [Sans.]   SD

L: Fate rules everywhere.
I: Fate cannot be resisted.
E: Fate rules everywhere.

27-12 ভাগ্যবানের কিনা হয়, অভাগার কিনা ভয়   SD

L: The lucky achieves everything, the luckless fears every - thing.
I: The lucky achieves everything, the luckless fears every - thing.
E: A lucky person is someone who plants pebbles and harvests potatoes [Grk.].
    His luck splits the stone [Ara.].

27-13 ভাগ্যবানের বউ মরে, অভাগার স্বামী মরে

L: Lucky man's wife dies, the unlucky woman's husband dies.

I: A widower can marry again, but a widow becomes a destitute.

27-14 ভাগ্যবানের বোঝা ভগবানে বয় SD

L: God bears the burden of the lucky person.

I: God bears the burden of the lucky person.

27-15 ভাঙ্গা হাঁড়ি জোড়া লাগে না   x **12-10**
RL,SD

L: A shattered claypot cannot be put together.

I: A broken marriage or joint family cannot be put together.

E: Credit lost is like a broken glass.
The cracked glass cannot be fixed *[Grk.].*

27-15   মাটির হাঁড়ি (Claypots)

27-16 ভাঙ্গে তবু মচ্‌কায় না x28-28 — SD

L: It would rather break than bend.
I: An unyielding person.
E: It will snap asunder rather than bend.

27-17 ভাজা মাছটি উল্টে খেতে জানে না — SD

L: (He) doesn't know how to turn over a fried fish and eat (the other side).
I: To feign ignorance of what is common knowledge.
E: To act dumb.

27-18 ভাত ছড়ালে কাকের অভাব নেই — RL,SD, SB

L: If you scatter rice (on the ground), there will be no shortage of crows.
I: You can attract a lot of people by throwing money around.
E: You can attract a lot of flies with honey

27-19 ভাত পায়না খেতে, সোনার আংটি হাতে x32-30 — RL,SD

L: He does not have enough rice to eat, but sports a gold ring on his finger.
I: Incongruous decoration on a destitute person.

27-20 ভানুমতীর খেল — SD

L: The magic of Bhanumati.
I: Fine magic. A magic-like sight.

27-21 ভাবিতে উচিত ছিল প্রতিজ্ঞা যখন x27-22

SD

L: You should have thought (of the consequences) when you made the promise.
I: You should have thought (of the consequences) when you made the commitment.
E: *Cf.* In the midst of great joy, do not promise anyone anything. In the midst of great anger, do not answer anyone's letter [Chi.].
   cf. Promises are meant to be kept [Fch.].

27-22 ভাবিয়া করিও কাজ্, করিয়া ভাবিও না ×27-21

L: Think and then do, don't do and then think.

I: Think and then do, don't do and then think.

E: Look before you leap. Think before you speak.
Before you are thirsty, dig a well *[Chi.]*.
Your mouth will not smell if you do not eat garlic *[Tur.]*.
He who goes near soot smells soot *[Fin.]*.
Thinking first is an asset, regret later is useless *[Indo.]*.

27-23 ভাল কথা পড়ল মনে আঁচাতে আঁচাতে,
ঠাকুরঝিকে নিয়ে গেল নাচাতে নাচাতে   RL, SD

L: As I was washing my mouth after the supper, good thing I remembered to tell you that my sister-in-law was snatched away (by the crocodile), looking as if she was dancing on the water.

I: Reflecting the strained relationship between the bride and the in-laws.

E: Well-married is when you have no mother-in-law and no sister-in-law *[Spa.]*.

27-24 ভালবাসার নৌকা পাহাড় বেয়ে যায়   ×24-63;29-47

L: The boat of love or affection can ascend mountains.

I: Strength of love can accomplish much.

E: Love conquers all.
Cf. Being in love, one may not see the true nature *[Fin.]*.

27-25 ভাল্লুকের জ্বর   SD

L: Bear's fever (a fever that is accompanied by great shivers, and subsides quickly).

I: A short-lasting condition of illness.

27-26 ভিক্ষায়াং নৈব নৈব চ *[Sans.]*   SD

L: Never by begging.

I: Never by begging. However you get it, don't do it by begging!

27-27 ভিক্ষার চাল কাঁড়া আর আকাঁড়া   SD

L: Why be choosy as to whether the rice got from begging has stone chips in it or not?
I: Beggars can't be choosers.
E: Beggars can't be choosers.
    Don't look a gift horse in the mouth.
    Little is better than nothing *[Fin.]*.

27-28 ভিটায় ঘুঘু চরানো   RL,SD,SB

L: To make doves roam in the ruins of one's ancestral home.
I: To totally ruin someone financially.
E: To take someone to the cleaners.

27-29 ভিমরুলের চাকে ঢিল ছোঁড়া x28-122   RL,SD

L: To pelt a stone at a hornet's nest.
I. To unleash great pandemonium and danger.
E: To stir up a nest of hornets.
    Do not roast baobab kernels and leave those who have teeth chewing (on them) *[Afr.]*.

27-30 ভীমরতি ধরেছে   SD

L: To be possessed by senility.
I: To start to show old-age related idiosyncracies.
E: Young people don't know what old age is, and old people forget what youth was.
    An old man does not fall out of step - he slides *[Afr.]*.

27-31 ভুলের মাশুল দেওয়া

L: To pay the price for one's mistake.
I: To pay the price for one's mistake.
E: Pay the piper.

27-32 ভুশুণ্ডীর কাক/ কাকভুশুণ্ডী x2-47   SD

L: A wise, very old crow with vast experience of the past that lives in the mythical field of Bhushandi.
I: An ancient, wise and very old man.
E: *cf.* Yoda.

27-34 ভূতের নাচ

27-34 ভূতের নাচ
L: The dance of ghosts.
I: An unruly and ungainly melee.

27-35 ভূতের বাপের শ্রাদ্ধ   SD
L: Funeral service for the father of the ghost.
I: Great and gross waste.

27-36 ভূতের মুখে রাম নাম   SD
L: The name Rama being chanted by a ghost.
I: A most incongruous homage.

27-37 ভেড়া বানানো   SD
L: To turn someone into a sheep.
I: To subjugate someone. Make someone docile.

27-38 ভেড়ার পাল x9-3   SD

L: A flock of sheep.
I: A group in which everyone follows the one in front blindly.
E: If one sheep leaps over the dyke, all the rest will follow.

27-39 ভেতো বাঙ্গালী x28-44   RL,SD,SB

L: Rice-eating Bengali.
I: The weak and timid Bengali (said in humour or sarcasm).

27-40 ভেবে তল না পাওয়া

L: To think and think but not be able to fathom.
I: To face something difficult to understand.
E: Unable to fathom.

27-41 ভেরেণ্ডা ভাজা   3D

L: To roast Bharenda (castor oil) seeds.
I: To engage in useless and unproductive effort.
E: To carry the day out in baskets *[Dut.]*.

27-42 ভোগের কর্তা ভগবান   SD

L: God decides if and when you will eat.
I: God alone provides.
E: God giveth . . .

27-43 ভোজনং যত্রতত্র, শয়নং হট্টমন্দিরে *[Sans.]*

L: He eats wherever he can, and sleeps in the marketplace.
I: A vagabond without any roots.
E: Home is where I put down my luggage.

27-44 ভ্যাবা গঙ্গারাম   SD

L: Gangaram the dolt.
I: A silly person. An utter fool.

৬০২

28.

28-1 **মগের মুল্লুক** *

RL.SD

L: The land of the Mogs.
I: A lawless frontierland/ country.
E: "Wild West."

28-2 **মণিকাথ৯ন যোগ**

SD

L: A conjunction of gems and gold.
I: An ideal combination of glitter and gold.
E: Glitter and gold.

28-3 **মধুরেণ সমাপয়েৎ** [*Sans.*]

RL,SD,BDG

L: End (the meal) with (a course of) honey.
I: A sweet ending.
E: All's well that ends well.

28-4 **মন চাঙ্গা তো ঘাটে গঙ্গা**

SD

L: If your mind is strong, you could see the Ganges flowing to your doorstep.
I: If your mind is pure, all else is peaceful.
E: A clear conscience is a soft pillow.

28-5 **মন দিলে মন পাওয়া যায়**

L: Give your heart to somebody and you will get theirs.
I: If you are devoted to someone, he/ she will also be devoted to you.
E: Love begets love [*Dan.*].

28-6 **মন না রাঙ্গায়ে যোগী রাঙ্গালি শুধু কাপড়**

L: Yogi, you have coloured your robe (saffron), but not your mind.
I: Changing the outward appearance does not necessarily change a person on the inside.

E: The cowl does not make the saint.
A mule can go to Mecca, but it will not come back as a pilgrim [Ara.].

28-7   মনসা চীয়তে বাক্য বচসা মা প্রকাশয়েৎ [Sans.] x32-7

L: Think (first) what you want to say, don't say it out loud.
I: Think before you speak.
E: Think before you speak.

28-8   মনের অগোচরে পাপ নেই/ মন্দ ভাবলে মন্দ হয়   SD

L: There is no sin that is not known to the mind.
I: Thinking makes something good or bad, evil is in the mind.
E: Evil to him who evil thinks [Fch.].

28-9   মন্ত্রমুদ্ধ (হয়ে শোনা)

L: (Listening) spell-bound.
I: To listen with rapt attention.
E: Spellbound.
Hanging on every word.
Clinging to someone's lips [Dut.].

28-10   মন্ত্রের সাধন কিংবা শরীর পাতন   SD

L: Either achieve the fruits of your worship, or give your life trying.
I: Worship as if your life depends on it.
E: Do or die.

28-11   মন্দ খবর বাতাসের আগে চলে

L: Bad news travels ahead of the wind.
I: Bad news travels fast.
E: Ill news runs apace.
Trouble rides a fast horse [Ita.].

28-12   মন্দের ভাল   SD

L: The positive in a bad situation.
I: The good element in an overall bad situation.
E: Every cloud has a silver lining.

28-13 মরণকালে জিঅন কাঠি   RL,SD

L: Wand of life at the time of death.
I: A measure that comes too late.
E: It is no time to go for the doctor when the patient is dead.

28-14 মরণকালে ঔষধ নাই

L: When death is imminent, there is no medicine for it.
I: Death is not preventable.
E: Death defies doctors.

28-15 মরণকালে হরিনাম

L: Take the name of Lord Hari at deathbed.
I: Taking the name of God only in time of need.
E: We forget even incense in easy times; come hard times, we embrace the Buddha's feet *[Chi.]*.
  When your horse is on the brink of a precipice, it is too late to pull the reins *[Chi.]*.
  A sinking vessel needs no navigation *[Afr.]*.
  Cf. When the danger is past God is cheated *[Ita.]*.

28-16 মরণ–বাঁচন সমস্যা

L: A life-and-death situation.
I: A very critical condition.
E: A life-and-death situation.

28-17 মরণের সময় অসময় নাই

L: Death does not recognize if the hour is convenient to you.
I: Death can come at any time.
E: Death keeps no time.

28-18 মরবার ফুরসৎ/ সময় নেই   RL,SD,SB

L: I can't even take a break to die.
I: A very busy person.
E: The busy bee has no time for sorrow.

28-19 মরমে মরে যাওয়া   x 22-5

L: To die at the very core of one's heart.

I: To be greatly embarrassed or ashamed.
E: I wish I could vanish.

28-20 মরা মানুষে কথা কয় না   SD
L: A dead man does not speak.
I: The secret is safe with a man who is dead.
E: Dead men tell no tales.
   A dead man cannot make war *[Fch.]*.

28-21 মরা হাতির দাম লাখ টাকা   RL,SD
L: A dead elephant can still fetch one lakh rupees.
I: The ruins of something great is still valuable.
E: The very ruins of greatness are great.

28-22 মরার উপর খাঁড়ার ঘা   SD,BDG,SB
L: Striking a corpse with a sword.
I: An unnecessary vengeful measure. To add insult to injury.
E: To slay the slain.
   To flog a dead horse.

28-23 মরিয়া না মরে রাম এ কেমন বৈরী SD
L: What kind of an enemy is Rama! Even when I kill him, he does not die!
I: A hard-to-defeat enemy.
E: A cat has nine lives.

28-24 মরীচিকার পিছনে ছোটা
L: To run after a mirage.
I: To chase an illusion. To pursue an unattainable goal.
E: To chase the rainbows.
   The horizon will not disappear as you run towards it *[Afr.]*.

28-25 মশা মারতে কামান দাগা x3-5 RL,SD,BDG,MW
L: Fire a cannon fusilade to kill a mosquito.
I: To employ a disproportionately large measure to a small problem.
E: Take not a musket to kill a butterfly.

Take a sledge hammer to crack a nut.
Shooting sparrows with a cannon *[Hun.]*.
To shoot a mosquito with a cannon *[Dut.]*.

28-26 **মশা মেরে হাত কালো** x12-8 SD

L: To stain one's hand by swatting a mosquito.

I: To spoil one's reputation by doing something that was not worth it.

E: Sue a beggar and get a louse.

28-27 **মশার কামড় না সয় পায়, ছোটলোকের কথা না সয় গায়** SD

L: A mosquito-bite is intolerable to one's feet, the verbal bite of a low-caste individual is intolerable to one's person.

I: The rich detest even the well-meaning words from a poor, lowly person.

28-28 **মহতের বাত, হাতির দাঁত, পড়ে ত নড়ে না** x5-5;27-16

L: Word of the noble and tusk of the elephant - they can be dislodged but not shaken loose.

I: The word of a noble person can be trusted implicitly.

E: An honest man's word is as good as his bond.
Cf. The bull should be taken by the horns, a man at his word *[Afr.]*.

28-29 **মহাভারত অশুদ্ধ হওয়া** RL,SD

L: To (do something to) place the accuracy of the epic *Mahabharata* in question.

I: Said in humor when a small matter is posed as a very serious fault or lapse.

E: Making a Federal case of something.

28-30 **মহাজনো যেন গতঃ স পন্থাঃ** *[Sans.]*

L: Follow in the footsteps of great men.

I: Follow in the footsteps of great men.

E: "Footprints on the sands of time."

28-31 **মহিষাসুরমর্দিনী** *

L: Slayer of the Buffalo demon (usually, Goddess Durga).

I: Said in jest of a very strong and domineering female.

28-31 মহিষাসুরমর্দিনী

28-32 মন্থরার কুমন্ত্রণা *
L: Seditious advice of Monthora.
I: Ill advice from a crafty person.

28-33 মৎস্য মারিব খাইব সুখে, লিখিব পড়িব মরিব দুখে

L: If I catch fish, I can eat happily. If I study, I will die in misery.

I: Humor about children avoiding homework.

28-34 মা ফলেষু কদাচন [*Sans.*]   SD

L: You never have any rights to the rewards (of your labour).

I: Do your duty for duty's sake, and not for its rewards.

28-35 মা নেই যার, বিফল জনম তার

L: It is a sad life for one who has no mother.

I: It is a sad life for one who has no mother.

28-36 মাকড় মারলে ধোকড় হয় *   RL,SD,SB

L: (My son,) if it is a spider you have killed, then there is no punishment.

I: To conveniently excuse one of your own by cooking up spurious defense.

E: Double standard.

28-37 মাকাল ফল   SD

L: The makal fruit (beautiful but inedible).

I: A person who is handsome but without any virtue.

E: A lemon.

28-38 মাঙ্গি কিন্তু সাচ্চা, সস্তা কিন্তু পচ্চা   SD

L: Expensive but of good quality, cheap but of poor quality.

I: Pay a good price if you want good quality.

E: You get what you pay for.

28-39 মাঘের শীত বাঘের গায়ে

L: Even the tiger feels the cold in the month of Magh.

I: Biting cold affects everyone.

E: Winter either bites with its teeth or lashes with its tail.

28-40 মাছ আর অতিথি, দু'দিন পরেই বিষ x32-41 — SD

L: Fish and houseguest, both are poisonous after a couple of days.

I: Do not overstay your welcome.

E: Fish and guest smell in three days.
Visits always give pleasure, if not the arrival, the departure [Por.].
All miracles last three days [Hun.].

28-41 মাছকে সাঁতার শেখানো — SD

L: To teach a fish to swim.

I: To engage in a needless exercise.

E: Never offer to teach a fish to swim.
To teach your grandma to suck eggs.
You do not teach a giraffe to run [Afr.].

28-42 মাছি-মারা কেরাণী * — SD

L: A fly-swatting clerk/scribe.

I: A mechanical copyist.

E: A pen pusher.

28-43 মাছি মেরে হাত কালো x28-26 — SD

L: Soiling one's palm (black) by swatting a fly.

I: To spoil one's reputation by doing something that was not worth it.

28-44 মাছে ভাতে বাঙালী x27-39

L: The Bengali, brought up on a diet of fish and rice.

I: An iconic ethnic identity of Bengalis.

E: Cf. An American will go to hell for a bag of coffee.

28-45 মাছের কাঁটা গলায় লাগলে, বিড়ালের পায়ে পড়িতে হয় — RL

L: If you get a fishbone stuck in your throat, plead with the cat (to remove it).

I: If you are in a desperate situation, you may have to swallow your pride and ask a lowly person for help.

E: Desperate times call for desperate measures.

28-46 মাছের তেলে মাছ ভাজা x7-2   RL,SD,SB
L: Frying fish in its own oil
I: Leveraging a situation. Making something enhance itself.
E: A wedge from itself splits the oak tree.

28-47 মাছের মায়ের পুত্রশোক x7-101   RL,SD
L: Fish repenting the loss of her son.
I: False grief.
E: Crocodile's tears.

28-48 মাটিং চকার *[Mock Sans.]*
L: To go to the grounds.
I: To be all spoiled.
E: To bite the dust.

28-49 মাটিতে পা পড়ে না   SD
L: Feet do not touch the ground.
I: (Said of) an overly vain person.
E: A stuck-up person.

28-50 মাটির মানুষ   SD
L: A man made of the earth.
I: A simple, good person.
E: Salt of the earth.

28-51 মাঠে মারা যাওয়া   SD
L: (A project) failing right on the field.
I: A project that fails to take off.
E: Doesn't get off the ground.

28-52 মাণিকজোড় x29-79   SD
L: A well-matched pair.
I: A close pair; intimate friends.
E: Two of a kind.
       Two peas in a pod.

28-53 মাতঙ্গ পড়িলে দকে পতঙ্গতে কি না বলে X 35-20

L: When the elephant is mired in the bog, even the insects make fun of him.

I: When the mighty is in distress, even little people poke fun

E: Little birds may peck at a lion.
Even a hare will insult a dead lion.
When a fox walks lame, the old rabbit jumps *[AmInd.]*.
A mosquito can make a lion's eye bleed *[Ara.]*.

28-54 মাথা নেই তার মাথা ব্যথা RL,SD,SB

L: A headache without having a head.

I: You cannot be obsessed with a problem that does not exist. Anxious without cause or reason.

E: Don't tie garlic on your head if you don't have a headache *[Aze.]*.
A beggar cannot be a bankrupt *[Aze.]*.

28-55 মাথা যার বিষ তার

L: One who has the head has the headache.

I: One who is the head bears the responsibility to meet difficult situations.

E: The owner of the skin is the one to tan it *[Afr.]*.

28-56 মাথায় ঘোল ঢালা SD

L: To pour ghol (yogurt drink) over someone's head.

I: To insult someone in public.

E: To tar and feather somebody.

28-57 মাথায় আকাশ ভাঙ্গা SD

L: The sky splits open over one's head.

I: A great disaster befalls one.

E: A bolt out of the blue.

28-58 মাথায় ছিট

L: A bale of printed cloth is inside his head.

I: He is crazy. He is not all there.

E: He has got a screw loose.
He is one sandwich short of a picnic.
There is a stitch loose with him *[Dut.]*.

28-59 মাথায় বাজ পড়া

L: To be struck on the head by a thunderbolt.
I: Unexpected danger.
E: A bolt from the blue.

28-60 মাথায় লাথি মেরে পায়ে গড়

L: Kick one's head and then take his foot dust (bow to him in respect).
I: To insult one badly, then ask for his forgiveness fervently.

28-61 মাথায় হাত

L: The palm of one's hand placed on one's head.
I: One is dismayed, surprised, shocked etc.

28-62 মাথায় হাত বুলিয়ে নিয়ে যাওয়া

L: To get something by running one's palm over someone else's head.
I: To fool someone into giving up something.
E: Like taking candy from a kid.
     To shave the fool without lather *[Dut.]*.

28-63 মাথার ওপর খাঁড়া ঝুলছে

L: A sword hanging over one's head.
I: A great peril that can befall anytime.
E: Democles's sword is hanging overhead.

28-64 মাথার ঘাম পায়ে ফেলা   SB

L: Sweat from the head falling on the feet (due to hard work).
I: To earn one's bread by the sweat of one's brow.
E: To earn one's bread by the sweat of one's brow.

28-65 মাথার ঘায়ে কুকুর পাগল   RL,SD

L: The dog is being driven mad by the wound in his head.
I: One going mad from his own problems.

28-66 মানুষ অভ্যাসের দাস x32-15

L: A man is a creature of habit.
I: A man is a creature of habit.
E: A man is a creature of habit.

28-67 মানুষ গড়ে, দেবতা ভাঙ্গে   SD

L: Man creates, God destroys.
I: Man creates, God destroys.
E: Man proposes, God disposes.

28-68 মানুষ মরে গেলে থাকে শুধু কথা,
কাপড় ছিঁড়ে গেলে থাকে শুধু কাঁথা। x23-4   SD

L: Only words are left behind when a person passes away,
     only a kantha (old sari made into a spread) is left behind
     after a saree is tattered.
I: One is left with memories of someone when he/she is
     gone.
E: Time passes away but sayings remain.
     An elephant dies leaves his tusk, a tiger dies leaves his
     stripes, man dies leaves name *[Indo.]*.

28-69 মানুষের দেওয়া কুলায় না,   SB
ভগবানের দেওয়া ফুরায় না

L: The giving of a man is never sufficient, but the gift of God
     is inexhaustible.
I: *As above*
E: "Mercy of God, inexhaustible source of miracles, We trust
     in Thee." *—The Bible*

28-70 মান্ধাতার আমলে   SD

L: In very ancient times
I: Before historic times. In the days long gone by.
E: Days of yore.

28-71 মামার শালা পিসার ভাই, তার সাথে কোন সম্পর্ক নাই x26-13
                                                              SD

L: Your maternal uncle's brother-in-law and your aunt's
     husband's brother - these two are not your relatives.

I: A person is not your relative just because you can dscribe a link to him.

28-72 মা নিষাদ * [Sans.]
L: Cease, Huntsman!
I: Stop! Don't do the harm you are about to do!
E: I wouldn't!

28-73 মায়ের আঁচল ধরা
L: A son who clings to the spare end of his mother's sari.
I: A timid or shy person afraid to face the world.
E: Hide behind mother's skirt.

28-74 মা'র কাছে মাসির গল্প / মামা বাড়ির গল্প
L: Telling tales about your maternal aunt's or uncle's home to your mother.
I: To tell someone something he/she, most of all, already knows.
E: A silly daughter teaches her mother how to bear children [Afr.].

28-75 মা'র চেয়ে দরদ যার তারে বলি ডাইনী   SD
L: If a woman loves you more than your mother does, then the former has to be a witch.
I: If someone pretends to love you too much, his/her intention is in question.

28-76 মায়ের চেয়ে মাসির দরদ বেশী   SD
L: Maternal aunt showing more affection than the mother.
I: A degree of affection/concern that exceeds what is normal.

28-77 মা'র মতন শাশুড়ী, দাদার মতন স্বামী   RL
L: A mother-in-law like one's mother, a husband like one's elder brother.
I: What one would like in a new relation.

28-78 মারা তীর ফেরে না x 35.26   RL,SD

L: A shot arrow never returns.
I: What is done is done.
E: A word spoken is past recalling.
     Words have wings and cannot be recalled.
     When something has been said, a team of four horses
     cannot overtake it [Chi.].
     Four things come not back: the spoken word, the sped
     arrow, the past life and the neglected opportunity [Chi.].
     One can't take back his spit [Uyg.].

28-79 মারি তো গণ্ডার, লুঠি তো ভাণ্ডার   SD,SB

L: If I am going to kill something, I am going to kill a rhino;
     if I am going to rob something, I am going to rob a
     treasury.
I: Not satisfied with small jobs.
E: Either Caesar, or none.

28-80 মারের মতন ঔষধ নাই

L: There is no cure like a good thrashing.
I: There is no argument like the stick.
E: There is no argument like the stick.

28-81 মা লক্ষ্মী চঞ্চলা

L: The Goddess Lakshmi is fickle.
I: Riches do not last.
E: Riches have wings.

28-82 মিছরির ছুরি   SD

L: A knife made of sugar candy.
I: An insult disguised as praise. Sweet verbal stab.
E: The wound of the knife heals, the wound of the tongue
     festers [Tur.].

28-83 মিষ্টি কথায় চিঁড়ে ভেজে না x 28-84; 32-28   SD,SB

L: You cannot make chira (flattened rice) soft by (soaking it
     in) sweet talk.

I: You cannot get a job done only by trickery of words.
       Where action is needed, pleasant talking will not help.
E: Fine words butter no parsnips.
       Praise fills not the belly.
       Fair words do not fill the pocket.
       Praying kneads no dough *[Rus.]*.
       Talkin' 'bout fire doesn't boil the pot *[AfrAm.]*.

28-84 মিষ্টি কথায় পেট ভরে না   x28-83;32-28   SD

L: Sweet words cannot fill your stomach.
I: You cannot get a job done only by trickery of words.
       Where action is needed, talking will not help.
E: Praise fills not the belly.
       Fair words do not fill the pocket.
       Praying kneads no dough *[Rus.]*.
       Talkin' 'bout fire doesn't boil the pot *[AfrAm.]*.

28-85 মীরজাফর *

L: Mir Zafar, a legendary betrayer within the house.
I: A betrayer of trust.
E: Judas.

28-86 মুখচোরার অন্ন হয় না

L: A bashful person does not get to eat.
I: If you want something, you have to ask for it.
E: A bashful dog never fattens *[Ger.]*.

28-87 মুখ ঝামটা দেওয়া

L: To give someone a volley from the mouth.
I: To snap at somebody.
E: To snap.

28-88 মুখ ফস্‌কে বলে ফেলা

L: To let something slip out of one's mouth.
I: To inadvertently divulge a secret or say an unpleasant word.
E: Slip of tongue.

28-89 মুখ সামলে কথা বলা

L: To keep reins on one's tongue.

I: To talk carefully and civilly.

E: Watch your language.

28-90 মুখ সেলাই করে দেওয়া

L: To stitch one's mouth.

I: To silence. To seal one's lips.

E: To muzzle.

28-91 মুখে কথা নয়, কাজ কথা কয়   SB

L: Speak through your act, not through your mouth.

I: Speak through your act, not through your mouth.

E: Action speaks louder than words.
Elbow grease is the best polish.
Slow in word, swift in deed *[Chi.]*.

28-92 মুখে খই ফোটে   *x* 7-18   SD

L: As if corns are popping in one's mouth.

I: To be eloquent. To be chattering excessively.

E: Talking up a storm.
Chatterbox.

28-93 মুখে চুনকালি দেওয়া   SD

L: To smear lime and ink on somebody's face.

I: To disgrace somebody publicly.

E: To tar and feather somebody.

28-94 মুখে ছাই পড়ুক   SD

L: Let ash besmear your face.

I: Shame on you!

E: Shame on you!

28-95 মুখে ফুলচন্দন পড়ুক   RL,SD,SB

L: Let flowers and sandalwood paste shower into your mouth.

I: To have one's tongue blessed for having made a desirable or successful prophecy.

E: You are a sight for sore eyes!

28-92 মুখে খই ফোটে

28-96 মুখে মধু, হৃদে ক্ষুর RL,SD,SB

L: Honey on the tip of one's tongue, dagger in his heart.

I: A two-faced person who means you ill. A smooth-talking, vicious fellow.

E: An angel's face with devil's mind.
A honey tongue, a heart of gall.
Fair face foul heart.
A dimple in the chin, a devil within.
The meat-biting tooth is in the mouth, the man-biting tooth is in the soul *[Mon.]*.
In a good word there are three winters' warmth, in one malicious word there is pain for six frosty months *[Mon.]*.
A white glove often conceals a dirty hand.
Honey on the tongue, ice in the heart *[Rus.]*.
One who has honey on his tongue, has poison in his heart *[Fin.]*.

28-97 মুখে রা কাড়ে না

L: Not even the sound Ra comes out of his mouth.
I: He is tight-lipped/ bashful.
E: "Cat got your tongue"?
    "Did the flour go to your mouth"? *[Fin.]*.

28-98 মুখেন মারিতং জগৎ *[Mock Sans.]*   SD

L: To destroy the World with voluble speech.
I: Talk big.
E: Full of hot air.
    All mouth and no trousers.
    The person of the greatest talk is the person of the least work .
    It is better to have less thunder in the mouth and more lightning in the hand *[AmInd.]*.

28-99 মুখের গ্রাস কেড়ে নেওয়া   x11-32   SD

L: To take food away from one's mouth.
I: To deprive someone of his livelihood.
E: To take the bread out of somebody's mouth.

28-100 মুখের লাগাম নেই   SD

L: There are no reins on his mouth.
I: He is careless of his speech.
E: The tongue indeed has no bones.

28-101 মুখোমুখি বোঝাপড়া করা

L: To have a face-to-face understanding.
I: To settle some dispute or disagreement face-to-face.
E: To have it out.
    It is better say the words face to face, it is better to eat kebab on the shish *[Uyg.]*.

28-102 মজুরকে লাথি, হুজুরকে সালাম

28-102 মজুরকে লাথি, হুজুরকে সালাম RL,SD.SB

L: Kick your labourer, salute your boss.
I: Beat up on those beneath you, kiss up to those above.
E: A kick-down, kiss-up person.

28-103 মুড়ি মিছরির এক দর RL,SD

L: Puffed rice and sugar candy selling for the same price.
I: Said of a strangely disparate valuation.

28-104 মুনীনাং চ মতিভ্রমঃ *[Sans.]*   SD,BDG,SB

L: Even the saints can stumble.
I: Great men too are liable to err.
E: To err is human.
       Being wrong is a human trait *[Hun.]*.
       Even an old lady makes mistakes *[Rus.]*.

28-105 মুশলধারে বৃষ্টি x2-6

L: Raining down like sharp weapon falling.
I: Raining hard.
E: Raining cats and dogs.
       Raining pitchers-full *[Spa.]*.
       It's raining pipestems *[Dch.]*.

28-106 মূর্খ বন্ধুর চেয়ে জ্ঞানী শত্রু ভাল   MHP

L: It is better to have a learned enemy than a foolish friend.
I: A wise enemy is better than a foolish friend.

28-107 মূর্খের নেই হেতুবাদ, বাজি রেখে করে মাত

L: A fool cannot reason, and so he wagers.
I: A fool will bait you because he cannot reason.
E: Wager is a fool's argument.

28-108 মূর্খস্য লাঠ্যৌষধম্ *[Sans.]*   SD

L: Beating by a rod is a stupid person's just medicine.
I: Administer the remedy that is right for the subject.

28-109 মৃতসঞ্জীবনী সুধা

L: A potion that brings the dead back to life.
I: Something that rescues a person from a hopeless situation.

28-110 মেও ধরে কে? x26-46   RL,SD

L: Who is to bell the cat?
I: Who is to bell the cat?
E: Who is to bell the cat?

28-111 মেঘ না চাইতে জল ✗ 9-28   RL,SD,SB

L: You did not even ask for the cloud, but you got rain.
I: To get more than what you asked for.
E: Encountering a fallen Durian *[Indo.]*.

28-112 মেঘে মেঘে বেলা হয়   RL,SD

L: (Although you may not notice) the sun is advancing under the cover of a cloud and the day is ending.
I: Sometimes it is hard to tell that it is late. Someone who is aging.

28-113 মেয়ে ত' নয় যেন আগুনের ফুল্‌কি   SB

L: Some woman! – A real spark of fire!
I: Woman with a fiery personality.
E: A live wire.

28-114 মেয়ে হলে মুখ ঘোরাও, ছেলে হলে শাঁখ বাজাও   SB

L: If the newborn is a daughter, turn away; if it is a boy, blow the conch shell horn (to celebrate).
I: A son is an asset, a daughter is a liability.
E: *Cf.* Runaway son, a shining jewel; runaway daughter, tarnished *[Chi.]*.

28-115 মেয়েরা যতই লেখাপড়া শিখুক, খুন্তি তো নাড়তেই হবে   SB

L: Women – no matter how much education they get, they are going to have to drudge in the kitchen.
I: A woman's place is at home.
E: A woman's place is in the kitchen.

28-116 মেরে চামড়া তুলে দেওয়া

L: To thrash the skin off a person.
I: To beat someone severely.
E: To give somebody a good hiding.

28-117 মেরে ভূত ভাগিয়ে দেওয়া   *   SD

L: To beat someone hard enough to expel the ghost (as does an exorcist).

I: To beat someone severely to disabuse him of some bad habit.

E: To beat sense into somebody.

28-118 মোগল পাঠান হদ্দ হ'লো, ফারসী পড়ে তাঁতী x35-19   BDG

L: The Moghals and the Pathans failed (to read Farsi), but now a weaver comes forward to read Farsi.

I: Where the mighty have failed, an unlikely person takes a stab.

E: Fools rush in where angels fear to tread.

28-119 মোটে মা রাঁধে না, তা তপ্ত আর পান্তা

L: The woman of the house does not cook at all, what is the point in asking if the rice is warm or stale?

I: Where the main fare is lacking, what is the point of discussing its pluses and minuses?

28-120 মোর বুদ্ধি তোর কড়ি, আয় দুজনে ফলার করি   SD

L: My brains and your money - let us put them together and have a feast.

I: Let's use our strengths to our benefit.

E: Another man's horse and your own spurs outrun the wind *[Ger.]*.
      Help me so that I can help you, so that we can climb the mountain *[Grk.]*.

28-121 মোল্লার দৌড় মসজিদ তক্   RL,SD

L: The Mullah can run as far out as the primeter of the mosque.

I: Everyone's sphere of influence ends within his limits.

28-122 মৌচাকে ঢিল মারা   x27-29   SD

L: To pelt stone at a beehive.

I: To stir up trouble.

E: Throw stones at a beehive.

28-123 মৌনং সন্মতিলক্ষণম্   *[Sans.]*   SD,BDG

L: Silence is taken as consent.

I: Silence gives consent.

E: Silence means consent.

He who keeps quiet grants/consents *[Spa.]*.

28-122 মৌচাকে ঢিল মারা

28-124 মৌন্ব্রত অবলম্বন করা

L: To take a vow of silence.

I: To take a vow of silence.

E: Silence is the best.

Don't speak unless you can improve on the silence *[Spa.]*.

৩৩২

29-1 যঃ পলায়তি স জীবতি *[Sans.]* SD

L: Whoever flees, lives.

I: It is best to walk away from trouble.

E: He who fights and runs away, lives to fight another day.
To run away is not glorious, but very healthy *[Rus.]*.
Of all the thirty-six alternatives, running away is the best *[Chi.]*.
Do not lengthen the quarrel while there is an opportunity of escaping *[Lat.]*.

29-2 যকের ধন

L: Hidden treasure guarded by Jaksha, a demon.

I: Riches guarded by a ghost.

29-3 যখন যেমন তখন তেমন RL,SD

L: Whatever the moment demands is how it will be.

I: Go with the flow.

E: When in Rome, do as the Romans do.

29-4 যত বড় মুখ তত বড় কথা SD

L: Your words are big compared to your mouth.

I: You are insolent.

E: You are too big for your breeches.

29-5 যতই কর না কেন, পুরুষের নীচে থাকতে জেনো SB

L: (Advice to a woman:) No matter how much you accomplish, be sure to remain a little below your man.

I: A dictate of a male-chauvinistic society.

E: A woman is like an onion, she must have her head down *[Ara.]*.
A wife and a plough handle are best when shorter than the man *[Afr.]*.

29-6 যতক্ষণ শ্বাস ততক্ষণ আশ   RL,SD,BDG

L: As long as there is breath, there is hope.
I: While there is life there is hope.
E: Where there is life there is hope.
     Not having arrived at the Yellow River, the heart is not
     dead *[Chi.]*.

29-7 যত গর্জে তত বর্ষে না   x9-11   RL,SD,SB,MW

L: The little rain that follows does not match the mighty roar
     of the thunder.
I: Too much preamble, little result. Much in words, less in
     work.
E: Much cry and little wool.
     Great cry, little milk *[Fch.]*.
     Clouds that thunder do not always rain *[Arm]*.

29-8 যত দোষ নন্দ ঘোষ   x34-2   RL,SD,SB

L: Whatever it is, blame it on Nanda Ghosh.
I: Have a convenient person to blame everything on. To find
     a scapegoat.
E: There is no rain – the Christians are the cause.

29-9 যত মত তত পথ   SD

L: There are as many ways as there are opinions.
I: There are as many ways as there are ideas.
E: There are many ways of skinning a cat.
     So many men, so many minds *[Vie.]*.

29-10 যত হাসি তত কান্না, বলে গেছে রাম শর্মা   RL,SD

L: Ram Sharma has said this: As much as you laugh, so
     much shall you weep.
I: You are living it up now, but sad times will surely come.
E: If you laugh today, you will cry tomorrow.
     Even a clown sometimes weeps *[Rus.]*.
     Weeping will follow a long delight *[Fin.]*.

29-11 যত গুড়, তত মধুর

L: The more jaggery you add, the more sweet it will be.

I: You can influence more people with sweet talk than harsh words.

E: With the hat in the hand one gets through all the land [Dut.].

29-12 যতো ধর্মস্ততো জয়ঃ [Sans.] SD

L: Whoever has religion on his side wins.

I: Whoever is on the side of the right or virtue wins.

E: Where there is justice there is victory.

29-13 যতন নহিলে কোথা মিলিবে রতন

L: Unless there is hard work, you can not get a gem.

I: If you do not try hard you will not get happiness and wealth.

E: No sweat, no sweet.

29-14 যথা পূর্বং তথা পরম্ [Sans.] SD

L: As it was, so it is.

I: There is no change. Just as before.

E: Same old same old.

29-15 যদি বরে (বর্ষে) কাতি (কার্তিক), সোনা রতি রতি KH,RL

L: If it rains in Kartik, the harvest will turn to gold.

I: If it rains before winter, there will be a golden harvest.

E: cf. May rain is worth gold [Hun.].
ct. If in February there be no rain, 'tis neither good for hay or grain.
Windy March and rainy April, make May jolly and gracious [Fch.].

29-16 যদি বর্ষে মাঘের শেষ, ধন্যি রাজার পুণ্যি দেশ KH

L: If it rains at the end of Magh, the King's sacred kingdom is blessed.

I: If it rains after winter, both the king and the country are blessed.

E: cf. May rain is worth gold [Hun.].

29-17 যদি বিপদ গেল, তো সম্পদ্ এল   SD

L: Once the danger is over, wealth comes.
I: Bad times will be followed by good times.
E: After rain comes fair weather.
Weal and woe come by turns.

29-18 যদি হয় সুজন, তেঁতুল পাতায় ন'জন   SD,SB

L: If you are good people, nine can eat off a tiny Tentul (tamarind) leaf.
I: Companionable people can accommodate one another to a great extent.
E: It's easy to halve the potato where there's love.
Friends won't feel crowded even in one grave *[Rus.]*.
To eat from the same pot with another man, is to take an oath of perpetual friendship with him *[Afr.]*.

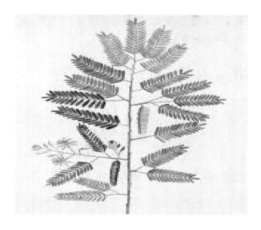

29-18   তেঁতুল পাতা (tamarind leaf)

29-19 যদির কথা নদীতে

L: Throw your 'ifs' into the river.
I: Let us discuss the realistic options.
E: "If there wasn't the little word *if*, my father would be a millionaire." *[Ger.]*.
If it's not here and now, who cares about what and when?

29-20 যদেতৎ হৃদয়ং তব তদস্তু হৃদয়ং মম।

যদিদং হৃদয়ং মম তদস্তু হৃদয়ং তব । [*Sans.*]

L: What is in my heart, may it be in your heart. What is in your heart, may it be in my heart.
I: The iconic lines from Bengali (Hindu) wedding vows.
E: "I do."

29-21 যমে মানুষে টানাটানি x|2-18;23-15| SD

L: A tug-of-war between Yama (Death) and men.
I: A person in extremely critical condition / death-bed.
E: In death-bed.

29-22 যমের অরুচি   RL,SD

L: Even Yama (Death) finds him repugnant.
I: A person/ thing so disgusting that even Death does not want to touch him/it.
E: "Everybody hates him!"

29-23 যমের বাড়ি

L: The home of Yama (Death).
I: The land of death.
E: Hades.

29-24 যশোদা ভাগ্যবতী, পরের পুত্রে পুত্রবতী   *   SD

L: Blessed Jashoda, someone else's son has made her a mother.
I: Someone who has gained a benefit without going through the trouble of acquiring it.

29-25 যস্মিন্ দেশে যদাচার [*Sans.*]   RL,SD,BDG,SB

L: In each country its own habits.
I: Behave according to local customs.
E: When in Rome, do as the Romans do.
Whatever ground is stood on, the sky is hold high [*Indo.*]
Trumpet in a herd of elephants, crow in the company of cocks, bleat in a flock of goats [*Mal.*]
In a land by its custom [*Fin.*]

If you drink the water, follow the custom *[Mon.]*.
One must howl with the wolves one is among *[Dan.]*.
Custom follows or country flee *[Dan.]*.
Different field has different insects, different ponds have different fish *[Indo.]*.

29-26 যাই দেখে কালা কালা, তাই ওর বাপের হালা

L: Whoever is black in complexion is suppose to be his father's brother-in-law.

I: An oversimplified categorization of a relative.

29-27 যা না হয় ন'এ, তা হবে না নব্বুই'এ

L: If it did not happen at age nine, it will not happen at age ninety.

I: What one does in early life, becomes his habit.

E: Morning shows the day.
     One who doesn't have a brain at 20, shouldn't expect one at 30 *[Grk.]*.

29-28 যা রটে তার কিছু বটে   RL.SD

L: In whatever rumour has spread, there must be a little truth.

I: Rumour has some element of truth in it.

E: Rumour has some element of truth in it.
     When the river makes noise, (it is because) it's carrying water *[Spa.]*.

29-29 যাক্ প্রাণ, থাক্ মান   SD

L: Preserve honour even if it means death.

I: Death is preferable to dishonour.

E: Death before dishonour!
     It is better to die on one's feet than on one's knees.

29-30 যাকে রাখ সেই রাখে

L: If you take care of someone/ something, he/ it will take care of you.

I: One should not waste or abuse things or persons.

E: Keep a shop and the shop will keep you.

29-31 যাত্রাদলের সং

L: The clown of the vaudeville troupe.
I: Some comically dressed person. A comic person amongst us.
E: The joker in the pack.

29-32 যার কাজ তারে সাজে

L: A job belongs to the expert.
I: A person should do what he is best at.
E: A cobbler should stick to his last.
There will be trouble if the cobbler starts making pies
[Rus.].

29-33 যার কেউ নেই তার ভগবান আছে   SD

L: One who has nobody has God behind him.
I: Nobody is completely alone in this world.

29-34 যার ছেলে যত পায়, তার ছেলে তত চায়   SD

L: The more a child has, the more the child wants.
I: The more one has, the more one wants.
E: Avarice increases with wealth.

29-35 যার জন্য করি চুরি সেই বলে চোর   RL.,SD

L: The one I am stealing for calls me a thief.
I: To be accused by them for whose benefit we transgress.
E: To be abused by them we do good.

29-36 যার জ্বালা সেই জানে   BDG

L: The afflicted knows best what hurt is.
I: The one who is suffering knows what it is.
E: The wearer knows best where the shoe pinches.

29-37 যার ধন তার ধন নয়, নেপোয় মারে দই   SD,SB

L: The owner of the wealth cannot enjoy it, but 'Nepo', the shrewd person is living high on yogurt.
I: The rightful owner cannot enjoy his wealth, but a rank outsider enjoys it.
E: One beats the bush, another catches the bird.

29-38 যার নাম ভাজা চাল, তার নাম মুড়ি   SD

L: What is called puffed rice is the same as muri.

I: Same thing, only different names.

E: Six of the one and half-a-dozen of the other.

29-39 যার নুন খাই তার গুণ গাই   x 23-55   RL,SD

L: I sing his praise of whose salt I eat.

I: Be true to your salt.

E: Never fall out with your bread and butter.
Everyone speaks well about the bridge which carries him over.
Whose bread you eat, his songs you will sing *[Fin.].*
Don't hack the branch you are sitting on *[Rus.].*

29-40 যার নিয়তি যেখানে, কে খণ্ডাবে সেখানে   x 7-26; 31-7   SD

L: When your fate dictates something, who can prevent it?

I: When your fate dictates something, who can prevent it?

E: Fate rules everywhere.

29-41 যার বিয়ে তার হুঁস নেই, পাড়াপড়শীর ঘুম নেই   RL,SD

L: The one getting married is supremely unconcerned while the neighbours are losing sleep over it.

I: One who is not at all concerned about his or her own urgent interest.

E: *Cf.* Rooster makes mo' racket dan de hen w'at lay de aig *[AfrAm.].*

29-42 যার মান আর হস আছে সেই মানুষ

L: One who has honour (maan) and good sense (hoosh) is a proper human being (maanoosh).

I: Honour and conscience make a real man. A fine human being is made of fine qualities.

29-43 যার যত খাঁই, তার তত নাই

L: The more you have, the more you want.
More one hankers after or demands, the more you feel you don't have.

I: The more you have, the more you want.

E: The more you have, the more you want.

29-41 বিয়ের প্যাণ্ডেল (a marquee for the wedding ceremony)

29-44 যার যেমন মতি, তার তেমন গতি   SD

L: One's direction matches his plan.
I: One works according to his plans. One decides his own
       fate.
E: You judge the way you live *[Mex.]*.

29-45 যার লাঠি তার মাটি x 13-32   SD

L: Whoever wields the stick holds the land.
I: Might is right.
E: Might is right.

29-46 যার সাথে যার মজে মন, কিবা হাঁড়ি কিবা ডোম

                                    x 24-63;27-24   SB

L: Once you fall in love who cares if the partner is a sweeper
       or an undertaker!
I: In case of love there is no bar between the lovers. Love is
       blind.
E: Love looks not with the eyes, but with the mind.

Affection blinds reasons.
Love rules without rules *[Ita.]*.
A man in love mistakes a pimple for a dimple *[Jap.]*.

29-47 যার শিল, যার নোড়া, তারই ভাঙ্গি দাঁতের গোড়া RL,SD,SB

L: It is with his mortar and his pestle that I crush his teeth.
I: Being ungrateful to the person who helped you. To harm someone with his own devices.
E: *Cf.* I'm not going to lend you a stick to break my head with *[AfrAm.]*.

29-47 শিল নোড়া (Indian mortar and pestle)

29-48 যারে দেখতে নারি তার চলন বাঁকা RL,SD,BDG,SB

L: If I cannot stand someone, he seems to walk funny.
I: One finds all kinds of faults with the one they dislike.
E: Faults are thick where love is thin.
Where there's no love, all faults are seen *[Ger.]*.

29-49 "যাহা চাই তাহা ভুল করে চাই, যাহা পাই তাহা চাই না"

L: I err in what I want, and what I get I do not want.

I: My desires and my rewards are not matched.

E: "We look before and after, and pine for what is not".

29-50 যাহা বাহান্ন, তাহা তিপ্পান্ন   x4-9   SD

L: If 52 will do, then 53 will do as well.

I: Little difference does not matter, nearly the same.

E: Nine is near ten [Afr.].
One is nineteen and the other one is less than twenty [Hun.].

29-51 যুদ্ধং দেহি

L: Give me a battle.

I: I am spoiling for a fight! Let us fight it out!

E: Bring it on!

29-52 যে আপনি খেতে জানে, সে পরকে খাওয়াতেও জানে   RL,SD

L: He who knows how to dine well also knows how to feed others.

I: He who is accustomed to dining well also knows how to treat others.

E: A merry host makes merry guests [Dut.].
Cf. The delicacy of the feast is the learned guest [Chi.].

29-53 যে গরু দুধ দেয় তার লাথিও ভাল   x21-32   SB

L: Even the kick of a milch cow is sweet!

I: One can put up with a lot from one's benefactor.

E: Give me the roast meat and beat me with the spit.

29-54 যে চলে সে রহে   SB

L: One who moves, survives.

I: Life is dynamic.

E: Rolling stone gathers no moss.
Insects do not nest in a busy door-hinge [Chi.].

29-55 "যে জন নিশ্চিত ছাড়ি অনিশ্চিতে যায়

নিশ্চিত অনিশ্চিত সে উভয়ে হারায়।"

L: Whoever leaves certainty to chase uncertainty loses both.

I: Don't gamble away your security.

E: Better the certainty of the straddle (packsaddle) than the mere loan of a saddle.

A chameleon doesn't leave one tree until he is sure of another *[Ara.]*.

29-56 "যে জন দিবসে মনের হরষে জ্বালায় মোমের বাতি,

আশু গৃহে তার জ্বলিবেনা আর নিশিথে প্রদীপ ভাতি।" x1-40

L: One who happily lights a candle during the daylight may not have even an oil lamp for the impending dark night.

I: Don't be a spendthrift. If you spend something when there is no need to do so, you will not have enough when you do need it.

E: He who of plenty will take no heed, shall find default in time of need.

If you sing before breakfast, you'll cry before night.

Put something away for a rainy day! *[Afr.]*.

Leave at least one egg in the nest *[Dut.]*.

29-57 যে জেগে ঘুমায়, তারে জাগানো দায়   x11-26

L: It is difficult to awaken a person who sleeps with his eyes open.

I: You cannot make a person see if he chooses not to. If one is already apprised you cannot further alert them to a situation.

E: None so blind as those who will not see.

You can't wake a person who is pretending to be asleep *[AmInd.]*.

Cf. The worst deaf is the one who doesn't hear. *[Grk]*.

29-58 যে ডালে বসে, সে ডাল কাটে   SD

L: To hack away at the same limb of the tree one is sitting on.

I: A foolish, self-destructive act.

E: Do not cut off the branch on which you are sitting *[Rus.]*.

29-59 যে দেবতা যে ফুলে তুষ্ট *x* 29-62

L: Each god is pleased with his own kind of flower/offering.
I: To please people with gift of their own choice.
E: Such priest, such offering.
Be righteous before God, be wealthy before a judge *[Rus.]*.

29-60 যে দেশে কাক নেই, সে দেশে কি রাত পোহায় না?   RL,SD

L: Does dawn not come to a land where there are no crows (to call the morning)?
I: Symbols do not control the actual course of events.

29-61 যে দেশে কাপড় নেই, সে দেশে ধোপার কি?   SD

L: What will a washerman do in a land where there are no clothes?
I: You cannot sell a service where there is no need for that service.
E: *cf.* Sell ice to Eskimos.

29-62 যে পূজার যে মন্ত্র *x* 29-59

L: Each type of worship has its own mantra/ chant.
I: The manner of expression to the bosses should be according to your self interest.
E: Such priest, such offering.
Different strokes for different folks.
The horse loves oats, the earth manure and the governor, tribute *[Rus.]*.
Like priest, like church *[Rus.]*.

29-63 যে যায় লঙ্কায় সেই হয় রাবণ *   RL,SD,SB

L: Whoever goes to Lanka turns into a Ravana.
I: Whoever gets to a position of power, misuses it.
E: Power corrupts.

29-64 যে রক্ষক, সেই ভক্ষক *x* 30-1   RL,SD,SB

L: The protector is the one who is consuming it.
I: The saviour is the devourer. The keeper is the thief.
E: Fox guarding the henhouse.
Putting the fox to mind the geese.

The dog's kennel is not the place to keep a sausage.
Turn a billy-goat into a gardener *[Ger.]*.
Trust a goat with a cabbage *[Hun.]*.

29-65 যে রাঁধে সে কি আর চুল বাঁধে না? RL,SD

L: Doesn't the one who cooks also braids her hair?
I: If you are charged with doing one thing, should this stop you from doing other things?

29-66 যে সহে, সে রহে RL,SD

L: He who bears endures.
I: He who bears adversity gains lasting power.
E: That which does not kill you makes you stronger.

29-67 "যেখানে দেখিবে ছাই, উড়াইয়া দেখিবে তাই,
মিলিলে মিলিতে পারে অমূল্য রতন"। SD

L: Wherever you spot a pile of ashes, blow it away, you might just find a priceless gem hidden underneath.
I: Wherever you see potential hidden opportunity, explore it.
E: Cf. If you want fire, look for it in the ashes *[Ger.]*.

29-68 যেখানে বাঘের ভয় সেখানে সন্ধ্যে হয় RL,SD,SB

L: Evening falls where an attack by tigers are feared.
I: Where danger is expected, danger comes earlier.
E: Danger often comes where danger is feared.
Where something is thin, that's where it tears *[Rus.]*.
Where the dike (or dam) is lowest the water first runs over *[Dut.]*.
Raindrops come heavy on a house unthatched.
ct. Where we least think, there goes the hare away.

29-69 যেখানে রাত, সেখানে পাত/ কাত SD

L: Wherever evening falls is where your meal/bed is.
I: Take things in your stride.
E: *Cf.* Pick your inn before the dark. Get on your road before the dawn.

29-68 যেখানে বাঘের ভয় সেখানে সন্ধ্যে হয়

29-70 যেখানে সুখ, সেখানে স্বস্তি   SD

L: Wherever there is happiness, there is peace.
I: Wherever there is happiness, there is peace.
E: *Cf.* May you have warmth in your igloo, oil in your lamp, and peace in your heart *[Inu.].*

29-71 যেন তেন প্রকারেণ

L: By any means at all.
I: To achieve the goal by any means.
E: By hook or by crook.
      If not by washing, then by rolling *[Rus.].*
      There are more than one way of achieving an objective *[Mao.].*

29-72 যেমন কর্ম তেমন ফল RL,SD,BDG,SB

L: As is your effort, so is your reward.
I: Your reward will be in accordance with your effort.
E: As you sow, so shall you reap.
  Do good, reap good; do evil, reap evil *[Chi.]*.

29-73 যেমন গাছ তার তেমনি ফল x 26-33 SD

L: As is the tree, so is its fruit.
I: The quality of the offspring is determined by that of the parents.
E: As is the tree, so is its fruit.
  Like father, like son.

29-74 যেমন দেবতা তেমন নৈবেদ্য x 29-59

L: As is the deity, so is the offering.
I: Behave with your superiors according to their stature.
E: Like saint, like offering.

29-75 যেমন দেবা তেমন দেবী x 29-79 SD

L: As is the male god, so is the female consort.
I: As is the man, so is his wife.
E: Like man, like wife.

29-76 যেমন বাপ তেমনি বেটা x 26-33 RL,SD

L: Like father, like son.
I: Like father, like son.
E: Like father, like son.

29-77 যেমন বুনো ওল তেমনি বাঘা তেঁতুল * SD,SB

L: As (poisonous) is the wild arum, so is the potent tamarind (to wash away the poison).
I: An antidote as strong as the poison.
E: As is the evil, so is the remedy.
  Measure for measure.
  Fight poison with poison *[Chi.]*.
  The remedy to fire is fire *[Afr.]*.
  One nail drives out another *[Ger.]*.
  A scald head need strong lye *[Dan.]*.

29-78 যেমন মনিব তেমন চাকর x26-33   SB

L: Like master, like servant.
I: Like master, like man.
E: Like master, like man.

29-79 যেমন হাঁড়ি তেমন সরা x29-75   SB

L: As is the earthen bowl so is the clay pot.
I: These two (people, e.g.) are really the same, don't take them to be different.
E: The wolf and the shaman are of one nest [*Inu.*].

29-80 যেমনি কুকুর তেমনি মুগুর   SD,MW

L: As is the dog, so is the cudgel (to control him).
I: As the villain, so is the terrible ruler/ punisher.
E: Like dog, like hammer.
        For the God who is doped, you need a priest who is drunk. [*Ind.*].

29-81 যৌবনে কুক্কুরীও ধন্যা   SD

L: Youth makes even a bitch look pretty.
I: Youth confers its own beauty even on an ugly woman.
E: Youth is beauty, even in cattle [*Egy.*].

৬০৩

30-1 রক্ষক যদি ভক্ষক হয়   x[29-64]   RL,SD,SB

L: If the keeper is the thief.

I: When a saviour is the devourer.

E: Fox guarding the henhouse.
Trust a goat with a cabbage *[Hun.]*.

30-2 রতনে রতন চেনে   SD,SB

L: A jewel recognizes another jewel.

I: It takes one to know one. A wise person recognizes another. A crook recognizes another crook.

E: It takes one to know one.
Like draws to like the whole world over.
Rats know the way of rats *[Chi.]*.
A fisherman recognizes another from afar *[Rus.]*.

30-3 রথ দেখা ও কলা বেচা   x[5-15]   RL,SD,SB

L: Selling bananas while enjoying the chariot festival.

I: Doing something profitable while enjoying oneself at the same time.

E: To kill two birds with one stone.
Mixing business with pleasure.
One shot, two birds *[Grk.]*.

30-4 রমণীর মন, সহস্র বর্ষের সখা সাধনার ধন

L: The mind (heart) of a woman, dear friend, is the reward of a thousand years of praying (for it).

I: Love of a woman is a most precious thing that must be earned.

E: A good woman is hard to find, and worth far more than diamonds. – *The Bible*

30-5 রম্যাণি বীক্ষ্য মধুরাংশ্চ নিশম্য [*Sans.*]

L: See what is beautiful, and also what is sweet...
I: See the World in all its good facets.
E: Who lives sees much.
Who travels sees more [*Ara.*].

30-6 রণে ভঙ্গ দেওয়া

L: To retreat from the battlefield.
I: To give up on a fight. To back off.
E: To say uncle.

30-7 রক্তের টান

L: Attraction of the blood.
I: Affinity for blood relations.
E: Blood is thicker than water.

30-8 রক্তের নেশা

L: An addiction that is in one's blood.
I: A very bad addiction.
E: What is bred in the bone will never be out of the flesh.

30-9 রাখে কৃষ্ণ মারে কে   RL,SD,SB

L: If Krishna protects someone, who can kill him.
I: If God protects, nobody can destroy.
E: No protector like God.

30-10 রাঘব বোয়াল   SD

L: A giant boal fish.
I: A man of high social standing who exploits people.
E: A fat-cat.
Big cheese.

30-11 রাজায় রাজায় হয় রণ, উলুখড়ের হয় মরণ   SD,SB

L: Kings fight a fierce battle, and the shrubs die (by being trampled on).

I: In the fight of two powerful groups or people, the unin-
       volved people can suffer.
E: Elephants wage war against elephants, deer die in the
       midst *[Indo.]*.
       When two bulls fight, it is the grass that suffers *[Afr.]*.
       Two camels fight and the fly in between dies *[Tur.]*.
       Tens of thousands of bones will become ashes when one
       general achieves his fame *[Chi.]*.
       Masters are fighting, (their) servant's forelocks are
       creaking *[Rus.]*.

30-12 রাজা-উজির মারা

L: Telling tales of vanquishing kings and their ministers.
I: Tell tall tales. Engage in braggadocio.
E: To solve all the problems of the World.

30-13 রাঁধতে রাঁধতে রাঁধুণী, নাচতে নাচতে নাচুনী   x 9-25

L: If you keep cooking, one day you will become a chef; if
       you keep dancing, one day you will become a danseuse.
I: Practice makes perfect.
E: Practice makes perfect.

30-14 রান্না খেতে কান্না পায়   SD

L: Her cooking brings tears to one's eyes.
I: She is a terrible cook.
E: *Cf.* When a woman prepares a dish which others find
       unpalatable, she says that she prepared it to suit her own
       taste *[Afr.]*.

30-15 রাবণের গুষ্টি   SD,SB

L: The clan of Ravana.
I: A highly proliferated family.
E: The mongol horde.

30-16 রাবণের স্বর্গের সিঁড়ি *   SD

L: Ravana's stairs to Heaven (the plan never materialized).

255

I: Don't plan too far ahead, it may never happen!
E: Tower of Babel.

30-17 রাম না জন্মিতে রামায়ণ * RL,SD

L: The Ramayana, composed even before Rama is born.
I: Getting ahead of the situation.
E: We have not saddled and yet we are riding [Port.].

30-18 রাম ভজি কি রহিম ভজি? SD

L: Do I worship Rama or do I worship Rahim?
I: Of the two masters, which one do I serve?
E: No man can serve two masters [Spa.].

30-19 রাম, শ্যাম, যদু, মধু

L: Rama, Shyam, Jodu, Modhu.
I: An inconsequential set of people.
E: Any Tom, Dick and Harry.

30-20 রামগড়ুরের ছানা *

L: The hatchlings of Ramgorur.
I: Unsmiling, humourless person.
E: Sourpuss.

30-21 রামরাজ্য SD

L: The Kingdom of Rama.
I: A utopian place.
E: Utopia.

30-22 রামের ধন শ্যামকে দেওয়া

L: To give the inheritance of Ram to Shyam.
I: Take from one person and give it to another. Unjust distribution or allocation.
E: Loading Tim's donkey with Jim's luggage.

30-23 রাহুর গ্রাস SD

L: What is gobbled up by Rahu (a demon who causes the eclipse).

I: A great loss ascribed to supernatural causes.

E: cf. Apocalypse.

30-24 রাহুর দশা x32-12

L: Under the (astrological) influence of Rahu.

I: In a luckless phase of life.

E: A bad spell.

30-25 রূপং দেহি জয়ং দেহি যশো দেহি দ্বিষো জহি [Sans.]

L: Grant us form, victory and welfare, and rid us of hostility (Prayer).

I: Give us the Good, rid us of the Bad.

E: Cf. "Give us this day our daily bread ..." – The Bible

30-26 রূপে কালো গুণে আলো SD

L: The complexion may be dark, but the qualities may well shine through.

I: The appearance of a person may not reflect his or her qualities

E: Cf. Beauty without virtue is like a rose without scent.

30-27 রূপে লক্ষ্মী, গুণে সরস্বতী SD,SB

L: As beautiful as (the goddess) Lakshmi, as talented as (the goddess) Saraswati.

I: An all-round accomplished and attractive woman. A modest and learned woman.

E: Cf. "Abigail ... was a woman of good understanding, and of a beautiful countenance..." – The Bible

30-28 রোদ হয় বৃষ্টি হয়, শিয়াল কুকুরের বিয়ে হয় SB

L: If it is rainy and sunny at the same time (a rare occurrence), a fox and a dog are getting married.

I: Fantasy tale (superstition) told to Bengali children.

E: *Cf.* If a cat washes its face and ears, it will rain *[Chi.]*.
      The devil is hitting his wife *[Hun.]*.
      You can't marry a hen and a fox *[Fch.]*.

30-29 রোকা কড়ি চোখা মাল SD

L: You have the cash ready, I have the finest goods ready.

I: Good value for ready money. If you pay cash you will get
      the best.

E: Paying cash on the barrelhead.

৩৫২

31-1 লক্ষ্মী চঞ্চলা x 15-1

L: Lakshmi (the goddess of wealth) is fickle.
I: Riches do not last.
E: Riches have wings.

31-2 লক্ষ্মীর ঝাঁপি

L: The chest of Lakshmi (A cane bowl where ladies keep coins for Lakshmi's worship).
I: A storing of a woman's cherished personal possessions.
E: *Cf.* Hope chest.

31-3 লঘু পাপে গুরু দণ্ড   RL,SD,SB

L: A heavy penalty for a light offense.
I: Severe punishment for a minor offence.
E: Severe punishment for a venial offence.

31-4 লজ্জাবতী লতা

L: A bashful creeper.
I: A bashful woman.
E: Like a mimosa plant.
   Shrinking violet.

31-5 লঙ্কাকাণ্ড   SD

L: The Lanka Affair (A chapter of the epic Ramayana, set in Lanka).
I: A great upheaval.
E: *Cf.* Armageddon.

31-6 লতায় পাতায় (শাখায় পল্লবে) আত্মীয়তা

L: Connected through a maze of creepers.
I: A distant or tenuous family relationship.
E: Distant relations.

31-7 ললাটের লিখন, না যায় খণ্ডন x7-26;27-3   SD

L: The writing on your forehead cannot be erased.
I: Fate cannot be overcome.
E: Fate rules everywhere.

31-8 লাখে না মিলে এক x5-39   SD

L: Not even one in a lakh (hundred thousand).
I: Not even one in a million (extremely rare).
E: One in a million.

31-9 লাগে টাকা দেবে গৌরী সেন *   RL,SD,SB

L: (Don't worry) If money is needed, Gouri Sen will provide.
I: Public money that can be freely and lavishly spent or squandered. Don't worry, someone will pay.
E: Uncle Sam will provide!
   Public money is like water, everybody helps himself to it
   [Ita.].

31-10 লাথের কাঁঠাল লাথে পাকে, বিনা লাথে ছ'মাস থাকে

L: The jackfruit that needs kicking to ripen will ripen only on kicking, otherwise it can stay green for six months.
I: Administer the remedy that is right for the subject.

31-11 লাভের গুড় পিঁপড়েয় খায়   SD,SB

L: The profit that is the stock of jaggery is consumed away by ants.
I: Draining out profits through spurious expenses.
E: Cheats never prosper

31-12 লেখাপড়া করে যেই, গাড়ীঘোড়া চড়ে সেই   RL,SD

L: Whoever studies hard rides in cars and on horses.

I: A good education will have its rewards.

E: Those who do not study are only cattle dressed up in men's clothes *[Chi.]*.
Learn to handle a writing-brush and you will never handle a begging bowl *[Chi.]*.

31-13 লেজে খেলানো SD

L: To play someone by the tail.

I: To delay providing a service with excuses.

E: To give someone the runaround.

31-14 লোটা কম্বল নিয়ে রওনা হওয়া

L: To set out with one's ewer and blanket.

I: To set out with all of one's belongings.

E: To strike the tent.

31-15 লোভে পাপ, পাপে মৃত্যু RL,SD

L: Greed leads you to sin, sin leads you to death.

I: In greed is sin, in sin is death.

E: Avarice begets sin, sin begets death.

31-16 লোম বাছলে কম্বল শেষ x16-1 MHP

L: If you are picking out the fluff in a blanket, you will end up with no blanket at the end.

I: If you are too particular about selecting only the best you may end up with nothing.

E: Sift him grain by grain, and you will find him all chaff.
Who sieves too much keeps the rubbish *[Bel.]*.

৩৩২

32-1 শকুনির দৃষ্টি ভাগাড়ের দিকে   x11-43   SD,SB

L: The vulture always keeps an eye on the waste ground (for dead animals).
I: An opportunist is always on the look-out.
E: Where the carcass is, there shall the eagles be gathered together.

32-2 শকুনির শাপে কি গরু মরে?   SD

L: Does a cow drop dead because the vulture cursed him so?
I: Things do not happen just because it is convenient to you.
E: *Cf.* A turkey never voted for an early Christmas.

32-3 শত্রু পাল্লায় পড়া

L: To fall in the clutches of a tough person or a tough situation.
I: To be in a tough situation.
E: Someone has got you under his thumb.

32-4 শত্তেুর ভক্ত নরমের যম   x28-104
RL,SD

L: Subservient to the strong, oppressor of the weak.
I: Submit to the strong, torment the weak.
E: Kiss up, kick down.

32-5 শঠে শাঠ্যং সমাচরেৎ [*Sans.*]   RL,SD,BDG,SB

L: The wicked must be met with wickedness.
I: Meet cunning with equal cunning.
E: With foxes you must play the fox.

32-6 শতমুখে প্রশংসা করা

L: To praise through a hundred mouths.
I: To praise profusely.
E: To praise somebody to high heaven.

32-7 শতং বদ মা লিখ *[Sans.]* x28-7   SD

L: Speak as much as you like, but never put it in writing.
I: Say it all you want, but don't commit it to writing. Don't keep a paper trail.
E: Put it in song, put it in drink, never ever put it in ink. Think much, speak little, write less *[Fch.].*

32-8 শত্রুতা ভুলিয়া গিয়া মিত্রতা করা

L: Forget enmity, embrace amity.
I: Bury the hatchet .
E: Bury the hatchet.

32-9 শত্রুর মুখে ছাই পড়ুক   SD

L: Let ash smear the face of the enemy.
I: Let the enemy suffer disgrace.

32-10 শত্রুর শেষ রাখতে নেই   SD

L: One should not let even a trace of the enemy survive.
I: When the opportunity comes, destroy the enemy very fully.
E: A snake deserves no pity *[Yid.].*

32-11 শনিবারের বারবেলায়

L: The noon hour of Saturday.
I: Not an auspicious time (for starting new things).
E: *Cf.* Neither marry nor travel on Tuesday or Friday! *[Ita.].*

32-12 শনির দশা x30-24

L: Under the curse of Shoni (The planet Saturn, astrologically speaking).

I: Going through bad times.
E: A bad spell.

32-13 শনির দৃষ্টি

L: Under the (malevolent) eyes of Shoni.
I: In a luckless state.
E: Evil eyes.

32-14 শবরীর প্রতীক্ষা *

L: Shabari's vigil (for god Rama).
I: A very long vigil. A long, almost unending wait.
E: *Cf.* "Waiting for Godot."

32-15 শরীরের নাম মহাশয়, যা সওয়াবে তাই সয় x 28-66   RL,SD,SB

L: The body can endure to the extreme if someone pushes it ot the limit.
I: The constant training, a soft body can become steely.
E: A body can get used to anything.

32-16 শর্ষের মধ্যে ভূত

L: The ghost (evil spirit) has penetrated right into the mustard seed (traditional antidote for evil spirits).
I: Virus in the antidote.
E: The enemy within.

32-17 শহরে কাক, বড় চালাক   SD

L: The urban crow is most crafty.
I: The shrewdness that comes from living in a city.

32-18 শাক দিয়ে মাছ ঢাকা * x 22-15   RL,SD,MW

L: Trying to cover up the fish (on the dinner plate) with spinach.
I: To cover up inadequately, ineffectively.
E: Paper over cracks.
       To try to hush something up when it is known to many.

That which has horns can not be wrapped *[Afr.]*.
The stench of something rotting can't be hidden with incense *[Afr.]*.

| 32-19 | শাঁখের করাত | RL,SD,SB |

L: A saw, which is double-edged, used to slice conch shell.
I: A no-win situation when you are up against it. Hurts in both ways.
E: Double-edged sword.

| 32-20 | শাপে বর হ'ল | RL,SD |

L: A curse turned out to be a boon.
I: Blessing in disguise.
E: Blessing in disguise.

| 32-21 | শিকারী বেড়াল, গোঁফ দেখলেই চেনা যায় | SD,SB |

L: One can identify a hunter cat by looking at his whiskers.
I: There are signs that tell of a person's life experience.

| 32-22 | শিকেয় তোলা | SD |

L: To store something away in a hanging basket.
I: To postpone something. Put something away for now.
E: To table.
To put on the backburner.

| 32-23 | শিব ঠাকুরের আপন দেশে | x5-34 |

L: In the very own country of Shib Thakur (Lord Shiva).
I: A fictional place where strange customs prevail.
E: In the land of Oz.

| 32-24 | শিবরাত্রির সলতে | SD,SB |

L: The wick (of an oil-wick lamp) of Shivaratri (a special evening of worship).
I: The only decendent of a family.

শিবের অসাধ্য

L: Not doable even by Shiva.
I: An impossible project or task or feat.

32-26   শিমুল ফুল   SD

L: Shimul flower.
I: Beautiful-looking but of no use.
E: Lemon.

32-27   শিয়রে শমন

L: Death standing near the headboard of one's bed.
I: Enemy is nearby.
E: Barbarians at the gate.

32-28   শুধু কথায় চিঁড়ে ভেজে না   x28-84   SD

L: Words alone cannot soften Chira (flattened rice).
I: You cannot get a job done only by trickery of words.
       Where action is needed, talking will not help.
E: Sweet words butter no parsnips.
       Bare words make no good bargain.
       Talk does not cook rice *[Chi.]*.
       Houses are built not with tongue but with rubbles and hatchets *[Rus.]*.
       With talking the cheese ship won't move *[Tur.]*.
       The mill won't turn with carried water *[Fch.]*.

32-29   শুধু কাজল পরলেই হয় না, চাউনি চাই   SD

L: It is not enough to line your eyes with kohl, you must have the eyes for it!
I: You cannot adorn something that is basically unadornable.
E: *cf.* An eye darkened with kohl is never equal to the one darkened with dust *[Ara.]*.

32-30 শুধু ভাত খায়, জরির জুতা পায়ে x24-46;27-19   SD

L: He eats only rice (without any side dishes), but sports a
     fine pair of gold-embroidered shoes.
I: A poor man pretending to be rich.
E: No one knows how the poor man dines *[Rus.]*.

32-31 শুভকার্যে অনেক ব্যাঘাত

L: When you try to do something good, you encounter many
     obstacles.
I: A good deed is never accomplished without any hitches.
E: A good deed is never accomplished without any hitches.

32-32 শুভস্য শীঘ্রম্ *[Sans.]*   SD

L: If something good is to be done, do it as early as possible.
I: If something good is to happen, do it as soon as possible.
E: Sooner the better.
     Never put off till tomorrow what you can do today.

32-33 শুয়ে চিত্ পরে কাত্, উপুড় হয়ে পোহায় রাত   SD
L: First prone, then on your side, then supine at the dead of
     night.
I: A prescription for a healthy night's sleep.
E: *Cf.* You should not sleep face down or face up, only on
     your side. The first part of the night you should lie on
     your left side, the latter part of the night on your right
     side *[Jew.]*.

32-34 শুয়ো রাণী দুয়ো রাণী

L: The chief queen and the second queen.
I: Unequal status given to two co-equals.
E: *cf.* The first wife my sandal, my second wife my turban
     [Tur.]

32-35 শুঁড়ির সাক্ষী মাতাল

L: A hooch-maker brings a drunkard as his witness.
I: An interested party is no witness.
E: The witness of the pot is the ladle *[Uyg.]*.

32-36 শুষ্কং কাষ্ঠং তিষ্ঠত্যগ্রে

নীরসতরুবরঃ পুরতো ভাতি। [*Sans.*]

L: (Two different ways of saying the same thing) A withered tree stands ahead.

I: A classic example of how the same thing can be said in dry prose or in beautiful poetry.

E: *Cf. Dutch/English languages:* Achtentachtig prachtige grachten/ Eightyeight beautiful canals.

32-37 শূন্য কলসীর শব্দ বেশী   RL,SD,SB

L: An empty pitcher makes loud sound.

I: Bragging of a person without much substance.

E: Empty vessel sounds much.
Where the stream is the shallowest, greatest is the noise.
Empty barrel clacks the most *[Fin.]*.
An empty drum gives loud sound *[Indo.]*.

32-38 শূন্যে সৌধ

L: A castle in the air.

I: Imagining unrealistic fortune.

E: A castle in the air.
Tower of Babel.

32-39 শূর্পনখার নাক কাটা *

L: The lopping off of the nose of Shurpanakha.

I: An evil person is properly punished. Well-deserved punishment.

E: Just dessert.

32-40 শ্মশান বন্ধু x1-69

L: A friend who accompanies you to the pyre-ground (when you go to cremate a close relative).

I: A genuine friend.

E: A friend in need is a friend indeed.

32-41 স্বশুরবাড়ি মধুর হাঁড়ি তিনদিন পর ঝাঁটার বাড়ি x28-40 SD

L: The in-laws' house is a like pot of honey until after three days (of stay) when you get shooed away with a broom-stick.

I: Do not be a houseguest for too long. Do not wear out your welcome.

E: Fish and houseguests smell in three days.
All miracles last three days [Hun.].

32-42 স্বাশুড়ী ম'ল সকালে, খেয়ে দেয়ে যদি বেলা থাকে তো কাঁদব আমি বিকালে SD,SB

L: My mother-in-law died in the morning. Let's see now - after I have lunched and rested, I will weep for her in the afternoon if I can find the time.

I: Indifference on the part of a daughter-in-law towards the mother-in-law.
Alt. One who is overburdened with household chores have no time to express even grief.

E: A mother-in-law may be good, but she is better when mother earth covers her up [Spa.].

32-43 শ্বেতহস্তী পোষা SD

L: To keep a white elephant as pet.
I: A very expensive hobby.
E: To keep a white elephant.

32-44 শ্যাম রাখি না কুল রাখি * SD

L: Do I maintain relations with Shyam (Krishna) or do I preserve the honour of my caste.
I: A person in a dilemma describes it thus.

32-45 শ্যামের বাঁশি *

L: The flute-call of Shyam (Krishna/ Shyam calling Radha).
I: A call to a romantic tryst. An irresistible call.
E: Siren call.

শ্যামের বামে রাই দাঁড়াইল

L: Radha stands to the left of Krishna.

I: A woman usually stands to the left of her man. Befitting match.

E: *Cf.* A woman who digs with her husband cannot be taken as weak *[Afr.]*.

32-47 **শ্রদ্ধাবান্ লভতে জ্ঞানম্** *[Sans.]*

L: The respectful attains knowledge.

I: Knowledge is best gained when your mind is respecful of it or of the teacher.

E: Render respect unto parents and teachers. Bear the words of your teacher ever in mind *[Bur.]*.

         Rice father, clothes mother, knowledge teacher *[Viet.]*.

৳৩৫২

33.

33-1 | যত্ব ণত্ব জ্ঞান নেই | SD

L: Being ignorant on the elementary rules of grammar.
I: Devoid of common sense.
E: Does not know the three Rs.

33-2 | ষাঁড়ের গোবর | SD

L: The dung of an ox (as distinct from cow-dung, which is a purifier in Hindu worship rituals).
I: Useless as a purifying item in rituals, and so just plain excrement.

33-3 | ষাঁড়ের গোঁ | SD

L: A bull-like obstinacy.
I: Great obstinacy.
E: Stuborn as a mule.

33-4 | ষষ্ঠীর কৃপা | SD

L: The blessings of goddess Shoshthi.
I: The omen that leads to the birth of children.
E: *Cf.* "Stork bring me a baby in a bundle." *[Pol.].*

33-5 | ষোল আনাই বৃথা / লাভ | SD

L: All 16 annas (16 annas = one rupee) are gone to waste/profit.
I: Everything up to this point has been for nothing/worth it.
E: All for naught.

33-6 | ষোলকলা পূর্ণ হওয়া |

L: The moon is full, with all the sixteen slivers in place.
I: The growing project or event is now complete.

Alt. To meet with complete disaster, to be utterly ruined.

E: All the pieces are in place.

Kolkata mid 1940s: Local street markets catering to the
                    daily needs were just as important
                    then as they are now.

ॐ

34-1 সকল কুকুর স্বর্গে যাবে, কারা তবে এঁটো খাবে RL,SD

L: If all the dogs go to Heaven, who will eat our left-overs.
I: If everyone wants the very best for himself, there is bound to be a problem.
E: You lady, I lady, who is going to milk the cow?
"I am a prince and you are a prince, who will lead the donkeys?" *[Ara.]*.

34-2 সকল পাখিতে মাছ খায়, মাছরাঙ্গার কলঙ্ক ×29-8 SD

L: Every bird hunts fish, but only the kingfisher gets the blame.
I: While everyone engages in a certain activity, only a symbolic group or person gets the blame.
E: There is no rain – the Christians are the cause.
An ox with long horns, even if he does not butt, will be accused of butting *[Mal.]*.

34-3 সকলে যদি ব্রত করে নৈবেদ্য খাবে কে? SD

L: If every worshipper pledges to fast, who will eat all the food consecrated by offering to the deity?
I: If no one has interest in the outcome, why undertake this effort?

34-4 সখের প্রাণ গড়ের মাঠ SD,SB

L: The free-and-fancy spirit is like the fields of Gar (a vast meadow around Fort William in Kolkata, now an open field).
I: Said of a person of effusive, expansive outlook on life.
E: Footloose and fancy-free.

34-5 সঙ্গ যেমন, রঙ্গ তেমন ₓ34-8

L: Your ways are determined by the company you keep.
I: Your actions are determined by the company you keep.
E: A man is known by the company he keeps.
Tell me who you hang around with and I'll tell you who you are [Spa.].

34-6 সততাই উৎকৃষ্ট পথ

L: Honesty is the best course.
I: Honesty is the best course.
E: Honesty is the best policy.

34-7 সত্য কথার ডালপালা নেই

L: (The tree of) truth has no branches or foliages.
I: Truth does not need adornments.
Alt. Truth is straightforward.
E: Truth needs not the ornament of many words.
Truth's best ornament is nakedness.
When you tell the truth, you don't have to remember what you said [Yid.].

34-8 সৎসঙ্গে স্বর্গবাস, অসৎসঙ্গে সর্বনাশ ₓ34-5   RL,SDG,SB

L: Keeping good company will get you to heaven, keeping bad company will lead to your ruination.
I: Good company will elevate you, bad company will ruin you.
E: A man is known by the company he keeps.
If you lie down with the dog, you get up with fleas.
A rotten sheep infects the flock.

34-9 সত্য সেলুকাস, কি বিচিত্র এই দেশ! *

L: "Truly, Seleucus, how marvellously strange this land is!"
I: A conversational interjection made upon hearing or seeing something strange or wonderful.
E: Cf. "Toto, I've a feeling we're not in Kansas any more."

34-10 সব তীর্থ বার বার, গঙ্গাসাগর একবার

L: Every other place of pilgrimage you visit again and again,
Gangasagar you visit only once.
I: The experience is so potent that once is enough.
E: *Cf.* He who drinks Nile water will return *[Egy.]*.

34-11 সব ভাল যার শেষ ভাল   SD

L: If every step goes well, the whole process will end well.
I: All's well that ends well.
E: All's well that ends well.
Well begun is half ended.
Of a good beginning cometh a good end *[Chi.]*.
A hard beginning makes a good ending.
The end crowns the work *[Rus.]*.

34-12 সব শিয়ালের এক রা   x 5-7   SD,SB

L: Every single fox calls out the same tune!
I: Everyone is testifying to exactly the same thing (usually
referred to a cover-up).
E: Dogs of the same street bark alike.

34-13 সবেধন নীলমণি x 11-35;34-34

L: The one and only precious gem.
I: A single, much-loved child in the family.
E: Apple of one's eyes.

34-14 সবে ত' কলির সন্ধ্যে   SD

L: It is barely the evening of Koli Yuga (a bad period of time
in the scriptures).
I: This is only the beginning of the peril, it is going to get lot
worse.
E: Drink and sing, the dark night is ahead of us *[Jap.]*.
You ain't seen nothing yet!

34-15 সবুরে মেওয়া ফলে RL,SD,BDG,SB

L: Patience will make fruit ripen.
   Alt. Waiting will make a dried fruit ready to eat.
I: Waiting is hard, but it will reward you.
E: All things come to those who wait.
   A green fruit gets ripe slowly *[Grk.]*
   If the cat sits long enough at the hole, she will catch the mouse.
   A patient man will eat ripe fruit *[Afr.]*.
   With time and pateince the mulberry leaf becomes a silk gown *[Chi.]*.

   Patience yields a rose *[Hun.]*.

34-16 সময় এবং কালের স্রোত কাহারও অপেক্ষা করে না ₓ34-1

SD,SB

L: Time and tide do not wait for anyone
I: You cannot stop the clock.
E: Time and tide for no man bide.

34-17 সময় কোথায় মেয়ে শিখবে লেখাপড়া,

সারবে কে সংসারের কাজ আগাগোড়া। SB

L: Where is the time for a daughter to study? Who is going to do all her household chores?
I: No point in educating a woman.
E: A woman's place is at home.

34-18 সময় বহিয়া যায় নদীর স্রোতের প্রায় ₓ34-16

L: Time flows along like a river current.
I: Time is unstoppable.
E: Time and tide for no man bide.
   Time is money.
   The Yangtze never runs backwards *[Chi.]*.

34-19 সময়ের এক ফোঁড়, অসময়ের দশ ফোঁড় ₓ2-18 SD,BDG,SB

L: (It needs) only one stitch if you do it in time, ten stitches if you wait.

I: A problem dealt with early on prevents it from getting worse, everything must be done in its proper time.

E: A stitch in time saves nine.

If you do not fill up a crack, you will have to build a wall *[Afr.]*.

If the roots are not removed while weeding,the weeds will grow again when the winds of Spring blows *[Chi.]*.

A stone thrown at the right time is better than gold given at the wrong time *[Per.]*.

Plough the earth in the fall, otherwise you need to plough it a hundred times *[Uyg.]*.

To prevent is better than to cure *[Dut.]*.

34-20 সমুদ্রে পেতেছি শয্যা, শিশিরে কি ভয়   SB

L: I have laid my bed on the ocean, why should I be afraid of dewdrops?

I: One who has suffered a big tragedy is not afraid of any smaller ones.

E: When the bush is on fire, the antelope ceases to fear the hunter's bullet *[Afr.]*.

He who has drowned is not troubled by the rain *[Chi.]*.

34-21 সমূলে উচ্ছেদ করা x 2-38

L: To pull out something, roots and all.

I: To evict somebody or remove something completely.

E: The best way to solve a problem is to attack the cause or root of it.

34-22 সর্বনাশং সমুৎপন্নে অর্ধং ত্যজতি পণ্ডিতঃ *[Sans.]*

L: When total loss is looming, the wise man gives up half (so as to save the other half).

I: It is better to give up something to save the rest.

E: Cut off the sick part while it is still small *[Afr.]*.

34-22a সর্বাঙ্গে ঘা, ঔষধ দিবে কোথায়   SD

L: When there are sores all over the body, where is the salve to be applied?

I: One wants to help somebody, but the latter is in no condition to receive help.

34-23 সর্বমতন্তগর্হিতম্ *[Sans.]*   SD,SB

L: Excess in anything is bad.
I: Never do even good things in excess.
E: Nothing in excess.
     If sweetness be excessive, it is no longer sweetness.

34-24 সশরীরে স্বর্গ লাভ   SD

L: To attain Heaven while still alive.
I: To have exceptional good luck or fortune in death.
E: May you live long, die happy, and rent a mansion in heaven.

34-25 সস্তায় পড়ায়/ সস্তার তিন অবস্থা   RL,SD,BDG

L: If you buy cheap, you will regret.
I: Cheap things may not last.
E: Cheap goods are dearer in the long run.
     If you pay peanuts, you get monkeys.
     If you buy quality, you only cry once.
     Cheap things turn out to be expensive *[Spa.]*.

34-26 সাতকান্ড রামায়ণ পড়ে সীতা কার ভার্য্যা   SD,SB

L: After reading all the seven cantos of the Ramayana, you're asking whose wife Sita is.
I: After a lengthy conversation, asking a question that reveals the listener has not followed any of it.
E: "Is the Pope Catholic?"

34-27 সাত খুন মাফ   SD

L: To absolve someone of seven murders.
I: To be excessively lenient with someone.
E: *Cf.* The King can do no wrong.

34-28 সাত ঘাটের জল খাওয়া   SD, SB

L: To drink from seven ports of call.
I: To gather wide and diverse life experience from compell-
   -ing circumstances.
E: He has been around a few times.

34-29 সাতঘাটের জল খাওয়ানো   x11-1;19-1;26-1   MHP

L: To make someone drink from seven ports of call.
I: To harass someone to the extreme.
E: To make someone jump through the hoops.

34-30 সাত চড়েও রা কাড়ে না   RL, SD

L: He does not say peep even after you have slapped his face
   seven times.
I: A subordinate under heavy workload who never protests.
E: Make him work as you like, he will keep mum.

34-31 সাত জন্মেও ভাবতে পারিনি

L: In seven lifetimes I couldn't have imagined it.
I: Something happened that is completely unexpected.
E: Beyond one's wildest dream.

34-32 সাতপাকে বাঁধা

L: Bound in seven turns.
I: Bound in the covenant of marriage (a part of the Hindu
   marriage ceremony).
E: Tie the knot.

34-33 সাত বলদের দুধ   RL, SD

L: The milk of seven oxen.
I: Something impossible.
E: Goose egg.
   You can pull and pull, but you can't milk a bull *[Rus.]*.

34-34 সাত রাজার ধন, এক মানিক x 34-13   RL,SD

L: One gem that equals the wealth of seven kings.
I: A very precious son of the family.
E: A prince among men.

34-35 সাত সমুদ্র তের নদীর পার   RL,SD

L: Beyond seven seas and thirteen rivers (in fairytales).
I: A mythical far away country. A place human being can
    hardly reach.
E: The back of beyond.
    Cf. Beyond the mountains there are mountains again
    [Hai.].

34-36 সাঁতার না জানলে ডোবাতেও ডোবে   SD

L: If you cannot swim, you can drown in a puddle.
I: If you haven't got the skills for a job, you will be in trouble
    right from the beginning .
E: *Cf.* He who cannot swim must not jump into a deep river
    [Afr.].

34-37 সাতেও না, পাঁচেও না   SD

L: He is neither in the matters of seven nor in the matters of
    five.
I: An indifferent person who does not get involved in every
    day matters, or in other people's affairs.
E: *Cf.* Buttinsky.

34-38 সাপকে দুধ খাওয়ালেও বিষ কমে না x 7-94   SD

L: Even if you feed milk to the snake, his venom remains just
    as potent.
I: An evil nature cannot change from kind treatment.
E: When the snake is in the house, one need not discuss the
    matter at length *[Afr.]*.
    A snake deserves no pity *[Yid.]*.
    However well you feed a wolf, he keeps looking to the
    woods *[Rus.]*.

34-39 সাপও মরে, লাঠিও না ভাঙে RL,SD

L: The snake is dead, and the stick remains intact.
I: To find a middle ground between destroying one's enemy and not harming oneself in doing so.

34-40 সাপে নেউলে x 1-71;2-43 RL,SD,BDG

L: As between a snake and a mongoose.
I: A fierce, deadly rivalry.
E: At daggers drawn.

34-41 সাপের পাঁচ পা দেখা RL,SD,SB

L: To (think you) see five feet on a snake.
I: To be extremely audacious.
E: Audacity, audacity, always audacity *[Fch.]*.

34-42 সাপের মাথায় ভেকের নাচ RL,SD

L: Frog dancing on the hood of a snake.
I: To station oneself right where the danger is maximum.
E: Do not dance on a volcano *[Fch.]*.
One doesn't follow a wild beast into its lair *[Afr.]*.

34-43 সাপের হাঁচি বেদেয় চিনে SB

L: The snake-charmer knows how the snake sneezes.
I: The two know each other inside out.
E: The fisherman knows where the octopuses are *[Afr.]*.

34-44 সাবধানের মার নেই RL

L: The cautious suffer no loss.
I: You must be extra careful to be safe.
E: An excess of caution does no harm *[Lat.]*.
Measure a thousand times and cut once *[Tur.]*.
Don't burn the kebab, neither the shish *[Uyg.]*.
Sure what is sure *[Hun.]*.

34-45 সারা ঘর লেপে দুয়ারে ছালা MHP

L: After cleaning the whole house, leaves a hessian sack on doorstep.

I: Working hard to complete something, but ruining it at the last minute.

34-46 সারাদিন গেল হেলায় ফেলায়, রাত্রিরে বুড়ি কাঁথা সেলায় SD

L: The old lady whiles away the daylight hours, and starts stitching the quilt after nightfall.

I: To while away time that is opportune to accomplish something. To do something when the time is not opportune.

E: Make hay while the sun shine.
Fill the Jars while it rains *[Tur.]*.

34-47 সাহসেই লক্ষ্মী হয়

L: Courage will get you Lakshmi (Goddess of Wealth).

I: Fortune favours the brave.

E: Fortune favours the brave.
Courage can bring fortune.

34-48 সিঁথির সিঁদুর অক্ষয় হোক্

L: May the vermilion mark in the parting of your hair be permanent.

I: May you never become a widow.

E: A long and happy married life.

34-49 সিংহের ভাগ

L: Lion's share.

I: The major share of something.

E: Lion's share.

34-50 সিংহের সন্তান শৃগাল হয় না SD

L: A lion can never bear a fox cub.

I: Impossible lineage. Don't assail the son of the powerful.

E: A wild goose never reared a tame gosling.
A tiger father has no canine sons *[Chi.]*.

34-51 সিকি পয়সা মা–বাপ x6-6

L: A quarter paise equals (in importance) both your father and your mother.

I: The sentiment of an extremely miserly person.

E: Penny pincher.

34-52 সীতা আর রাবণের নাচে বাম অঙ্গ

L: The left part of the body twitches for both Sita and Ravana (portents saying that Sita will triumph and Ravana will lose).

I: Twitching of left part of the body of a woman is a good sign but it is bad for a man.

E: *Cf.* The woman is the left eye, the man the right *[Dan.]*.

34-53 সীতার অগ্নিপরীক্ষা * x1-6

L: Trial by fire of Sita.

I: An ordeal of fire.

E: An ordeal of fire.

34-54 সুখ স্বপনে, শান্তি শ্মশানে

L: Happiness you find in a dream, peace you find in the funeral pyre.

I: You only get real peace when you are dead.

E: The grave is our mother *[Ara.]*.
Heaven lent you a soul, Earth will lend a grave *[Chi.]*.
Hope is the dream of a soul awake *[Fch.]*.

34-55 সুখে থাকতে ভূতে কিলোয় x10-7

L: When you are enjoying a well-settled life, ghosts start thumping on your back.

I: To develop some strange and irrelevant ideas that upset your smoothly functioning life.

E: Leave well enough alone.

| 34-56 | সুখের চেয়ে স্বস্তি ভাল | RL,SD |

L: Peace of mind is preferable to prosperity.
I: Peace of mind is preferable to prosperity.
E: A happy heart is better than a full purse *[Ita.]*.
   cf. To be happy in one's home is better than to be a chief *[Afr.]*.
   Contenment is an inexhaustible treasure *[Tur.]*.

| 34-57 | সুখের পায়রা | RL,SD |

L: The pigeon of happiness.
I: A happy-go-lucky person. A fun-loving, superficial person.
E: The lark of happiness.

| 34-58 | সুঁচ হয়ে ঢোকে, ফাল হয়ে বেরোয় | RL,SD,SB |

L: Goes in as a needle, emerges as a tilling plough.
I: A person who gains your confidence as an innocuous comer, later grow to be a formidable enemy and cause harm.
E: Give him an inch and he will take an ell.
   If the camel once gets his nose in the tent, his body will soon follow *[Ara.]*.
   Evil enters like a needle and spreads like an oak tree *[Afr.]*
   Little by little, the camel goes into the couscous *[Afr.]*.

| 34-59 | সুদখোর আর মদখোর সমান | SD |

L: The usurer and the drunkard are the same.
I: The usurer and the drunkard are the same (both bad).
E: A usurer, a miller, a banker, and a publican, are the four evangelists of Lucifer *[Dut.]*.

| 34-60 | সুন্দর মুখের জয় সর্বত্র | x2-22 |

L: A pretty face wins out everywhere.
I: A fine appearance goes a long way.
E: Young and beautiful, access to everything *[Kir.]*.
   Beauty is a good letter of introduction *[Ger.]*.

One hair on a pretty woman's head is enough to tether a big elephant [Jap.].

The whisper of a pretty girl can be heard further than the roar of a lion [Ara.].

34-61 সুয়ো হ'ল রাজরাণী, দুয়ো হ'ল ঘুঁটে কুড়ানী   SD

L: The favoured wife becomes the queen, the one out of favour goes collecting cow-dung cakes.

I: Consequences of being in favour and out of favour with the person who controls your welfare.

E: The butter is for Emm Zubeid and the thrashing is for Emm Obeid [Ara.].

34-62 সুযোগ পেলে সাধুও চোর   x 25-2   SD

L: Given an opportunity, even a monk will steal.

I: Opportunity to be corrupt can corrupt anyone.

E: Opportunity makes the thief [Hun.].
Cf. As honest as a cat when the meat is out of reach.

34-63 সুসময়ে বন্ধু বটে সকলেই হয়,
অসময়ে হায় হায় কেহ কারও নয়।

L: In times of great fortune, everyone wants to be your friend; in times of adversity, no one knows you.

I: Fair weather friends. One gets friends in his good days and not in bad times.

E: When good cheer is lacking, our friends will be packing. In times of prosperity friends are plentiful.

While the pot boils the friendship lasts [Tur.].
The day your horse dies and your money's lost, your relatives change to strangers [Chi.].
It's when in need that one recognizes his friends [Ara.].

34-64 সূর্য্য দেখতে বাতি লাগে না   MHP

L: You do not need a light to see the Sun.

I: Someone noble or famous is his own light.

E: Does one need a torch to see the sun? *[Jap.]*.
    The sun cannot be daubed by using wet clay *[Tur.]*.

`34-65` **সে গুড়ে বালি**   RL,SD,MW

L: That bit of jaggery is laced with sand (inedible).
I: That prospect is unlikely to materialize. Disappointment.
E: Don't count on it!

`34-66` **সেকরার ঠুক ঠাক, কামারের এক ঘা**   SD

L: The jeweller taps away gently at his work while the black-
    smith strikes only once.
I: The difference between a skilled craftsman and a hack.
E: The mason who strikes often is better than the mason
    who strikes hard.

`34-67` **সেকরা মাসের কানের সোনাও চুরি করে**   RL

L: The jeweller will shave off some gold even from his own
    mother's earrings.
I: A swindler does not spare anyone.
E: He can cheat a fish out of its skin *[Rus.]*.

`34-68` **সে রামও নাই, সে অযোধ্যাও নাই** x22-1   RL,SD,SB

L: Gone is Rama of yore, gone is Ayodhya yore!
I: O the times! How they have changed! Gone are the glory
    days!
E: Woe the times! Woe the manners!

34-69 সোজা আঙুলে ঘি ওঠে না

34-69 সোজা আঙুলে ঘি ওঠে না x|5-30| RL,SD,SB

L: You cannot scoop up ghee with a straight finger.
I: Don't be straight-laced when crookedness is called for.
E: One finger cannot lift a pebble *[AmInd.]*.
      One finger cannot remove lice from the head *[Afr.]*.
      A bird will not fly with one wing *[Tur.]*.

34-70 সোনায় সোহাগা   SD

L: Borax (a polishing/shining compound) applied to gold.
I: Quite the fine combination (said in jest or sarcasm).
      A happy match, a most desirable union, (sarcastically) an
      alliance of two vile persons.
E: Gilding the lily.
      Icing on the cake.
      Adding legs when painting a snake *[Chi.]*.

34-71 সোনার কাঠি, রুপার কাঠি RL,SD

L: The golden wand, the silver wand.
I: Things having magical qualities.
E: Magic wand.
    Cf. The glass slippers.

34-72 সোনার পারথবাটি x7-61 SD

L: A stone bowl made of gold.
I: An impossibility.
E: Iron wheel made of wood *[Hun.]*.

34-73 স্ত্রীবুদ্ধি প্রলয়ংকরী RL,SD,SB

L: A woman's advice leads to unhappy results, or upsets
    everything.
I: Following a woman's advice can be disastrous.
E: When an ass climbs a ladder, we may find wisdom in
    women.

34-74 স্বর্গ হাতে পাওয়া SD

L: To grasp Heaven in one's hands.
I: To attain great joy or pleasure or fortune.
E: To be in seventh Heaven.

34-75 স্বর্গের সিঁড়ি তৈরী করা SD

L: To build a staircase to Heaven.
I: To assure one's passage to Heaven. To accumulate credit
    for the afterlife through good deeds.
E: Stairway to Heaven.

34-76 স্বদেশে পূজ্যতে রাজা, বিদ্বান সর্বত্র পূজ্যতে *[Sans.]*

L: A king is revered in his own kingdom, a learned man is
    revered everywhere.
I: Learning and wisdom are more important than pomp and
    power.
E: Pen is mightier than sword.

34-78 স্বপ্নে ঘি ঢালা

34-77 স্বপ্নে ঘি ঢালা x 34-79

L: To add ghee (to your cooking pot) in dream.
I: Dream big of what you cannot afford.
E: Building castles in the air.

34-78 স্বপ্নে যদি মাংস রাঁধি, ঘি দিতে কার্পণ্য কেন x 34-78

L: If I am cooking meat in my dream, why would I not add (expensive) ghee generously?
I: If you are fantasizing, why limit yourself?
E: If wishes were horses beggars would ride.

34-79 স্বপ্নে সৌধ তৈরী করা   SD

L: To build a castle in one's dream.
I: Dream big of what you cannot afford.
E: Building castles in the air.
         You'll never plough a field by turning it over in your mind
         We live by hope, but reed never becomes an Iroko tree by
         dreaming *[Afr.]*.

34-80 স্বপ্নেও ভাবতে পারিনি

L: Could not imagine this even in my dream.
I: Something completely unexpected.
E: Beyond one's wildest dreams.

34-81 স্বভাব যায় না ম'লে   RL,SD,SB

L: One's habits don't die with his death.
I: Habit is hard to break.
E: Habit is second nature.
         The fox can lose his fur but not his cunning *[Ita.]*.
         Evil in people does not go away when they get buried*[Ara]*
         Habits don't expire until life expires *[Tur.]*.

32-82 সেয়ানে সেয়ানে কোলাকুলি   SD,BDG

L: The hugging of two sly men.
I: Encounter between two equally shrewd people.
E: Diamond cut diamond.

34-83 স্রোতে গা ঢালা   SD

L: To float with the flow of the river.
I: To effortlessly let oneself be carried by the flow of events.
E: To go with the flow.

৩০২

35-1 হংস মধ্যে বক যথা *[Mock Sans.]* SD

L: Like a heron amid swans.

I: Misfit. Out of place. Stands out.

E: A donkey is a donkey even if he is raised among horses *[Ara.]*.

A crow in peacock feathers *[Rus.]*.

35-2 হক্ কথায় বন্ধু বেজার, গরম ভাতে বেড়াল বেজার SD

L: Telling the (unpleasant) truth makes a friend unhappy, hot rice makes the cat unhappy.

I: Good words or good things are not necessarily welcome to everyone.

E: He that speaks truth must have one foot in the stirrup *[Tur.]*.

The truthful person is considered the difficult person in the community *[Afr.]*.

35-3 হবু ছেলের অন্নপ্রাশন x 1-10 SD

L: To arrange the first rice-eating ceremony for a yet-to-be-born child.

I: To plan an uncertain future event.

E: To count one's chickens before they are hatched.

35-4 হ য ব র ল x 2-63 SD

L: A random collection of Bengali letters.

I: Nonsense. Jibberish. Hodgepodge.

E: Mumbo jumbo.

35-5 "হরি দিন তো গেল সন্ধ্যা হ'ল, পার কর আমারে...."

L: (Lord) Hari, my days are done, the evening has fallen, please ferry me over now...

I: An old age prayer or lament or self-deprecation.

E: *Cf.* "Abide with me, O Lord, fast falls the eventide, the darkness deepens..." - *The Bible*

35-6 হরি ঘোষের গোয়াল   SD,SB

L: The cattle shed of Hari Ghosh.

I: A place of utter disarray. Pandemonium.

E: It's like a public bath with its water cut off [*Ara.*].

35-7 হরিমটর খাওয়া   SD

L: To dine on the bean offerings to Lord Hari.

I: To go without food or to starve.

E: Dine with Duke Humphrey.

35-8 হরিষে বিষাদ   SD

L: A sudden sorrow arising in the midst of rejoicing.

I: Sadness tinted with joy. Joy turning to sadness.

E: "Our sincerest laughter
      With some pain is fraught . . "

35-9 হরিহর আত্মা   SD

L: (Their) souls are as close as Hari and Hara.

I: When two people are very close.

E: Two peas in a pod.

35-10 হরির লুট   SD

L: The scattering (among the attendees) of the ceremonial offering (of sugar candies) after the worship of Lord Hari.

I: A giveaway.

E: Freebies.

35-11 হর্তাকর্তা বিধাতা

L: Lord and God – rolled in one.

I: The supreme master.

E: Lord High Executioner.

35-12 হয় একান্তরি নয় দেশান্তরি

L: Either soul mates, or live countries apart.

I: Said of a relationship that can be either very close or very distant.

35-13 হয় এস্‌পার নয় ওস্‌পার

L: Either this way or that way.
I: (Settle this at) one extreme or the other. Do something finally.
E: Don't sit on the fence.
You can't dance at two weddings at the same time, nor can you sit on two horses with one behind *[Yid.]*.

35-14 হলফ করে বলছি / মাইরি বলছি

L: I am giving you my word (that this is true).
I: I promise it is true.
E: Cross my heart and hope to die...

35-15 হাকিম নড়ে তো হুকুম নড়ে না   RL,SD,SB

L: The judge may change but not the order.
I: The decision cannot be changed by the person now in charge.
E: *Cf.* Who is well seated, let him not budge [*Spa.*].

35-16 হাটিমাটিম্‌ টিম্‌ *

L: An imaginary humorous creature.
I: An amusingly odd person.
E: *Cf.* Jabberwocky.

35-17 হাটে হাঁড়ি ভাঙা   SD

L: To crack open a sealed earthen pot in the middle of the village marketplace.
I: To suddenly divulge someone's dark secret in public (and thus embarrass him to the extreme).
E: To wash one's dirty linen in public.
To spill the beans.
The potty gets knocked over *[Hun.]*.
One cannot say family talk in the bazaar *[Uyg.]*.

One needs to wash one's dirty laundry with family around *[Fch.]*.

35-18 হাত ঘুরিয়ে নাক দেখানো x7-62   SD

L: To point to one's nose with one's arm circled back round the head.

I: An unnecessary roundabout way of expressing something simple.

E: Shall we kill a snake and carry it in our hand when we have a bag for putting things in?

35-19 হাতী ঘোড়া গেল তল, বেঙ বলে কত জল? x28-118 RL,SD,SB

L: Elephants and horses are capsized (trying to cross the river), and the frog asks, 'How deep is the water'?

I: Referring to the audacity of a person who wants to try something where the more able have failed

E: Fools rush in where angels fear to tread.

35-20 হাতী যখন ফাঁদে পরে, বেঙেও লাথি মারে x28-53   RL,SD

L: When the elephant is caught in a trap, even the frog kicks him.

I: When the mighty has fallen, even a weakling gets his digs in.

E: Even little birds may peck at a dead lion.

35-21 হাতে কালি মুখে কালি বাছা আমার লিখে এলি

L: Ink on your hands, ink on your face. My son, you've really done some studying!

I: Parents can be blind.

E: A child may have too much of his mother's blessing.

35-22 হাতে কলমে শেখা

L: Learning by hand and pen.

I: Learning hands on. Learning practically.

E: Life's a dance, you learn as you go, sometimes you lead, sometimes you follow.

35-23 হাতে দই পাতে দই, তবু বলে কই কই x 29-84   SB

L: Yogurt in hand, yogurt on plate, even so you are asking for more.
I: One who is never satisfied.
E: Eaten bread is forgotten.

35-24 হাতে নাতে ধরা পরা   MW

L: Caught in the act.
I: Catch somebody red-handed.
E: Caught red-handed.
Catching someone with his hands in the cookie jar.
Catching somebody with the hide and the horns *[Thai]*.

35-25 হাতের ফাঁক দিয়ে জল গলে না   SB

L: Water does not leak through his closed fingers.
I: A very close-fisted (miserly) person.
E: Like coins between a dying miser's fingers.

35-26 হাতের ঢিল ছুঁড়ে দিলে আর ফেরে না x 28-78   RL,SD

L: A pelted stone does not return.
I: An irreversible act of misjudgment.
E: Spoken words and shot arrows cannot be taken back.
It is easier to catch an escaped horse than to take back an escaped word *[Mon.]*.

35-27 হাতের লক্ষ্মী পায়ে ঠেলা x 10-6   SD,SB

L: To kick away Lakshmi (Goddess of Wealth) who was within your grasp.
I: To throw away one's fortune.
E: He whose garment has a long trail will surround his waist with it *[Ara.]*.

35-28 হাড়জ্বালানি ডাকিনী

L: A woman who irritates you right down to your bones.
I: A pestering woman.
E: She devil.

35-29 হাম পন্ছি এক ডালকে *[Hin.]*

L: All us birds are sitting on the same branch.
I: We are all alike. We are all in it together.
E: We are all in the same boat.

35-30 হাম সে বড়া কৌন্ হ্যায়? *[Hin.]*

L: Who is greater than I?
I: Words of feigned boasting.
E: I am the King of the Mountain!

35-31 হাসলে মাণিক পড়ে, কাঁদলে মুক্তা ঝরে   SD

L: If she smiles, gems drop from her lips; if she cries, her tears become pearls.
I: Said of a fairytale princess.
E: "She walks in beauty . . ."

35-32 হাসিও পায়, দুঃখও হয়   SD

L: It evokes both laughter and sorrow.
I: A situation that is sad and humorous at the same time.
E: *Cf.* Learn from your tears and you will win laughing *[Spa.]*.

35-33 হিন্দু যদি মুসলমান হয় গরু খাওয়ার যম হয়

L: When a Hindu converts to Islam, he becomes a great lover of beef (which the Hindu religion forbids).
I: Refers to a convert's overenthusiasm.
E: Zeal of the convert.
     To be more Catholic than the Pope.

35-34 হিতে বিপরীত

L: (Someone is) trying to do good, but the opposite happens.
I: An adverse outcome of something undertaken with good intentions.
E: I tried to draw the eyebrow, but I ended up poking the eye *[Aze.]*.

35-35 হিংটিং ছট্

L: Hing Ting Chhot.

I: (Humorous) meaningless jibberish resembling in sound the chanting of Sanskrit mantras.

E: *cf.* Hocus-pocus (meaningless jibberish derived from Latin *Hoc est corpus meum* – meaning, Here is my body).

35-36 হোঁদল-কুতকুত

L: A fictional, ungainly man-like beast.

I: A corpulent and dark-complexioned man.

E: *Cf.* "Jabba the Hut".

35-37 হেড অপিসে গণ্ডগোল

L: There's something wrong in his Head Office.

I: He is crazy.

E: He has got screws loose.
He has not got his head screwed on tight.
He is not playing with a full deck.

৩০২

Appendix

Context and background

In the following, the context or the background story for many of the proverbs and idioms is presented. Only enough information is given to enable the reader to make sense of the proverb or the idiom. Also, and naturally, these stories may differ in matters of detail from one narrator to another.

1-6; 34-53 (সীতার) অগ্নিপরীক্ষা

When Rama returned from his exile and sought to claim the throne of Ayodhya, he cast doubt on the chastity of his wife Sita who had long been a captive of Ravana. Devastated by her husband's doubt, Sita then offered to undergo the trial by fire. A fire was lit in the Royal Court and Sita entered the fire. The flames left her completely unscathed, proving that Sita was the purest of the pure (From the *Ramayana*).

1-11 অর্জুনের বিশ্বরূপ দেখা

On the eve of the epic battle of Kurukshetra, Lord Krishna – who served as the charioteer of the warrior Arjun – gave the latter a lengthy sermon. This is the subject of the Hindu scripture the *Bhagavad Geeta*. During this sermon, Krishna showed the many appearances (manifestations) of himself to Arjun. In these manifestations, Arjun saw all the shapes and forms of the Universe (From the *Mahabharata*).

1-16 অতিদর্পে হতা লঙ্কা

The epic battle of the *Ramayana* between Rama, the exiled Prince of Ayodhya and Ravana, the King of Lanka resulted largely from the haughty and hubris-ridden arrogance of Ravana regarding his own superiority and the superiority of his military power. It is this excessive arrogance that finally did him in.

অশ্বথামা হত ইতি গজ

In the epic *Mahabharata*, the Pandava and the Kaurava clans fought against each other, with other noted warriors taking sides. The undefeatable warrior Guru Dronacharya took the Kaurava side, as did his son Ashwatthama, of whom his father was most fond. The Pandavas realized that Dronacharya could not be defeated in battle fair and square, and so they devised a subterfuge. It was proclaimed to Dronacharya in the battlefield that Ashwatthama was dead ('Ashwatthama hata'), whereas in fact an elephant named Ashwatthama ('iti gaja': 'an elephanet so named, that is') had died. However, Dronacharya was most distraught on hearing the first part of the news that he did not hear the second part which was said in a low voice so as to be inaudible in the din and bustle of battle. So, technically speaking, no lies were told. A grief-stricken Dronacharya was then easily felled.

2-33 "আজ নগদ কাল ধার, ধারের পায়ে নমস্কার।

যে বাবুকে দিলাম ধার, এ পথে সে চলে না আর।"

A framed sign often seen in shops and café in Bengal. It is basically an emphatic way of saying: Please don't ask for credit.

2-74 (শুভ) আষাঢ়স্য প্রথম দিবসে

In the sanskrit long-poem *Meghadutam* by Kalidas, a man isolated on the northern mountains - who is far away and long seperated from his love - pines for her. On the first day of the Bengali month Ashar, he espies a group of clouds overhead, floating south. He implores the clouds to carry a message from him to his love. This way, the day achieves a special, auspicious significance. In colloquial Bengali, the expression commonly used is "Shubho Asharasya prathama diboshe". But the word shubho (auspicious) is not there in the original Sanskrit text.

5-40 একলব্যের গুরুদক্ষিণা

Ekalabya was a low-caste tribal prince. He had a great desire to study archery under the great guru Dronacharya who was teacher to the Pandavas on weapons and martial arts. Dronacharya refused to accept Ekalabya as a student. Crestfallen, Ekalabya nevertheless did not lose his great regard for this guru. He set up a clay image of Dronacharya, and started a course of self-training in full view of this statue. Ekalabya became a very accomplished archer, and a formidable competition to Arjun, the Pandava brother who was the most accomplished student of the guru in archery. Arjun requested Dronacharya to remove (get rid of) the competition. Taking advantage of Ekalabya's reverence for him, Dronacjarya demanded Ekalabya's right thumb as a teacher's fee. Ekalabya severed his thumb and presented it to the guru. This of course made him useless as an archer (From the *Mahabharata.*)

5-32 একা রামে রক্ষা নেই সুগ্রীব দোসর

Rama alone was a fitting enemy of Ravana. But he got some help, to boot. Sugriv, king of the monkey kingdom, then joined forces with Rama. His monkey brigade fought against Ravana (From the *Ramayana.*)

5-44 "এতক্ষণে, অরিন্দম কহিলা বিষাদে"

A somewhat fuller context, from *Meghnad Badh Kabya* by Michael Madhusudan Datta, is the following:

'এতক্ষণে' – অরিন্দম কহিলা বিষাদে –
'জানিনু কেমনে আসি লক্ষণ পশিল রাক্ষসপুরে'!– – –

It says:

"At last--," said Arindam sadly –
"I understand how Lakshman managed to enter the inner
sanctum of the demons!---"

In the epic battle of the *Ramayana*, the "good guys" were led by the brothers Rama and Lakshman. The bad guys were led by the demon King Ravana, aided by many, including his son Indrajit, a formidable warrior also known as Arindam. Ravana's brother Bibhishan was a betrayer who secretly joined Rama's camp. One day, he sneaked Laksmana into the innermost sanctum of Ravana's palace, with intent to do harm. Bibhishan showed Lakshman into the place where Indrajit was engaged in meditative worship. Indrajit opened his eyes and was startled to find his worst enemy from the battlefield, right in his own private sanctum. Presently, however, he saw his uncle Bibhishan lurking in the dark some distance away. Suddenly, the entire betrayal by his uncle became clear to him. He then spoke as above. (Also see 10-8).

7-48 কাকতালীয় ব্যপার

A crow flies in and sits on a Taal tree heavy with the load of ripe taal fruits. At the same time, a fruit happens to fall to the ground. One hastens to the cause-and-effect connection that the crow has caused the fruit to fall. This is the *Kaaktaaliyo Byapar*: The Crow-Taal fruit connection.

7-41 কাঙ্গালী-বিদায় করা

When a Hindu homesteader performs some religious rite, destitute people gather round. After the ceremony is finished, the homesteader distributes food or money among the destitute. Then they leave.

7-60 কাঠবিড়ালীর সাগর বাঁধা

When Rama decided to build a bridge between the mainland (India) and the island of Lanka (to attack and vanquish the evil king Ravana), an army of monkeys started to throw stones into the ocean. Likewise, the squirrels helped by carrying small pebbles to the waters edge and dropping them there (From the *Ramayana*).

কালনেমির লঙ্কা ভাগ

The demon Kalnemi was an uncle to Ravana, the King of Lanka. The latter asked him to vanquish the great monkey warrior Hanuman. Kalnemi agreed in return for the promise of half of the Kingdom of Lanka. Hence the expression Kalnemi's Share of Lanka. But little did Kalnemi know that he was no match for Hanuman. However, as Kalnemi proceeded on his mission, he was greatly lifted by his fantasies of possessing half of Lanka and everything in it, including half of Ravana's wives. He was particularly pleased with the thought of Ravana's main queen, Mandadori. Kalnemi of course would be defeated by Hanuman and would be in no position to enjoy *Kalnemir Lankabhag*. (From the *Ramayana*.)

7-76 কালবৈশাখীর ঝড়

It is the fierce storm in the monsoon rainstorm season in Bengal around the Bengali month Baishakh (April-May). It is preceded by portentous dark clouds and lightning and thunder, making the day seem like night. Then the heavy sheet of rain descends. It floods, it washes, it soaks you to the bones. And suddenly, after a hot, sultry, sweaty day, you even feel a little refreshing chill.

7-89 কিষ্কিন্ধ্যাকাণ্ড

Kishkinda Kando is an important and elaborate book of the *Ramayana* where Rama makes a military alliance with prominent leaders of the monkeys, Hanuman and Sugriv, in order to invade Lanka and rescue his wife Sita who had been abducted by Ravana, the King of Lanka.

7-100 কুম্ভকর্ণের নিদ্রা ভঙ্গ

Kumbhakarna was a great warrior and a brother of Ravana, the King of Lanka. The gods cursed him to sleep six months of the year. When the battle raged between Ravana and Rama and things were not going so well for the former, Kumbhakarna was asleep. Ravana ordered his soldiers to create tremendous din and bustle and noise and pandemonium to try to awaken

Kumbhakarana, and also to physically push him and jerk him and shake him. Even with all this, it took a tremendous effort before Kumbhakarna would wake up. Immediately, he had to be given mountains of food, for he was ravenously hungry. Only then did Kumbhakarna proceed to battle and gave a good account of himself. He killed the enemy in great numbers before Rama slew him. (From the *Ramayana*.)

The illustration on page 81 is that of a statue at a construction site on the Andhra-Karnataka border in India.

The statue tells a story, of course, but there is another story inside it. This is an auditorium. The head is the stage, the belly is the gallery, and the legs are the entry and exit points.

The statue was conceived by former Anantapur Collector Someshkumar and given shape to by Visakhapatnam-based Architect Venkat three years ago to make people alive to issues like HIV/AIDS, corruption and environmental pollution. "Though the 'concrete' Kumbhakarna will continue to sleep, we want people to awaken and shed their indifference to the problems facing the society" . . . District Tourism Officer Biju George.

7-102 কুরুক্ষেত্র কাণ্ড

Kurukshetra was the vast, sprawling main battleground of the epic *Mahabharata*. Great battles were fought here and great tragedies unfolded.

10-8 ঘরের শত্রু বিভীষণ

Bibhishan was a brother of Ravana, the King of Lanka. In the war council where the advisors of Ravana were urging him to wage an unjust war against Rama, Bibhishan demurred. He counselled against the war. At this, Ravana became very angry and expelled him. Bibhishan then joined Rama's camp and advised them on how to defeat Ravana. Hence the expression Bibhishan, the Enemy Within (from the *Ramayana*.)

11-17 চিত্রগুপ্তের খাতা

Chitragupta is a scribe to Yama, the god of death. It is the scribe's duty to maintain the ledger in which the sins and virtues of each human being are meticulously recorded. When someone arrives at Yama's door, the recknoning of his deeds – as recorded in the ledger – takes place. Accordingly, he is sent to Heaven or Hell.

14-1 ঝড়ে কাক পড়ে, ফকিরের কেরামতি বাড়ে

A Fakir was reputed to have special mental powers with which he could make things happen. One day he sat near a pond, looking at a crane. Suddenly, a storm came and felled the crane. Everyone thought that the Fakir felled the crane with his mental prowess. His reputation then grew apace.

16-5 ঠুঁটো জগন্নাথ

The famous deity without any limbs is in a temple in Puri, Orissa, India.

21-45 দৈত্যকুলে প্রহ্লাদ

In the Hindu scriptures, Prahlad is the son of Hiranyakashipu, of the Asuras or the demon clan. However, Prahlad managed to overcome all efforts of his father to indoctrinate him to the evil ways of the demons and became a pious devotee of Lord Vishnu. (From the *Ramayana*).

21-49 দ্রৌপদীর বস্ত্র হরণ

The *Mahabharata* is an epic story of conflict between the Pandava brothers (Yudhisthira being the eldest) and the Kaurava brothers (Duryadhan and Duhshasan). The very pious Yudhisthira had but one fault: An addiction to gambling. Taking advantage of this, the Kauravas invited him to sit at a game against their uncle Shakuni, who was in fact an accomplished cheat. Yudhisthira kept betting one thing after another, and losing it all. At last, when he had nothing else to bet, the Kauravas suggested he bet his wife Draupadi. Yudhisthira did so and lost again. Upon this, the Kauravas dragged Draupadi out into the open and insulted her in various ways. Finally, Duhshasan started to disrobe her in public by pulling at one end of the sari. Daraupadi then prayed to her mentor Lord Krishna. He granted her prayer. The more Duhshasan pulled on the sari and uncoiled it, the more length was added to the sari. An inexhaustible bale of sari continued to descend from Heaven. Eventually, completely exhausted by his labour, Duhshasan fainted and Draupadi's ordeal ended.

22-4 ধর লক্ষণ

Through cruelty of fate, Rama had to go to a fourteen-year exile in the forest, accompanied by his wife Sita and his half-brother Lakshman. Lakshman was exceptionally devoted to his sister-in-law, and shrank before her from great reverence. Everyday, Sita gathered whatever food she could from the forest, and gave a third of this to Lakshman, saying: "Hold this Laksman," meaning, clearly, "Eat this, Lakshman." But since she did not literally spell out the instruction verbally, Laksman simply took the food and set it aside ('held it!'). He never ate. (From the *Ramayana*.)

22-8 ধর্মপুত্র যুধিষ্টির

Yudhisthira, the eldest of the five Pandava brothers (the "good guys" of the epic *Mahabharata*) was a very pious person, the very embodiment of the highest ethical and moral and religious qualities - so much so that he is referred to as Yudhisthira, the Son of Dharma.

23-32 নাটোরের বনলতা সেন

Natorer Banalata Sen (Banalata Sen from Natore) is perhaps the best known poem of the prominent Bengali poet Jibanananda Das. It is a mysterious and mystical poem about a young woman who is the object of sublime desire. She is the ultimate Bengali romantic heroine. The poem has been compared to the poem "To Helen" by Edgar Allan Poe.

24-64 পুকুর চুরি

Theft of a pond or lake by extending a trench in your land to slowly merge with your neighbour's pond.

24-71 পুনর্মূষিক ভব

A mouse was being harassed by a cat and was in danger of being killed. So he went to a holy man and asked for a boon: To be turned into a cat. The holy man granted his wish. But when the mouse became a cat, a dog began to harass him. And when he became a dog by means of a second boon, a tiger began to harass him. When he became a tiger, he came to the holy man. The latter asked: "What would you like now?" The tiger said: "To eat you." Then the holy man said: "*Punarmushika bhava* – Turn into a mouse again!"

24-84 প্রথমরাত্রে মারিবে বিড়াল

A bridegroom was intent on establishing once for all his own turf with respect to his new bride, on the very night of the wedding. A cat strayed into the wedding chamber. The bridegroom pretended to be very angry, and killed the cat with one strike. The bride understood that this was not a man to be got angry. She understood on the very first night who "wore the trousers" in the family! Hence the advice to all bridegrooms: "Kill the cat on the first night!"

24-87 প্রহারেণ ধনঞ্জয়

Dhananjaya was a son-in-law who was living in his father-in-law's house. After a long stay, unwilling to leave, he was ousted from that home by severe beating.

ফুল্লরার বারমাস্যা

Phullora, a woman in *Chandimangal* (paean to the goddess Chandi) has to go through the yearlong cycle of the daily grind: drudgery and the like. Hence *Phullorar Baromasya*, or The year-round woes of Phullora.

26-30 বানর ও তৈলাক্ত বাঁশের অঙ্ক

A typical beginner's mathematics problem goes like this: A bamboo pole has been made very slippery by rubbing oil on it. A monkey is trying to get to the top of the pole. Every time he jumps 5 feet, he slips 2 feet. How many jumps will it take for him to climb a 20 feet pole? This has become symbolic of a hard-to-make-progress situation.

26-48 বিদুরের ক্ষুদ

Bidur was a man of low birth, the son of a maidservent in the employ of the Royal Palace in Hastinapur. But he was a great devotee of Lord Krishna. When the latter came visiting Hastinapur, the Royal Palace prepared to greet this most revered guest. But instead of coming to the palace, Krishna went to visit Bidur's meager hovel. Bidur was so poor that all he could offer Krishna was a little bit of khood (the broken rice grains rejected at husking, and usually eaten by the poorest of the poor), with not even a pinch of salt to make it edible. Krishna accepted and savoured this gift with great delight, for it was the quality and the depth of Bidur's devotion that had brought him there. (From the *Mahabharata*)

26-85 বৈতরণী পার

Vaitarani is a river of the Hindu mind, and also an actual matter-of-fact river. As a concept, it is the river that bounds the kingdom of Yama, god of death. Upon death, one has to cross Vaitarani to reach the land of the dead. In Greek mythology, there is a river Stygian. When people die, they will have to cross that river to go to . . . .

28-1 মগের মুল্লুক

This expression literally means 'the lawless Mog frontierland'. 16th Century Portugese water/ ocean pirates used to torture the natives of eastern and southern parts of Bengal. Still referred to this as an example of torture/ oppression.

28-32 মন্থরার কু মন্ত্রণা

Monthora was the private maid of the queen Koikeyi, one of King Dasharath's three wives. The maid was most mean-spirited and evil, and she advised Koikeyi to plot to gain the throne for her own son at the exclusion of her stepwives' sons. Much of the complexity and the tumult of the epic *Ramayana* stemmed or flowed from this bit of scheming.

28-31 মহিষাসুরমর্দিনী

Mahishashuromardini, literally the female slayer of the buffalo demon, is another name of the goddess Durga. In her most common depiction, she is shown standing victoriously over a vanquished demon who takes the shape of a buffalo.

28-72 মা নিষাদ

The sage Valmiki, who would write the *Ramayana,* was once meditating in the forest when he saw a hunter shoot an arrow at a pair of herons engaged in love-making. The arrow felled one of the herons. This greatly angered the sage. But when he cursed the hunter, his words came out of his mouth as beautiful verse (the type of verse that would be used to compose the epic). The expression Ma Nishad ("Never, O Hunter") comes from what the sage said to the hunter: "Never, O Hunter, ever in eternity, will you know rest. For you have felled one heron of a pair in enchanted love-making in their nest".

28-36 মাকড় মারলে ধোকড় হয়

The story goes thus: a subject came to his Brahmin master and asked what would be the punishment for killing a spider. The master, thinking it must be one of his subject's children, mentioned a heavy punishment. The subject said, then punish your son because he is the one who has killed the spider. The master then said: But when a brahmin's son kills a spider there is no punishment.

28-42 মাছি মারা কেরাণী

This story about a kerani, or a lowly office scribe goes thus: He was given the menial task of copying an old ledger into an empty book. As he was doing this work, he saw that a dead fly was stuck to one page of the old ledger. He then went to great lengths to find and swat a fly, and paste it onto to the new ledger at exactly the same location. This story has come to signify mechanical activity without any thought.

28-85 মীর জাফর

Mir Jafar Ali Khan was a high official in the court of Sirajuddaula, the Nawab of Murshidabad. He betrayed the Nawab by stirring up trouble within the Nawab's army, and later by aligning himself secretly with the British. In the fateful battle of Plassey, he gained trust of Sirajuddaula and adviced him to deploy the army against the British in a certain way. This deployment actually facilitated things for the British army, who thus easily vanquished the army of Sirajuddaula. For this and many other betrayals and treacheries and cowardice, Mir Jafar lives on in infamy.

28-118 মেরে ভূত ভাগিয়ে দেওয়া

Exorcism is performed by a functionary called the Ojha. Many times, he would try to exorcise the evil by severely beating the possessed, as though he was beating the devil himself. So the more severe the beating, the more effective the exorcism is expected to be.

29-18 যদি হয় সুজন, তেঁতুল পাতায় ন'জন

It was common custom in festive Bengali gatherings to eat the meal off a square sheet of a freshly cut, large banana leaf. Sometimes, two family members could eat together, off the same banana leaf "plate". The tentul or tamarind leaf, however, is very small, perhaps less than half the size of a penny. So, nine people eating together off one tentul leaf represents a humourously extreme symbol of companionability.

29-24 যশোদা ভাগ্যবতী, পরের পুত্রে পুত্রবতী

In the epic *Mahabharata*, Lord Krishna as a baby was raised by his foster mother Jashoda (or Yashoda). The newborn Krishna was secretly removed from his real mother Devaki and deposited with Jashoda in order to save the baby from evil Kangsha who was slaying every offspring of Devaki (because of a divine curse that Kangsha would be slain by a son of Devaki). Jashoda loved Krishna as her own son, and bestowed great affection on him. Hence the expression: Joshoda the Fortunate, fulfilled as a mother by someone else's son.

29-63 যে যায় লঙ্কায় সেই হয় রাবণ

Ravana was the vile and corrupt king of Lanka. The saying goes that whoever goes to Lanka, becomes (corrupt like) Ravana.

29-77 যেমন বুনো ওল তেমন বাঘা তেঁতুল

Wild arum root is edible when cooked, but one must first remove its strong horseradish-like, sometimes poisonous pungence. It is so strong that to neutralize it, you need the extract of a most potent 'Tiger-strength' tamarind (bagha tentul) to soak the vegetable in. Thus the saying: The tiger tamarind is the just match for the wild arum root.

30-1   রামগড়ুরের ছানা

Ramgorurer chhana (a hatchling of Ramgorur) is an imaginary character from Sukumar Roy's collection of nonsense rhymes called *Abol Tabol*.

30-16   রাবণের স্বর্গের সিঁড়ি

Ravana, the evil King of Lanka, is said to have tried to build a staircase to Indralok (Heaven) so that, in spite of all his evil deeds, he would simply walk up to Heaven on his death. That did not materialise as he was killed by Rama before he could build his staircase. (From the *Ramayana*)

30-17   রাম না জন্মিতে রামায়ণ

It is said that the entire epic *Ramayana*, the eventful life and the tumultous times of Rama, was written by the sage Valmiki 60 years before Rama was even born.

31-9   লাগে টাকা দেবে গৌরী সেন

Gouri Sen is a fictional financier (generally, the Government or the Public Treasury) who is wasteful with money. If you want easy money to do whatever you wish , go to Gouri Sen.

32-14   শবরীর প্রতীক্ষা

Shabari was a low-caste girl who fled an oppressive home and found shelter in a forest hermitage. There she joined the monks in their vigil for Lord Rama who, it was rumored, would be passing this way soon. Shabari prepared herself for the vist of Rama, making herself pure of mind and body, and preparing offerings of the finest fruits for Rama. This she did everyday, day after day. All the time, she remained apprehensive that Rama might not deign to speak to her because of her low caste. The vigil continued and Shabari lost her youth and greyed. One day, Rama did finally come, and sat with Shabari and had great discourse with her. He tasted her fruits and granted her moksha, or eternal bliss. Shabari went to heaven. Such was the long and intense Vigil of Shabari. (From the *Ramayana*)

32-18 শাক দিয়ে মাছ ঢাকা

Trying to cover up the fish on your dinner plate with the serving of spinach so that no one will know that a vegetarian is enjoying in non-vegetarian fare on the sly.

32-19 শাঁখের করাত

A saw used to slice conch shell has sharp edges on both sides. It is a reciprocating saw that cuts both going forward and backward. This accelerates the process and is less likely to break the shell.

32-39 শূর্পনখার নাক কাটা

When Rama lived in exile with his wife Sita and half-brother Lakshman in a forest hermitage, the demoness Shurpanakha spotted the two handsome brothers and was overcome with desire to possess one of them. She assumed the form a beautiful young lady and approached them. But when the brothers repeatedly rejected her, she realized that Sita was the obstacle in her way. She then attacked Sita, intending to kill her. But Lakshman intervened and cut off Shurpanakha's nose and ears. (From the *Ramayana*)

32-44 শ্যাম রাখি না কুল রাখি

Do I marry Shyam (Krishna) or do I preserve the honour of my caste (and forsake the lower-caste Shyam)? - Dilemma of Radha, in *Mahabharata*)

সত্যি সেলুকাস, কি বিচিত্র এই দেশ!

First line of the first scene of the first Act of the drama 'Chandra Gupta' by famous Bengali dramatist, poet and singer Dwijendralal Roy.

After conquering India, Alexander the Great is said to have exclaimed to Seleucus, a high officer in Alexander's army, thus: "Truly Seleucus, what a marvellously strange land this is...".!

হাট্টিমাটিমাটিম্ টিম্

Hattimatim tims are imaginary, humorous composite-animal characters from Bengali nursery rhymes.

ছবে

Bibliography

The following is a selected chronological list of works on Bengali proverbs consulted during the preparation of this book:

Long, Rev. James	*Prabadmala* Part I (1868), reprinted by Proshun Basu, Naba Prokashan, Kolkata, 1979
Long, Rev. James	*Prabadmala* Part II (1868), reprinted by Proshun Basu, Naba Prokashan, Kolkata 1979
Long, Rev. James	*Prabadmala* (1868), Re-printed by Proshun Basu, Naba Prokashan, Kolkata 1979
De, Sushil Kumar	*Bangla Prabad*, Kolkata, (1952)
Ferguson, Charles A. and Preston, W. D.	*Journal of American Folklore;* Vol. 59, No. 234, Dec.1946
Das Gupta, Bidhubhushan	*Learn Bengali yourself* (1956), Kolkata
Pathan, M. Hanif	*Bangla Probad Porichiti;* Bangla Academy, 1985
Basak, Sudeshna	*Banglar Probad;* Ananda Publishers Pvt. Ltd., Kolkata (2007);
Warrington, Matt	*Crocodile in the water, tiger on the land;* 2008 University Press Ltd., Dhaka
Khana	*Khanar Bachan*, date unknown

Additionally, the following dictionaries contain sections on Bengali proverbs:

	Bangla Wikipedia
Dev, Ashu Tosh	*Dev's Concise Dictionary* (Bengali – English) 1968, Kolkata
Samsad	*Bengali - English dictionary*

Resources for equivalent proverbs

For proverbs from the English-speaking cultures, the following book were consulted:

Oxford Dictionary of English Proverbs by William George Smith, Clarendon Press, 1980

Oxford concise dictionary of Proverbs

Penguin Book of Proverbs

Proverbs and their origins by Linda and Roger Flavell 2000

A book of Proverbs by Raymond Lamont-Brown

The following are some of the Internet resources that were consulted:

http://www.giga-usa.com/index.html

http://www.worldofquotes.com/index.php

http://www.legendsofamerica.com/NA-Proverbs.html

http://www.quotationspage.com/

http://www.quotationspage.com/

http://chinese-sayings.com/

http://en.wikiquote.org/wiki/Category:Proverbs

http://www.world-of-proverbs.com/index.html

http://www.special-dictionary.com/proverbs/

http://www.famous-proverbs.com/

Additionally, the following online book was found most valuable:

Schipper, Mineke — Never trust a woman with big feet: Women in proverbs from around the World, Yale University Press (2004).

Subject Index

(by ID number)

A

Aashar   2-73,74.

Ace   15-11.

Achieve 29-71.

Action 28-91.

Advice 28-32.

Affection 2-48.

Alms 9-44; 13-26.

Anger   24-58.

Antidote   29-77.

Ants   24-61; 31-11.

Appearance   2-22.

Arjun   1-11.

Arrow   28-78.

Ash   12-2,3; 27-6; 28-94; 29-67.

Atonement   24-47.

Aubergine   19-14,30.

Auspicious 26-68.

B

Baby   21-30.

Back   24-75.

Bad times   2-8.

Baishakh   7-76.

Bamboo   7-43; 7-80; 23-16; 26-23.

Banana plant   2-29.

Banyan tree   6-1; 26-8.

Bargain   21-11.

Bark of a tree   5-8.

Battle   29-51.

Beating (hiding) 4-7; 14-14; 19-23; 20-117,118; 24-79,87; 28-80,107,117; 34-30.

Beauty   1-14; 13-31; 23-48; 24-7,9; 31-1,2,3,4; 34-60.

Bed   32-27; 34-20.

Beehive   27-29; 28-123.

Begging   27-26,27.

Bengalees   26-25; 27-39.

Belong   22-24.

Betel leaf   24-43.

Betray   28-85.

Blow   7-86.

Bindi   1-26

Bird   5-14,15; 24-31; 34-2.

Birth   13-6.

Bitter   2-2; 24-51.

Bitter-sweet   19-10.

Blanket   31-14,16.

Blind   1-33,34,35; 7-65,66.

Blessing   32-20.

Blunder   24-35.

Boasting   10-5.

Blow   7-86.; 14-6.

Boat   10-10; 21-25.

Body   9-34 to 37; 32-15; 34-24.

Bow   22-3.

Boy   12-12,13.

Brahmin   4-3; 7-65; 7-72; 11-23; 24-83; 26-37,38.

Break   23-17

Breath   23-37,41.

Brothers   27-8

Bribe   10-16.

Brick   3-3.

Bribe   10-16.

Bride   5-41; 7-22.

Bull   7-34, 22-11, 33-4,5; 34-33.

Bush 14-6.

Business   26-28; 28-120; 29-30.

C

Camel   4-5.

Cards (playing)   19-9.

Castle   32-38; 34-80.

Cat   1-30; 3-4; 5-43; 9-12, 20,45; 24-84; 26-45, 46, 47; 28-45; 28-111; 32-21; 35-2.

Catch   35-24.

Cattle shed   35-6.

Cause & effect   7-73; 23-53.

Cautious   2-36; 34-44.

Character   1-49; 23-32; 34-81.

Charka   23-42.

Cheap   34-25.

Child   2-71; 24-68,69; 35-3.

Clap   5-30.

Clergy   28-122.

Clever   1-14,15; 26-75.

Cloud   1-20; 10-3; 26-57; 28-112,113.

Company   7-110; 34-5.

Conscience   26-54.

Coconut   14-5.

Control   7-31.

Cook/ cooking   1-18; 1-60; 5-31; 12-12; 24-65; 28-120; 29-65; 34-79.

Count 7-6.

Cover-up   18-1; 22-15.

Cow   2-18,32; 5-10; 9-16, 17,22; 10-3; 13-26; 13-7; 21-14, 32, 36; 27-9; 29-53.

Crane/ heron   7-51; 35-1.

Crazy   35-37.

Creeper   31-4,6.

Credit   2-33.

Crocodile   7-99,101; 8-10; 13-11,13.

Crow   7-46 to 49, 51,52; 14-1; 26-84; 27-18, 32; 29-60; 32-17.

Crowd   19-15.

Cry   12-11; 30-14.

Cuckoo   7-108; 26-16.

Curry   24-33.

Curse   32-20.

Custom   21-42; 29-25.

Cut   7-58; 22-17.

D

Dam   26-6.

Dance   19-2, 24; 23-1, 28.

Danger   26-59; 29-17.

Dark   1-32; 2-49; 7-82; 24-85; 29-68.

Day   16-4; 21-19,20,21;29-60.

Deaf   7-78.

Dead/ death   1-41; 4-8; 13-6,22; 19-11,18; 22-1; 23-15; 24-6; 28-13 to 23,68; 17-23; 24-6; 29-21 to 23; 31-15;32-40.

Deceit / deceive   5-26.

Decision   5-19; 35-13.

Deer   2-56; 5-11.

Delhi   21-22,23.

Destiny   7-25; 27-3; 31-7.

Dew   34-20.

Dhobi   29-61; 22-24.

Diamond   12-13.

Disgrace   28-93.

Dishonest   34-8.

Dishonour   1-41.

Dismiss   25-7.

Doctor   23-51.

Dog 7-91 to 94; 28-65; 34-1.

Doll   7-35.

Donkey   9-30.

Donor   10-17.

Dream   5-1; 12-9; 34-54,77 to 80.

Drum   23-43.

Drunkard   32-35; 34-59.

Ducks   35-1.

Dumb   26-88.

Dung-cake   10-14, 15; 24-35.

Durga/ Mahishmardini 28-31.

Dust   2-10.

Duty   28-34.

E

Ear   7-62,63,64,68,69; 21-38.

Earn   13-24.

Earth   22-5,6; 26-67.

Eat   13-17; 24-44; 26-18, 89; 29-52; 35-7.

Egg   17-3; 10-20.

Endure   26-69.

Enemy   10-8; 24-21; 28-1, 10; 31-2,10; 32-8 to 10.

Elephant   1-68; 9-2, 8; 21-35; 28-21, 53, 79; 32-43; 35-19,20.

Elixir of life   28-110.

Error   28-10.

Ethical   23-62.

Evil   21-36,37; 23-14.

Expert   9-25.

Eye   11-3,4,12,25 to 35; 21-29; 32-29.

F

Face   20-3; 28-93 to 96; 35-21.

Faith   26-60.

Family   16-8; 26-20.

Famous   5-13; 19-4.

Farmer   11-15.

Fate   7-24,25,26,74; 19-22; 26-52,53; 27-3,14; 27-11 to 14; 29-40,44; 31-7.

Father   29-76.

Favours   24-15.

Fault   9-48; 24-24; 27-31; 29-8,48.

Fear   27-5.

Feelings   24-20.

Feet   5-19; 21-44; 23-45; 24-48,49, 50.

Festivals   26-40.

Fever   9-32; 10-11; 27-25.

Field   19-26.

Fig   17-5.

Finger   24-32; 34-69.

Fire   1-5,6; 2-16,17; 10-4; 13-16; 24-18; 34-53.

Firewood   7-59.

Fish   1-30,60; 7-3,27; 9-9; 10-23; 13-9; 22-7; 24-65,66, 67; 27-17; 28-33,40,41, 45 to 47; 32-18.

Flattery   8-19.

Flattened-rice   32-28.

Flower   25-4,5; 32-26.

Fly   5-9; 28-43.

Food   7-4; 8-13; 20-4; 28-99; 29-52; 35-7.

Fools   23-50; 26-77; 27-44; 28-106; 29-58.

Friend   1-17,69; 5-18 to 21, 33; 9-21,33; 21-10; 28-52, 105; 29-18, 47; 34-63; 35-2, 9,12.

Frog   7-104; 26-81,82; 34-42; 35-19,20.

Fruit   28-37; 29-73.

G

Ganesh   9-50.

Ganges/ Ganga   9-2; 23-18; 27-10.

Gem   2-49; 35-31.

Ghee   1-36; 24-22,45,46; 27-6; 34-69,78.

Ghost   24-82; 27-33 to 36; 32-16; 34-55.

Gibberish   2-63; 35-4.

Ginger   2-42,43,44; 24-3.

Girl   12-12,13; 28-114.

Give and take   5-29; 23-47.

Goat   24-37; 26-14.

God   1-23; 3-7,10; 8-16,17; 13-21; 21-5,6,39,40; 22-13; 27-1,42,43; 28-67,69; 29-33, 59,74,75; 34-72; 35-11.

Goddess   29-75; 33-4.

Gold   7-57; 11-1; 27-19; 28-2; 34-70, 71.

Goldsmith   34-66,67.

Good   2-51.

Good deed   32-31,32.

Goods   28-38; 30-29.

Good sense   2-13.

Gossip   24-14; 29-28.

Grapes   2-30.

Grass   10-12,18; 19-25.

Grateful   23-55; 29-39.

Gratitude   23-55.

Gravy   2-54.

Greed   1-13,22,24; 2-68; 31-15.

Green banana/plantain 7-42.

Grief   28-47; 34-20.

Groom   1-36.

Guest   1-23; 28-40.

Guilt   16-3.

Guru   23-30; 5-40; 9-42.

H

Habit   1-50; 24-18; 29-27; 34-81.

Hair   11-21,22; 29-65; 31-16.

Half   1-57,58.

Hand   35-18,21 to 27.

Hanging   2-27.

Happiness   2-25,50,77; 22-2; 24-56; 29-70; 34-55, 56.

Harassment   23-20,29.

Harm   24-27; 26-63.

Hay 8-3.

Head   7-71; 28-54 to 65.

Headache   28-54,55.

Heart   1-31.

Heaven   2-5; 19-37; 23-9; 30-16; 34-8,24,74,75.

Hell   2-5; 13-18; 23-12.

Heron / crane   26-1.

High Court   26-25; 35-1.

Hilsa fish   3-7.

Hindu   35-33.

Home   2-20.

Honest   34-8

Honey   2-2; 28-3,96.

Honour   1-42; 29-29.

Horse   9-30; 10-17,18,19, 20.

House   10-3.

Humility   1-19; 21-49; 26-50.

Humour   1-54.

Hunger   8-14; 24-79.

Husking pedal   2-6; 4-9; 18-6; 26-77.

I

Ideas   29-9.

Idle   1-62

In-laws   26-75; 28-77; 32-41, 42.

Indulgence   2-45,46; 7-92.

Ink   9-39; 28-93; 35-21.

J

Jackal   4-15; 24-77; 26-9; 34-12.

Jackfruit   3-1; 7-61,87; 9-26; 24-28; 31-10.

Jagannath   16-5.

Jewel / jewellery   13-15.

Jilebi   13-20; 24-80.

Journey   5-23.

Judgement   2-13,14; 21-1; 35-15.

K

Kajal (kohl)   11-32; 32-29.

Khoi (puffed rice)   4-4.

Kick   28-60.

King   26-9; 34-76.

Knife   28-82.

Knot   26-2.

Knowledge   23-3; 24-39; 26-77,78.

Koee   7-2,3; 14-2.

Kohl (kajal)   11-32; 32-29.

Krishna   7-61,105.

L

Ladder   9-27.

Lakshman   22-4.

Lakshmi   1-40; 10-6; 28-81; 30-27; 31-1,2; 34-47; 35-27.

Lame   24-2.

Lamp   24-22,85; 27-2; 34-64.

Language   5-16; 9-41.

Lanka (Srilanka)   1-16; 7-75; 29-63; 31-5.

Lantern   2-26.

Last rites   24-60.

Laughter   29-19; 35-32.

Lazy 1-4,62; 7-55,95,97.

Leach   13-30.

Leader 9-24; 24-53.

Learning   1-64; 7-1; 9-42; 12-12; 13-7; 16-7; 22-12; 23-40,49; 24-70,81; 26-49, 50; 28-119; 31-12; 34-76.

Lies   14-8.

Life   2-59,65; 3-8; 11-2,11, 12,17,36;   13-7,21;   17-2,36; 16-8; 17-2; 18-2,3; 19-20, 21, 31,34,35; 21-2, 16,46,47,48; 22-18,20,21,22, 25; 23-2,15, 47, 53,58; 24-4, 5,30,34,78; 26-7,58,74;   27-16,30,43; 28-4,5, 33; 29-6, 54,66; 34-31.

Lime paste   9-39.

Lion   34-49,50.

Listen   5-6; 28-9.

Liver   24-57.

Lotus   7-66; 9-51.

Love   26-6; 27-24.

Luck   7-23,24.

M

Mad   24-37.

Maestro   6-5.

Magic   11-16; 27-20.

Mahabharat   28-29.

Man   2-47; 5-5; 7-111; 8-5; 19-33; 22-16,25; 23-13,60; 26-7; 28-30, 50, 67,68,69; 34-40.

Married life 34-48.

Master 29-78.

Meal 29-52.

Meddle 25-10.

Medicine 34-22.

Mess   14-7; 19-6.

Milk   9-38; 21-31 to 33; 29-53; 34-38.

Million 31-8.

Mirage 28-24.

Miser   19-5.

Misunderstood   4-16.

Molasses 29-11; 31-11; 34-65.

Mole 12-7,8.

Money   1-55,56; 2-23,24, 70; 7-5,7,8,9,110; 12-9; 13-1 to 9; 15-1 to 10; 25-9; 31-9.

Monkeys   7-89; 26-21,22, 30, 31.

Monks   1-28; 21-24; 23-33; 28-6,104.

Mooli / raddish   4-6.

Moon   1-51; 2-9; 3-9; 11-8 to 10.

Moori   29-38.

Mosquito   25-27; 28-25,26, 27.

Mother   2-31; 7-98; 26-10; 28-35,47,73, to 77,81, 120; 29-24.

Mountain   24-16,17,18.

Mourn   7-45

Mouse   3-4,5.

Moustache   9-45,46; 32-21.

Mouth   28-86 to 100.

Murder   34-27.

Muslim 35-33.

Mustard /oil   11-30; 23-24;
32-16.

N

Nectar of immortality   1-52.

Needle   11-13; 12-5,6; 34-58.

Neighbour   24-40.

News   7-103; 8-18; 28-11.

Night   26-69.

Non-sense   2-15.

Non-violence   1-72.

Nose   23-19 to 27,44;
32-39; 35-18.

O

Obstacle   24-11; 32-31.

Ocean   34-20,35.

Occurrence   23-10.

Offence   31-3.

Offerings   35-10.

Oil   13-8,12; 19-27 to30;
24-48; 25-9.

Opposite   35-34.

Opportunist   8-9; 23-46;
24-28,29; 26-15.

Opportunity   29-67; 34-62.

P

Pancakes   24-26.

Patience   34-14.

Patriot   5-42,45; 13-4.

Paper   7-50.

Parents   2-62; 6-6; 24-55,
66; 34-51.

Pearls   4-14; 26-31; 35-31.

Pen   35-22.

People   8-4; 26-12,72,73,
74; 28-28; 29-31,33; 32-3,
4,5.

Pigeon   10-13; 26-41;
27-28; 34-57.

Pilgrimage   19-19.

Pitcher   7-33; 8-11; 10-2;
12-13; 22-6; 27-7; 32-37.

Place   22-14; 34-9.

Plant   9-47

Poison   21-29; 26-5,61,63,
64.

Politeness   27-2.

Pond   23-35; 24-64.

Poor   1-61; 7-40,41; 9-13,
14,15,31.

Posture 19-36.

Pots 29-79.

Poverty 1-39,49; 17-1; 21-5,
17.

Power   21-2.

Praise   29-39; 32-6.

Problem   9-49; 27-40;
28-109.

Precious   34-13,44.

Pretence   19-16.

Pride   1-16,19; 2-39; 9-19.

Promise   27-21; 35-14.

Protector 29-64.

Punishment 31-3.

Purchase 7-84.

Pure 22-25.

Puffed-rice 29-38.

Q

Quarrel 26-29.

Queen 32-34; 34-61.

R

Radish / mooli 4-6.

Rain 1-20,65; 2-6; 9-11; 28-108,112; 29-7.

Rama 5-32; 23-18; 28-23; 34-68.

Ramayana 30-17; 34-26.

Ravana 29-63; 34-52.

Relationship 24-84; 26-33; 32-41; 35-12.

Relatives 19-13; 23-8; 26-13; 27-23; 28-71,74,77; 29-26; 32-41.

Religion 22-9,10,11; 26-1; 22-10, 11; 29-12.

Remark 13-10; 25-11.

Repent 9-4.

Respect 2-57; 32-47.

Responsibility 21-15.

Result 25-1.

Reward 29-49.

Rhinoceros 9-6.

Rice 1-37,38; 4-11; 5-43; 7-10; 9-12; 10-7; 22-12,13; 23-54; 24-36,45,73; 25-8; 26-48; 27-18,19,27; 28-86, 103; 32-28,30; 35-3.

Rice pudding 24-51.

River 8-1; 23-5,6,7; 24-8; 26-85; 34-35,83.

Robbery 21-21.

Rose 9-52.

Rules 5-34; 24-86; 26-51.

Rush 24-19.

S

Sadness 2-25; 35-32.

Salt 8-14; 13-30 ; 23-55; 29-39.

Saraswati 30-27.

Saturday 32-11.

Saturn 32-12,13.

Saviour 29-64.

Seeds 4-10; 26-42,66.

Sense 33-1.

Self 2-40,62.

Servant 29-78.

Shave 5-7.

Sheep 9-3; 27-37,38.

Shell 32-19.

Shield 18-4.

Shiva 22-13; 32-23 to 25.

Shiver   20-2.

Shoes   13-26 to 29; 32-30.

Shy   28-86.

Shyam   32-44, 45,46.

Silence   28-124,125.

Silver   34-71.

Simul   32-26.

Sin   9-10; 24-47; 28-8; 31-15.

Sing   9-31.

Sita   34-26,52,53.

Situation   1-46.

Skin   11-33; 28-117.

Sky   2-4 to 12; 28-57.

Slander   24-59

Slap   34-30.

Sleep   7-100; 29-57; 32-33.

Smell   9-36; 10-24.

Snake   1-71; 7-107; 21-31, 34; 34-38 to 43.

Snake charmer   34-43.

Son   29-24,76.

Sorrow   1-66; 35-8.

Soul   2-41.

Sound   32-37.

Speak   32-7.

Speech   21-3; 28-7,87,88, 89,92,98; 29-4; 35-2.

Spider   28-36.

Spinach   26-87; 32-18.

Spleen   24-62.

Squirrel   7-60.

Stab   24-76.

Stealing   11-20.

Step   5-18.

Stitch   26-56; 28-90; 34-19

Stick   29-45; 34-39.

Stomach   24-78 to 81; 27-5.

Stone   1-32; 10-9; 13-1;18-5; 27-29; 34-72; 35-26.

Storm   14-1.

Story   2-73.

Street   24-12.

Strong   13-32.

Student   12-4.

Suffering   21-27,28; 29-36.

Sugar   11-18.

Sugar candy   28-32

Sun   11-8; 13-16; 34-64.

Sweat   9-18; 28-64.

Sweet   2-21; 29-11

Swim   34-36.

Swindler   16-1,2.

T

Taal   1-2; 23-35.

Tail   31-13.

Talk   5-22; 24-38.

Taste   2-52.

Teach   2-58.

Teeth   21-12,13; 29-46

The Trinity   26-90.

Thief   1-20; 11-37 to 46; 23-59; 25-2; 29-35; 34-62.

Thorn   7-21,44; 24-11.

Thought   27-22.

Thumb   26-79.

Thrift   29-56.

Thunder   26-57; 28-59; 29-7.

Tiger   2-19; 4-12; 7-9; 13-11; 16-6; 21-14; 24-52; 26-26, 27; 29-68.

Time   7-81; 21-17,19,20,24; 34-15 to 19,46.

Tin soldier   19-7.

Too much   1-20,24,25.

Torn   12-9,10.

Tortoise   9-2

Torture   26-71

Town   32-17.

Traveller   5-17; 24-10.

Treasure   29-2.

Tree   9-26,27,28,29; 26-3, 11; 29-73.

Trial   2-27.

Truth   1-58; 22-9,10; 34-6,7.

Try   5-27; 11-24.

U

Umbrella   26-81.

Unborn   1-10; 35-3.

Uncle   11-11; 23-57.

Undecided   19-3.

Ungrateful   7-56.

Unlucky   1-47,48.

Uninvited   1-27.

Unity   5-25.

Unique   5-39.

Utensils   19-12; 25-3; 29-79; 35-17.

V

Vain   21-41; 28-49.

Veil   1-21.

Vice   19-8.

Vigil   32-14

Village headman   9-24.

Villager   21-43.

Virtue   2-22; 22-8; 27-9.

Vow   22-3.

Vulture   27-9; 32-1,2.

W

Wall   21-38.

Wash   22-23.

Waste   1-39,40.

Water   5-19; 7-33,77,109; 8-12; 13-8 to 14; 17-4; 19-29; 22-7; 25-3; 26-32; 34-28; 35-25.

Weak   1-70.

Wealth   13-23; 22-1,2; 24-25; 26-18,39,62; 29-34, 37, 43.

Weather   29-15,16; 30-28.

Weaver   8-6.

Weaving machine   23-42.

Wedding   6-2,3; 10-1; 26-5,43; 29-20,41; 34-32.

Wick   32-24.

Wife   9-27; 26-80; 34-26.

Wilderness   1-53.

Will   3-2.

Wind   26-29; 28-11.

Wind-up   24-41,

Winter   5-21; 13-16; 28-39.

Wisdom   26-75,76.

Woodcutter   1-19.

Woman   1-44,45; 13-31; 28-115,116; 29-5; 34-17,73; 35-17,28.

Words   5-20; 7-11 to 20; 12-14; 19-17; 26-24; 28-68, 83,84; 32-28.

Work   2-75; 5-37; 7-30,36, 53 to 56; 8-8,15; 21-7,9,18; 23-56; 26-81; 27-41; 28-102; 29-13, 32,72.

World   27-4.

Worship   28-10; 29-62; 34-3.

Worthless   33-5.

Wound   7-58; 34-22.

Y

Year   2-37.

Yogurt   21-1; 25-8; 35-23.

Z

Zero 9-54.

ॐ

Lightning Source UK Ltd.
Milton Keynes UK
25 February 2010
150600UK00001B/48/P